Indochina Monographs

The Khmer Republic at War and the Final Collapse

Lt. Gen. Sak Sutsakhan

U.S. ARMY CENTER OF MILITARY HISTORY

WASHINGTON, D.C.

Library of Congress Cataloging in Publication Data

Sak Sutsakhan.
    The Khmer Republic at war and the final collapse.

    (Indochina monographs)
    1. Cambodia--History--Civil War, 1970-1975.
I. Title. II. Series.
DS554.8.S24   959.704'34   79-607776

This book is not copyrighted and may be reproduced in whole or in part without consulting the publisher

Reprinted 1984

CMH PUB 92-5

Indochina Monographs

This is one of a series published by the U.S. Army Center of Military History. They were written by officers who held responsible positions in the Cambodian, Laotian, and South Vietnamese armed forces during the war in Indochina. The General Research Corporation provided writing facilities and other necessary support under an Army contract with the Center of Military History. The monographs were not edited or altered and reflect the views of their authors--not necessarily those of the U.S. Army or the Department of Defense. The authors were not attempting to write definitive accounts but to set down how they saw the war in Southeast Asia.

Colonel William E. Le Gro, U.S. Army, retired, has written a forthcoming work allied with this series, Vietnam: From Cease-Fire to Capitulation. Another book, The Final Collapse by General Cao Van Vien, the last chairman of the South Vietnamese Joint General Staff, will be formally published and sold by the Superintendent of Documents.

Taken together these works should provide useful source materials for serious historians pending publication of the more definitive series, the U.S. Army in Vietnam.

JAMES L. COLLINS, JR.
Brigadier General, USA
Chief of Military History

INDOCHINA MONOGRAPHS

TITLES IN THE SERIES
(title--author/s--LC Catalog Card)

The Cambodian Incursion--Brig. Gen. Tran Dinh Tho--79-21722	CMH PUB 92-4
The Easter Offensive of 1972--Lt. Gen. Ngo Quang Truong--79-20551	CMH PUB 92-13
The General Offensives of 1968-69--Col. Hoang Ngoc Lung--80-607931	CMH PUB 92-6
Intelligence--Col. Hoang Ngoc Lung--81-10844/AACR2	CMH PUB 92-14
The Khmer Republic at War and the Final Collapse--Lt. Gen. Sak Sutsakhan--79-607776	CMH PUB 92-5
Lam Son 719--Maj. Gen. Nguyen Duy Hinh--79-607101	CMH PUB 92-2
Leadership--General Cao Van Vien--80-607941	CMH PUB 92-12
Pacification--Brig. Gen. Tran Dinh Tho--79-607913	CMH PUB 92-11
RLG Military Operations and Activities in the Laotian Panhandle--Brig. Gen. Soutchay Vongsavanh--81-10934/AACR2	CMH PUB 92-19
The RVNAF--Lt. Gen. Dong Van Khuyen--79-607963	CMH PUB 92-7
RVNAF and U.S. Operational Cooperation and Coordination--Lt. Gen. Ngo Quang Truong--79-607170	CMH PUB 92-16
RVNAF Logistics--Lt. Gen. Dong Van Khuyen--80-607117	CMH PUB 92-17
Reflections on the Vietnam War--General Cao Van Vien and Lt. Gen. Dong Van Khuyen--79-607979	CMH PUB 92-8
The Royal Lao Army and U.S. Army Advice and Support--Maj. Gen. Oudone Sananikone--79-607054	CMH PUB 92-10
The South Vietnamese Society--Maj. Gen. Nguyen Duy Hinh and Brig. Gen. Tran Dinh Tho--79-17694	CMH PUB 92-18
Strategy and Tactics--Col. Hoang Ngoc Lung--79-607102	CMH PUB 92-15
Territorial Forces--Lt. Gen. Ngo Quang Truong--80-15131	CMH PUB 92-9
The U.S. Adviser--General Cao Van Vien, Lt. Gen. Ngo Quang Truong, Lt. Gen. Dong Van Khuyen, Maj. Gen. Nguyen Duy Hinh, Brig. Gen. Tran Dinh Tho, Col. Hoang Ngoc Lung, and Lt. Col. Chu Xuan Vien--80-607108	CMH PUB 92-1
Vietnamization and the Cease-Fire--Maj. Gen. Nguyen Duy Hinh--79-607982	CMH PUB 92-3
The Final Collapse--General Cao Van Vien--81-607989	CMH PUB 90-26

Preface

On the chessboard that is the world of today, the geographical position of a country plays an all-important role. Whether rich or poor, at war or at peace, a country will be taken seriously only by its neighbors or by those with whom the country has dominating political and economic interests. By the rest of the world, such a country should expect nothing more than to be forgotten, misunderstood, or treated with indifference. Cambodia (the Khmer Republic from 1970 to 1975), immersed for five years in the conflict known in that region as the Indochina War, was in the category of a forgotten country. The war we carried on during that period has been violently criticized by our enemies, ignored by some, and poorly understood by our friends. It is my hope that this monograph will serve to put these events into better perspective and to make clearer the Khmer point of view.

As Commander-in-Chief of the Armed Forces, as Chief of the General Staff, FANK, as Ambassador, and as the last Chief of State of the Khmer Republic, I participated in making many of the major decisions of that country and was a witness to still others. In addition to my personal involvement, I have relied on documents in my possession and numerous conversations with the Khmer military community now in this country.

In the preparation of this monograph, I am particularly indebted to Colonel Harry O. Amos, U.S. Army Retired, twice a Military Attache in Phnom Penh and long-time friend of Cambodia, for his help in translating and editing my original draft. My thanks go as well to Ms. Pham Thi Bong, a former Captain in the Republic of Vietnam Armed

Forces and also a former member of the Vietnamese Embassy staff, who spent long and arduous hours, in typing and editing, and in the administrative requirements for putting my manuscript into final form.

McLean, Virginia
20 November 1978

Sak Sutsakhan
Lieutenant General, FANK

Contents

Chapter		Page
I.	INTRODUCTION	1
	The Sihanouk Era	1
	The Political Strategy of Neutrality	6
	Neutrality of the Left	9
	The Origins of the Khmer Republic	12
II.	CAMBODIA AND THE COMMUNISTS	18
	Vietnamese Communist Use of Khmer Territory	18
	Khmer Communist Political Origins	22
	Khmer Communist Military Development	26
III.	THE ARMED FORCES OF THE KHMER REPUBLIC	32
	Origins	32
	The Initial Expansion After March 18, 1970	38
	Military Organization	46
	The U.S. Military Assistance Program	50
	The Khmer Krom Units	55
IV.	THE FIRST TWO YEARS OF THE WAR	59
	The Initial Communist Attacks	59
	The Evacuation of the Ratanakiri Garrison	63
	FANK Strategy	67
	CHENLA I	69
	CHENLA II	72
	Cooperation and Coordination with the RVNAF and the U.S.	80
V.	THE POLITICO/MILITARY SITUATION IN CAMBODIA, 1972-1974	87
	The Political Situation	87
	Enemy Strategy	90
	General Mobilization -- The Plan for the Countryside	91
	Condition of the FANK	94
	The End of U.S. Bombing	96

Chapter	Page

VI. MAJOR MILITARY OPERATIONS, 1972 THROUGH 1974 99

    Operations in Military Regions 1 and 2, and Against Phnom Penh, March-June 1972 101
    FANK Efforts to Keep Lines of Communications Open, July-December 1972 106
    The Enemy Dry-Season Offensive, January-July 1973 . . . 114
    The First Months Without U.S. Air Support, August-December 1973 122
    Dry Season Operations, January-July 1974 125
    The Wet Season, August-December 1974 140

VII. CLOSING MONTHS, JANUARY-APRIL 1975 149

    Peace Initiatives 150
    Enemy Strategy 153
    FANK Change of Command 154
    Military Operations 155
    The Departure of Lon Nol 158

VIII. THE FINAL DAYS OF THE KHMER REPUBLIC 162

    Departure of the U.S. Embassy 162
    The Last Government 164
    One More Effort to Negotiate 167
    The 17th of April 1975 168

IX. ANALYSIS AND CONCLUSIONS 172

Appendix

  A. The Delegations to the Summit Conference of the Indochinese Peoples, April 25, 1970. 177
  B. The Members of FUNK and GRUNK 179
  C. Major Items of U.S.-Furnished Equipment in FANK 182
  D. FANK Order of the Day, 5 October 1971 184

GLOSSARY 186

Charts

No.
1. FANK General Staff Organization After 1972 47
2. FANK Organization After 1972 51

Maps

No.		Page
1.	Cambodia and its Southeast Asian Neighbors	4
2.	Cambodian Government Information on Locations of Principal NVA/VC Base Areas in Cambodia in 1969	19
3.	FANK Information as to Deployment of VC/NVA in Cambodia, 1970	29
4.	Locations of Principal FARK Ground Units Prior to 18 March 1970	34
5.	Locations of Principal FANK Infantry Units on 1 May 1970	44
6.	The Military Regions of the Khmer Armed Forces in 1971	49
7.	Initial Communist Attacks, March-April 1970	62
8.	FANK-Held Areas in Cambodia in August 1970	64
9.	Area of FARK OPERATION TEST VC/NVA, November 1969	65
10.	FANK Strategic Concepts for Defense of the Khmer Republic	68
11.	OPERATION CHENLA I and Area of Operations	70
12.	Concept for OPERATION CHENLA II and Area of Operations	73
13.	Enemy Attacks Against OPERATION CHENLA II Column, 26-31 October 1971	76
14.	Locations of FANK Operations ANGKOR CHEY and PREK TA	100
15.	Areas of Operations, March-June 1972	102
16.	Points of Military Interest in Phnom Penh	104
17.	Objective Area, OPERATION SORYA, July-August 1972	108
18.	Area of Operation Along Route 2, July-December 1972	109
19.	Angkor Wat/Angkor Thom Temple and Ruins Complex	110
20.	Areas of the Mekong Controlled by the Enemy, February-Arpil 1973	117
21.	Combat Areas Near Phnom Penh, July 1973	121
22.	Defense Sectors for Phnom Penh, January 1974	126
23.	Oudong Area of Operations, March 1974	131
24.	The Battle for Kampot, March-April 1974	135
25.	Operations Along the Bassac River, April-July 1974	137
26.	Operations in the Bassac-Mekong Corridor, September-December 1974	145
27.	Final Assault on Neak Luong and Closing of the Mekong, March 1975	157
28.	The Battle for Phnom Penh, April 1975	159

Illustrations

Destruction in Tonle Bet (on Mekong Opposite Kompong Cham) Following Communist Attacks in April 1970	31
Ceremony at Phnom Penh in 1971 to Mark Return of FANK Special Forces Detachments from Training in Thailand	57
Khmer Krom Unit, Newly Arrived from South Vietnam and Armed with the U.S. M-16 Rifle, Salutes 1st Military Region Commander During a Visit to Tonle Bet, November 1970	58
A Planning Session for OPERATION CHENLA II	84
Brigadier General Fan Muong, Commander 1st Military Region, Inspects a Squad in Kompong Cham Armed with the U.S. M-1 Carbine, November 1970	85

Page

FANK Recruits Move to the OPERATION CHENLA I Area on a Requisitioned Civilian Truck, Armed with the Communist Assault Rifle, AK-47, November 1970 86

Marshal Lon Nol, President of the Khmer Republic, April 1972 . . 98

CHAPTER I

Introduction

The Sihanouk Era

Cambodia's participation—or to put it more accurately its being dragged into the Indochinese conflict—dated rather far back in the political history of Cambodia. The dominant personality of this entire period was unquestionably Prince Norodom Sihanouk who, first as reigning King, and then as Chief of State, held nearly absolute power for more than 30 years in this tiny kingdom which shares over one half of its national boundaries with South Vietnam.

WW II, and its origins, brought the Franco-Japanese conflict to Indochina, and the Japanese occupation from 1940 to 1945, the year of Japanese defeat. This was followed by the reconquest of Indochina by the allied forces, bringing with it the triumphal return of the French to that region.

During the year of 1940 it should be noted that, after the brief struggle between the French protectorate and Thailand, which the latter country had arranged—as usual—to be on the winning side, Cambodia lost its entire province of Battambang and a part of the province of Siem Reap. The Thai occupation in these provinces lasted from 1941 to 1945.

From 1945 to 1954, Cambodia had to face two great problems. The first was the political struggle with France for complete independence, a struggle led, it must be remembered, by Prince Sihanouk who was then King of Cambodia. This struggle against France had the near-total support of all segments of the population. The second problem was the danger from the expansion of the Vietnamese forces known by the name of Viet Minh, who carried out guerrilla operations against the French presence in Vietnam.

The Viet Minh troops in Cambodia continued to expand gradually as the political and military situation of the regime in power deteriorated. Under the pretext of bringing military assistance for independence in Cambodia, these Viet Minh forces established themselves more and more deeply in Cambodia. Their method was to move into certain frontier regions to facilitate taking over particular areas in the interior of Cambodia just before the signing of the Geneva agreements in 1954. These areas of Viet Minh control were then expanded according to the "oil spot" or "leopard spot" concept.

At that time, the warring parties were divided into three camps:
1. The combined Franco-Cambodian or purely Cambodian Forces
2. The Viet Minh forces
3. The *Khmer Issarak* or free Khmer, forces which were both anti-Sihanouk and anti-Viet Minh.

Out of the events described above, there was born a new feeling among the Cambodians, an awakening of belief in nationhood and a fear of the "expansionist" tendencies of its neighbors.

The period from 1954 to 1970 saw three stages in the history of Cambodia, this newly independent state of the 20th Century:
1. Its efforts to recover and consolidate its national institutions.
2. Its struggles against the vicissitudes of national and international politics.
3. Its denouement or unwinding. By denouement I mean the change of the Kingdom of Cambodia into the Khmer Republic and its fall. What happened in Cambodia after 17 April 1975 in "Democratic Kampuchea" (the new name for present-day Cambodia) history itself will have to tell us.

From the international point of view, the problem of the first Indochinese conflict was settled by the Geneva Accords of 1954, and the parties are to be congratulated on the results of that conference whose sessions lasted only from the 26th of April to the 21st of July 1954. The rapidity and efficiency of the effort presaged a durable peace under the triple guaranty of the major power participants, Great Britain, the

Soviet Union, and the People's Republic of China. (The U.S. participated but chose not to adhere to the final declaration). An International Control Commission (ICC) consisting of India, Canada, and Poland, was placed in each of the three states of Indochina to ensure respect for the cease-fire.

Cambodia lost no time in having the foreign troops evacuated from its territory. French war ships transported them to North Vietnam, and the evacuation was carried out within the time limits set by the accords. Unfortunately, it was realized a little too late that hundreds of Cambodian cadre affiliated with the Viet Minh had also been transported to the same destination. The final count indicated that there were more than three thousand of these Cambodian cadre who had escaped the vigilance of the Cambodian authorities. This was both the start of Communism in Cambodia and the secret establishment of the Khmer Communist Party.

What then was the reaction of the interested countries to this new Indochina problem?

Faced with the Khmer national will, the majority opinion of its own people, and that of the rest of the world, France could not do otherwise than to withdraw from Cambodia and accord independence to a country where she had been the law for almost a century.

One of the countries participating in the Geneva Conference of 1954 was the great People's Republic of China (PRC), well known for its total support of North Vietnam and the Pathet Lao. Beginning in 1955 the PRC began to act. While each of the newly independent countries (Laos, Cambodia, Vietnam) undertook to make friends and worked actively in the political and diplomatic arenas, the inevitable nonetheless came to pass. To no great surprise the world witnessed the birth of two blocs, ideologically opposed: pro-Communist bloc, consisting of North Vietnam and the Pathet Lao; a pro-free world bloc, consisting of Cambodia, South Vietnam and Laos. It is not known what was going on in the Communist camp, but on the side of the free world France and the U.S. no longer concealed their rivalries, which brought them into opposition with each other on political, economic and military questions. Each country courted the three countries of Indochina. *(Map 1)* France, unwilling

Map 1 – Cambodia and its Southeast Asian Neighbors

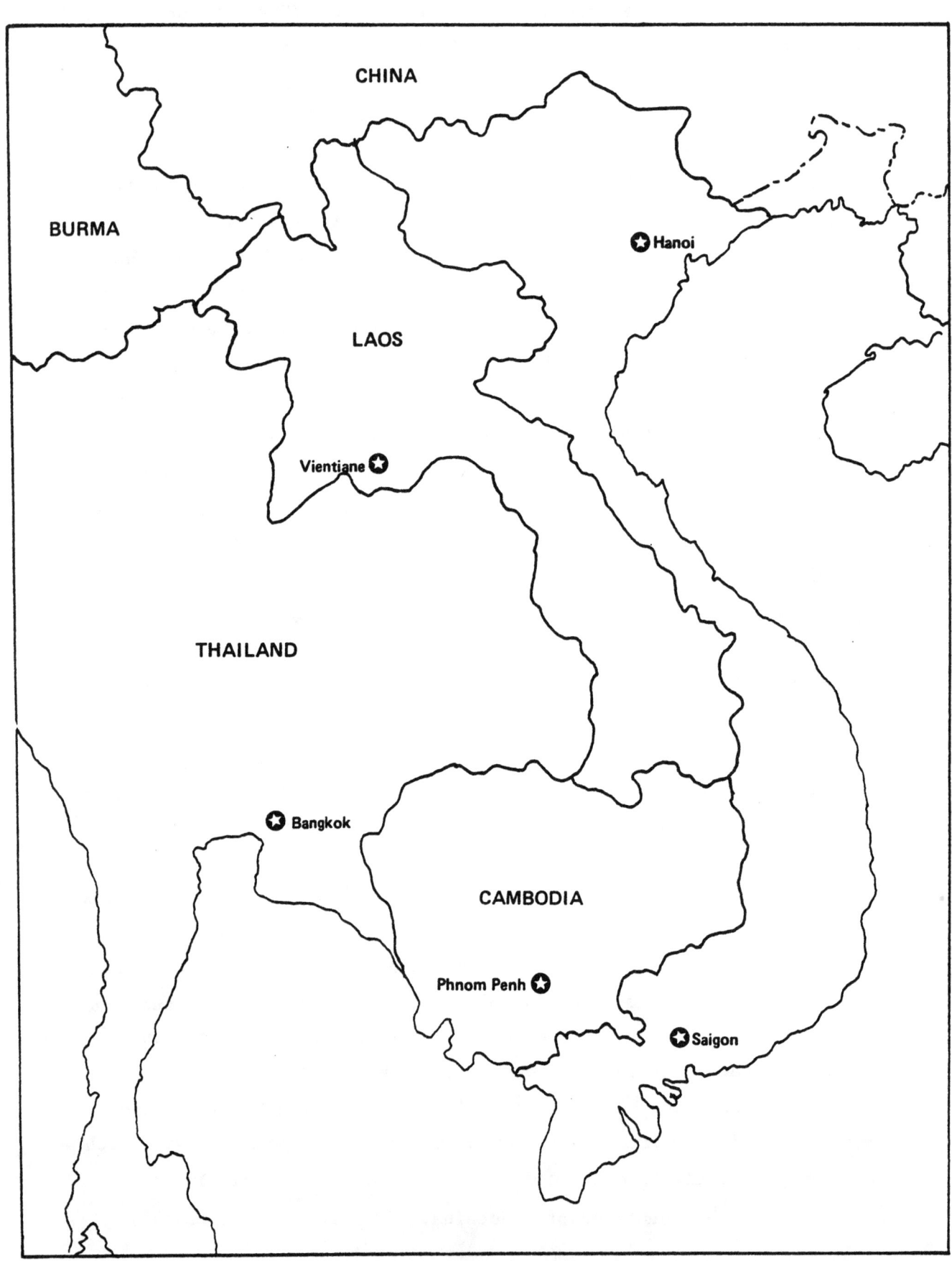

to accept the loss of everything without a struggle, sought by every means to regain the friendship of its former proteges. However, the U.S., richer and more powerful, held all the trumps. Laos and Vietnam perceived perfectly this difference in strength and wealth and arrayed themselves on the side of the more powerful.

Cambodia, being more shrewd, said neither "yes" nor "no." Not wishing to risk the liberty it had gained with such difficulty, Cambodia preferred to keep its distance while extending the hand of friendship to each of the two rival nations. Thus it was that Cambodia ensured its peace and stability. The experience of South Vietnam and Laos was otherwise; by their sudden movement into the American camp, these two countries had found themselves engaged immediately in a cold war which seemed to have no end. The great China, acting as discreetly as possible, equipped and trained the North Vietnamese and the Pathet Lao and pushed its two allies to wage a struggle without mercy against their own compatriots. Armed movements were created and given the names "Movement for National Liberation" or "Front for National Liberation" (FNL). They urged liberation of their countries from the yoke of imperialism (free world bloc). In time, these movements became better and better organized, spreading their offensive, recruiting new elements, and in the space of several years they passed from the status of simple guerrilla cells to that of regular units (battalion, regiment, division) having either territorial or maneuver capabilities. There was no ignoring their quality and operational capacity.

The Republic of Vietnam (South Vietnam) profited from its enthusiasm for the free world by consolidating its foundations. The most remarkable was the development of its military institutions, a development so spectacular that it provoked admiration and jealousy. Its armed forces became one of the most powerful in Southeast Asia.

As time passed, the acts of armed rebellion became more and more serious and more widespread. With its well-calculated and perfectly orchestrated system of propaganda and "psychological warfare," the Communists were able to establish "oil spots" throughout the population and among the different segments of society.

Although on good terms with South Vietnam, Cambodia was disquieted nonetheless by the dimensions to which Communism had grown in that country; this was all the more so that within Cambodia itself two currents of opposition to the policies adopted by Sihanouk were beginning to surface. The first accused Sihanouk of being "pro-free world"; the second criticized his dictatorial methods of governing the country. Political stirrings began with the dissolution of the original Democrat Party and the abdication of Sihanouk. The former king had chosen to be only the Chief of the Cambodian National Socialist Party. The Cambodian Communist movement took form in certain parts of the country, and in the 1960's one heard mention for the first time of the "Khmer Serei" or Free Khmer, created under the aegis of Son Ngoc Thanh and supported by the U.S. CIA.

Thus, Cambodia found itself at this time facing two dangers: from the exterior in the form of the Khmer Serei movement and the expansion toward the south of North Vietnamese Communism; the other danger was from the outlawed Khmer Communist party, a movement made up of opponents of Sihanouk, the malcontent, the abused, and the persecuted of the various segments of society from government worker to student.

During all of this troubled period when his antagonists deployed all of their skill and cunning in parallel with the eruption of local Communism, Prince Sihanouk was the only one in power to foresee events, and he seized on the slightest occasion to take the pulse of the two blocs or to measure the gulf which separated them in order to adopt an appropriate policy.

The Political Strategy of Neutrality

The general trends of political events in both Cambodia and its neighboring countries following 1955 pushed Cambodia to adopt the path of "neutrality" or "fair play" as a political strategy for dealing with all sides. It was a policy that Cambodia maintained until 1962. This strategy was calculated to not only calm the political stirrings within the country but also to permit Cambodia to maintain intact the separate

benefits to be drawn from dealing with the two power blocs. The
blunders of the western bloc, whether intentional or not (and we will
address them later), were among the factors causing the Cambodian ship
of state to change course and take another direction.

During the first years of experimenting with neutrality, the fact
should be admitted that Cambodia was having numerous and quite serious
difficulties with its immediate neighbors, Thailand to the west and
South Vietnam to the east. These difficulties stemmed from border disputes that Prince Sihanouk described as "annexationist in design" on
the part of our neighbors. Of these many disputes, the affair of Preah
Vihear was the best known because the drawn-out legal battle for it was
terminated only by a formal decision of the International Court of
Justice at The Hague.[1] Relations with the Republic of Vietnam had also
known some bad moments caused by many border incidents, themselves the
result of pursuit operations carried out by the RVNAF against the VC
and NVA.

It should be noted that with each of these incidents, whether on
the Thai or RVN border, the Royal Cambodian Government directed representations and protests not only to the government concerned but at the
same time to the United States. This latter was done because Cambodia
considered that the U.S. could exercise its political influence on Thailand and the RVN to halt the border incidents. Only nothing ever
came of the Cambodian protests, and these border incidents, by then
becoming more and more frequent, constituted one of the causes for the
change in policy adopted by Prince Sihanouk during the years preceding
the entry of Cambodia into the Indochina conflict.

Encouraged by the visit to Phnom Penh of Prime Minister Nehru in
1954 and by the conference of Ban Dung in April 1955, where he met Chou

---

[1] Prea Vihear is an ancient Khmer Temple located on the Cambodian-Thai border, almost directly north of Phnom Penh. For a number of years, there was a dispute between the two governments as to whether the temple was, in fact, in Cambodia or Thailand. Submitted to the International Court of Justice, the Court ruled in favor of Cambodia in early 1962. Dean Acheson represented Cambodia.

En Lai, Prince Sihanouk saw, from the Cambodian point of view, indisputable advantages in a policy of strict neutrality, and in order to demonstrate the authenticity of the newly achieved Cambodian independence, a policy dictated by neither France nor the United States, Sihanouk denounced the Southeast Asia Treaty Organization (SEATO). Created in 1954, it was seen as a political instrument of the Free World which was anti-Communist not only in political and economic ideology but in deed as well; thus it was that certain members were seen directly engaged in the armed conflict in South Vietnam. Cambodia renounced the protection of the SEATO umbrella and to please the Communists denounced before the world the harmful effects of SEATO on the war in Vietnam and on Cambodia. For example, there was the attempted coup d'etat fomented by Brig. General Dap Chhuon, Commander of the 4th Military Region (Siem Reap) in 1959. The Ambassador of South Vietnam to Cambodia, Mr. Ngo Trong Hieu, was directly implicated, and by association, the U.S. There were also the numerous border incidents between the Cambodian forces on the one hand and the forces of the Khmer Serei, of South Vietnam, and of Thailand on the other.

Cambodia believed itself to be sheltered from all danger by its policy of neutrality. This neutrality, however, ran counter to the interests of the South Vietnamese, the Thai, and the U.S., who sought to tear Cambodia away from its position of "wait and see" and its leaning toward Communism. As for the leaders of the red bloc, they did not remain inactive either; they did not fail to wave in the face of Cambodian authorities the dangerous game plan of the imperialists. Within Cambodia, anti-imperialist sentiment among the masses of poor reached the proportions of a cult and was reflected in the first-ever exchange of gun fire between the Khmer Rouge (Khmer Communists) and Cambodian authorities, this incident occurring in Battambang Province in 1967.

In the eastern part of the country the same sort of confrontations were taking place in the new provinces of Mondolkiri and Ratanakiri where the majority of the population was comprised of the ethnic minorities known as *Meo, Kha, Phnong, Jarai.*

Neutrality of the Left

During the 1962 Geneva Conference on Laos, Prince Sihanouk recommended a neutralized zone made up of Cambodia and Laos. The outcome of this conference left him disappointed, however, because not only was his idea rejected, he also saw Laos partitioned. The prospect of Cambodia turning into another Laos in the future deeply worried him and led him to adopt a new policy line which sought to strike a certain balance between the east and the west in Cambodia.

During this same period, the situation in South Vietnam continued to deteriorate. And when the military coup against Ngo Dinh Diem's regime occurred in November 1963, during which the South Vietnamese president was killed, Prince Sihanouk was faced with a political dilemma of having to choose between two alternatives: Communism or the Free World. He found neither sufficiently reassuring for his regime and Cambodia's future.

Sihanouk had been led to believe in the growing danger of U.S. aid from his visit to Peking in early 1963, during which the Chinese expressed their concern about the increasing American presence in Cambodia on the one hand and the presence of CIA-supported Khmer Serei troops on the other. As a result, at the conclusion of the Special National Congress which he convened on 19 November 1963, Sihanouk renounced U.S. aid altogether, apparently to avoid American interference in Khmer domestic affairs.

Two days later, Prince Sihanouk unsuccessfully tried to initiate a limited international conference—with the participation of the U.S., South Vietnam and all countries directly involved in Cambodia's security—designed to guarantee Cambodia's sovereignty within its current national boundaries. His attempt was dictated by the uncertainty of South Vietnam's future and the more disquieting foreign aid that Vietnamese Communists were receiving.

In his reasoning, Prince Sihanouk had said in effect:

> Quite frankly, it is not in our interests to deal with the West, which represents the present but not the future. In 10 years time, there will probably be in Thailand, which always responds to the dominant wind, a pro-Chinese neutralist government, and South Vietnam will certainly be governed by Ho Chi Minh or his successor. Our interests are served by dealing with the camp that one day will dominate the whole of Asia —and by coming to terms before its victory—in order to obtain the best terms possible.[2]

Despite the fact that Prince Sihanouk saw his real enemies to be the Communists, his change of policy, and especially his derogatory remarks about the U.S., exasperated the U.S. government to the point that one day Secretary Dean Rusk reportedly summoned the Cambodian ambassador to his office and told him, "Mr. Ambassador, you've got to remember that small countries are not the only ones capable of outrage. Big countries can get mad too."

Since the U.S. had not supported a conference such as the one suggested by Sihanouk, the Prince, it was reported, authorized a popular demonstration in March 1964 during which the U.S. and British embassies in Phnom Penh were seriously damaged.

During his visit to Peking in September 1964, Sihanouk met with Pham Van Dong, North Vietnam's prime minister, and asked him to recognize Cambodia's territorial integrity. Dodging the issue, Dong in his turn asked Sihanouk to refer to the National Liberation Front (NLF) which could represent South Vietnam in this matter.

In December 1964, American and Cambodian officials met in New Delhi, through the good offices of the Indian government. Although very cordial, this encounter failed to improve the already tense relations between Cambodia and the U.S.

In early 1965, Great Britain and the U.S. finally decided on an international conference to guarantee Cambodia's national boundaries in an apparent effort to slow Cambodia's slide toward Communism. Unfortunately, this was too late because Sihanouk, who was now firmly on

---

[2]Leifer, Michael, Cambodia, <u>The Search for Security</u>, New York, F.A. Praeger, 1967.

Peking's side, insisted that the NLF represent South Vietnam in this conference. Obviously, this was unacceptable to the western powers. And so a further step had been taken, and on 3 May 1965 Sihanouk severed diplomatic relations with Washington.[3]

In this period of Sihanouk's very active political maneuvering, during which he sought to keep in line with current international trends, in order ultimately to align Cambodia on the Communist side, several military events occurred in this part of Southeast Asia, particularly in South Vietnam, which seemed to justify Sihanouk's attitude if a parallel is drawn between them and the actions he had taken.

By that time, the very famous Ho Chi Minh Trail which crossed the 18th parallel had already been well established along the entire length of Laos. The rights of the Pathet Lao in this country had been recognized since the 1962 Geneva Conference. In South Vietnam, the VC/NVA presence, which had caused serious turmoil and was barely under control by the government, continued to increase and expand its influence in most provinces. All of these events tended to confirm Sihanouk's thesis as to South Vietnam's fate in the first place and by way of Cambodia, that of the Indochinese peninsula in general.

At the same time that the spirit of regional organization and solidarity was growing, the movement of "non-alignment" began to manifest itself on the international scene. The first conference of non-aligned nations opened in Belgrade in 1962. Cambodia was one of the first to identify itself with this movement and soon found itself in numerous company, as the newly independent states of Asia and Africa, the states of Eastern Europe, the underdeveloped states, and the emerging nations joined in. The movement grew in such a way as to admit the countries of the Communist and Socialist blocs. This political leap on the part of

---

[3] Sihanouk had broken relations with Thailand in October 1961 and the Republic of Vietnam in August 1963.

the Communists gained points for them everywhere, whether on the local, regional, or international scene. The war in the Republic of Vietnam came to be qualified as "the ordering of Vietnamese internal affairs." The theatre of military operations passed into the hands of the great powers. The two camps began to match each other by providing materiel support for the battlefield with inevitable consequences. Each side paid the heavy price of its sacrifices.

The slide of Cambodia into the Communist side of the international political balance was apparent from 1962 forward; in that year, Sihanouk initiated intense political contacts with the PRC. As a result the PRC agreed to aid Cambodia in all areas, economic, military, etc., without any prior conditions. The PRC asked only that in return Cambodia disassociate itself from the Free World for good, particularly from the U.S., and demonstrate its sympathy for the cause of anti-imperialism.

The Origins of the Khmer Republic

The political leadership of the Cambodia of 1970 clearly had one foot firmly planted in the Communist camp. The policy of "double-dealing" practices by Prince Sihanouk favored the Vietnamese and Khmer Communists with disastrous results for Cambodia, a fact not lost on Sihanouk who did not fail to vehemently denounce before all the world and on many occasions the continuous infiltrations and subversion of the Communists and the peril for Cambodia which they posed. The divorce of Cambodia from the U.S. and its subsequent marriage with the PRC constituted before the world and within Southeast Asia a new level of Communist penetration into the Indochinese peninsula. It changed significantly the face of the war in South Vietnam and provoked in Cambodia's neighbors a sense of the danger of Communist expansion. Within Cambodia this marriage signified the victory of Communist factions, who began to appear little by little from their hiding, and the defeat of the pro-imperialist factions.

The trickery of the political games played by Sihanouk from 1954 to 1970 earned for him a certain standing on the international scene as "leader of his country"; but in his own country these tactics met with total defeat. What was unpardonable in Khmer religious and intellectual circles was Sihanouk's practice of abruptly changing loyalties or a policy of "consistent inconsistency" (*politique de constance dans l'inconstance*) an expression used by Lt. General Sisowath Sirik Matak in an open letter to his cousin, Prince Sihanouk, dated August 27, 1973. This gap between reputation at home and abroad widened with time for the situation within Cambodia gave scarcely any reason for satisfaction. Actually, Vietnamese Communist forces had already occupied large portions of Khmer territory in the east, southeast, and south. The Cambodian population of these regions, weary of bearing the violent persecutions and exactions of the invading forces, were forced to abandon everything and seek refuge farther in the interior, away from the Vietnamese Communists.

A silent rage began to spread through the population as the people came to realize the political trickery of Prince Sihanouk, a trickery which led to an aggravation of the situation. That peace of which Cambodia had prided itself on being the sole beneficiary in Southeast Asia was rapidly fading. In vain, Sihanouk publicly and repeatedly denounced the exactions of the Vietnamese Communists. Finally he announced to the nation that he would depart on January 6, 1970 for France to take the cures dictated by his physical condition, following which he would travel to the Soviet Union and the People's Republic of China to discuss economic and military aid. In intellectual circles in Cambodia there was general agreement that the two latter visits had no other real purpose than to find some way to resolve the political difficulties caused on the one hand by the Vietnamese Communists and by the activities of the Khmer Communists on the other, activities which were becoming more widespread all the time.

Sihanouk's absence from Cambodia provided the pretext for several demonstrations. On the 8th and 9th of March 1970 there were demonstrations in the capitals of the provinces of Svay Rieng and Prey Veng. Even in Phnom Penh there were frankly violent demonstrations organized by university students against the Embassies of North Vietnam and the PRG and supported among intellectual circles. Mr. Cheng Heng, acting

Chief of State, and General Lon Nol, Chief of Government (Prime Minister), tried in vain to make Prince Sihanouk aware of a situation which was worsening day by day in Cambodia. When the Prince refused to receive the delegation sent to brief him, Lon Nol and Cheng Heng turned to the National Assembly and the Council of the Kingdom.

The two legislative bodies assembled to consider the problem of Sihanouk's conduct and absence. They were the same two bodies which had ten years earlier, in 1960, designated the Prince as Chief of State. On March 18, 1970, after a long and historic debate, the two bodies by unanimous vote withdrew their confidence in Prince Sihanouk and removed him from office. The members accused him, among other things, of having authorized North Vietnamese and Viet Cong troops to illegally occupy Khmer territory and establish bases (sanctuaries) during the latter half of the 1960's, an occupation in flagrant violation of Khmer neutrality as provided by the Geneva Accords of 1954. The occupation was characterized as well, as an attack on the independence, sovereignty, and territorial integrity of the country.

Following action by the legislative bodies, the Prince Chief of State was tried by the High Court of Justice and condemned to death in absentia for high treason.[4]

Two important events which followed the removal of Sihanouk deserve noting at this point. The first was the meeting on March 16, 1970 between representatives of the Cambodian Government (Ministry of Foreign Affairs and the General Staff of the Armed Forces) and representatives of the Embassies of North Vietnam and the PRG, a meeting which had as its purpose the securing of Communist agreement to evacuate their forces from Cambodia in accordance with the demand contained in the Cambodian government's official note of March 12, 1970. Unfortunately, the two-hour meeting at the Ministry of Foreign Affairs produced no results. The second event was the initiative of the PRC after having broken

---

[4]In French: *Condamné à mort par contumace par le Tribunal de la Haute Justice pour haute trahison.*

diplomatic relations with Cambodia on May 5, 1970. Chinese Communist emmissaries sent from Peking for the express purpose declared to General Lon Nol, by then head of the government, that the "matter between Sihanouk and the Khmer government was nothing more than an internal problem" and that Peking could overlook personalities involved so long as the Cambodian side accepted the following three conditions:

1. Permit China to continue to use Khmer territory to resupply the NVA/VC with weapons, munitions, and materiel so as to continue the war against South Vietnam.

2. Authorize the NVA/VC to establish their bases in Cambodia as before.

3. Continue to support North Vietnam and the Viet Cong with propaganda.

This demarche by China met with total rejection on the part of the Cambodian government.

In a note dated March 25, 1970 the Khmer invited the North Vietnamese to discuss for a second time the problem of the evacuation of their forces. The meeting was set for the 27th of March. But on the 25th of March the Republic of Poland advised the Khmer officially of the departure from Phnom Penh of the Embassies of North Vietnam and the Viet Cong, to take place on 27 March when the two groups would travel by ICC aircraft to Hanoi.

Immediately after the armed aggression by NVA/VC forces, which was launched against Cambodia from their sanctuaries along the South Vietnamese border, the Khmer Republic government made countless appeals to the United Nations (UN) Security Council for an end to that aggression. Instead of taking action on the Cambodian request, this international organ (the UN Security Council) merely replied that in view of Cambodia's being governed by the 1954 Geneva Accords, the Khmer Republic had better apply to the co-chairmen of the 1954 Geneva Conference (Soviet Union and Great Britain).

On 31 March 1970, therefore, in a memorandum addressed to the ambassadors of the Soviet Union and Great Britain, the Cambodian government expressed its deep concern about increasingly flagrant and repeated violations of the 1954 Geneva Accords by the armed forces of the Democratic Republic of Vietnam (DRV) and those of the PRG of South Vietnam. These forces, the memorandum said, not only refused to withdraw from the Cambodian territory, they were now launching overt attacks against Khmer outposts and defense forces within the Khmer national boundaries. The Cambodian government then demanded the reinstallment of the International Control Commission on an urgent basis.

On 6 April 1970, the United Nations Secretariat announced that Secretary General U Thant had decided "to deal with the authorities who effectively controlled the situation in Cambodia"; in other words, with the Phnom Penh government and not with the former Chief of State. This first and only positive response by the UN constituted, in effect, an answer to the claims made by Prince Sihanouk who, in a message addressed to His Excellency U Thant, represented himself as the only legal holder of Cambodian authority.

In addition to the events described above, the chronology of political activities in Cambodia after March 18 can be established as follows:

1. March 26 and 27. Trouble provoked by the Vietnamese Communists in Kompong Cham Province, and particularly in the provincial capital, where two deputies who tried to calm the demonstrators were knifed to death in broad daylight and in the midst of the crowd. The office of the governor was partially burned.

2. March 29. The North Vietnamese and Viet Cong Embassies announced the unilateral rupture of diplomatic relations with Cambodia and their refusal to resume discussions concerning the withdrawal of their forces.

3. March 29. Launching of North Vietnamese and Viet Cong aggression in several Cambodian provinces. (The details are covered in the next chapter.)

4. April 11. Popular manifestation called "The March of National Concord" at the National Sports Complex in Phnom Penh as a sign of support for the government of Lon Nol; the manifestation also demanded the establishment of a Republican regime for the country.

5. April 14. Lon Nol appealed to the countries of all world blocs to aid him in the fight against Vietnamese Communism.

6. April 30. American and South Vietnamese troops launched their attacks against NVN and VC sanctuaries located along the frontier in the eastern provinces of Cambodia.

7. May 5. The PRC broke diplomatic relations with Cambodia.

8. May 13. Reestablishment of diplomatic relations with Thailand, which had been broken in 1961.

9. May 16 and 17. Indonesia brought ten nations together at a conference in Djakarta, aimed at finding a way of restoring peace in Cambodia.

10. May 19. Restoration of diplomatic relations with South Korea, broken since 1966.

11. May 27. Restoration of diplomatic relations with the Republic of South Vietnam, broken since 1963.

12. June 25. "General Mobilization" of Cambodia in order to deal with the invasion.

13. June 30. Final date set for ending the cross-border operations of U.S. forces against NVA/VC sanctuaries in Cambodia.

14. August 28. Mr. Spiro Agnew, Vice President of the U.S., made an official visit to Cambodia.

15. September 15. Mr. Emory C. Swank, the first U.S. envoy of ambassadorial rank since resumption of diplomatic relations in 1969, presented his credentials to Mr. Chang Heng, Chief of State. Before that date, the U.S. Mission was presided over by Charge d'Affairs Lloyd M. Rives.

16. October 9. Proclamation of the Khmer Republic.

The above chronology explains in itself the initial reaction of certain nations to the entry of Cambodia into war.

CHAPTER II

Cambodia and the Communists

Vietnamese Communist Use of Khmer Territory

The penetration of Cambodia by Vietnamese Communist forces, complete with their logistic systems, took place along two separate axes. The first was across the Vietnamese borders with Laos and South Vietnam, with the complicity of Khmer communist cells, cadred by the North Vietnamese. The second was by way of the Port of Sihanoukville or Kompong Som.

As a matter of fact, communist forces began, as early as 1962, to infiltrate into the northern and eastern border provinces of Cambodia, particularly in Stung Treng, Ratanakiri, Kratie, Prey Veng, Svay Rieng, Takeo and Kampot. By 1969, these infiltrated forces were estimated at 50,000 men installed in "sanctuaries" whose importance varied from a simple transit center to all types of bases, having complete military, logistic, and rest facilities, such as the bases in Ratanakiri, Mondolkiri, and Snoul. *(Map 2)*

Because of his "double dealing," Prince Sihanouk simply omitted, in all of his public statements, references to the existence of these infiltrations, and most particularly, the sanctuaries. He did this apparently to cover up his complicity with North Vietnam and the Viet Cong on the one hand, and to reject the pretext of "enemy pursuit" by U.S. and South Vietnam forces on the other.

The incorporation of Cambodia into the communist supply system kept pace with the development of the flow of VC/NVA infiltration into Cambodia, and the development of political relations between Cambodia and the Provisional Revolutionary (Viet Cong) Government (PRG).

From the communist viewpoint, the Ho Chi Minh Trail constituted in fact the only strategic route leading south. Under constant

Map 2 — Cambodian Government Information on Locations of Principal NVA/VC Base Areas in Cambodia in 1969

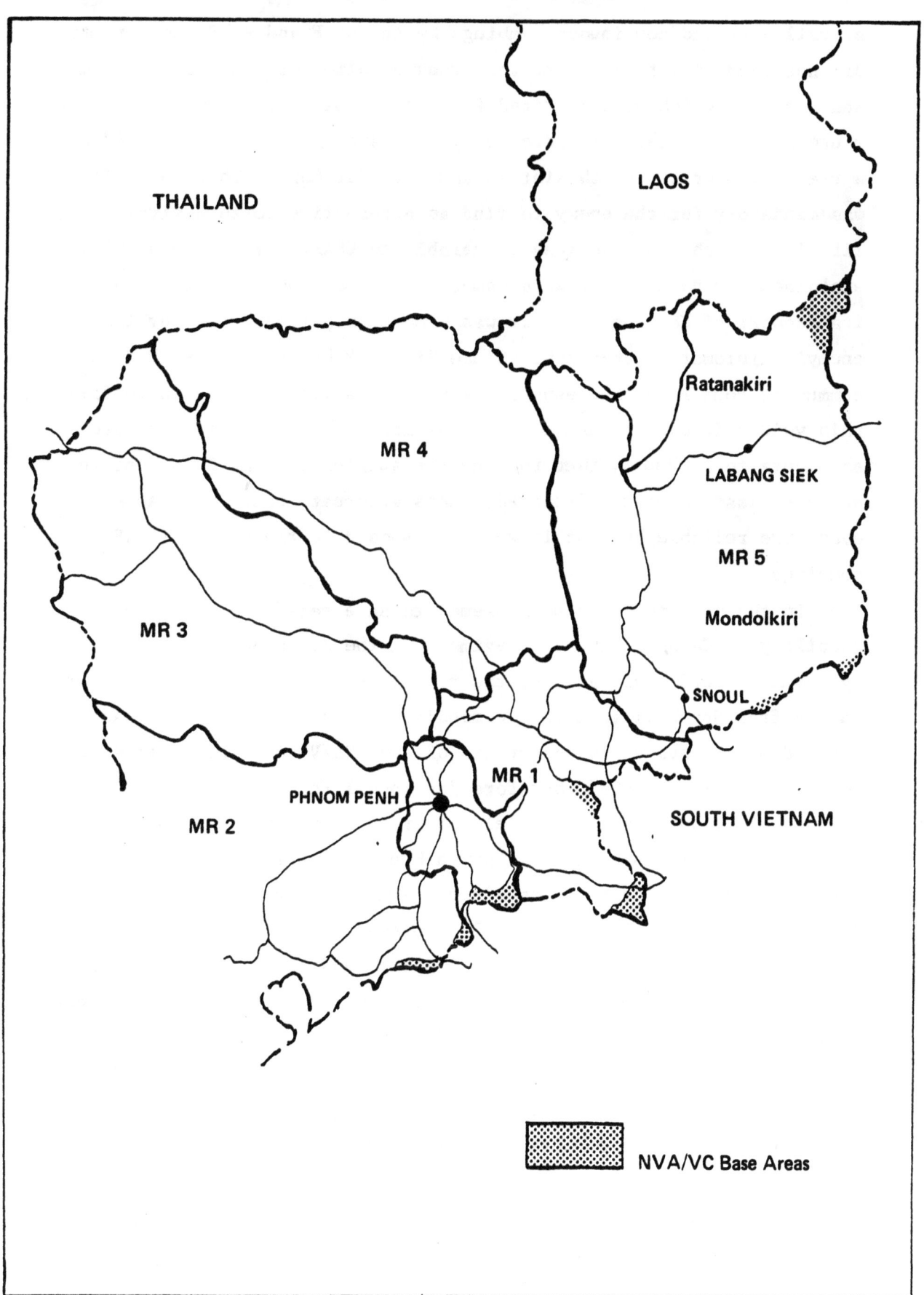

surveillance and continuous bombings by the USAF and VNAF, this route did not lend itself easily to the transportation of the heavy equipment and materiel which were required for NVA troops in the south. If this route were completely interdicted by U.S. and RVN forces, it would be a real disaster for North Vietnam and the Viet Cong. Therefore, it was mandatory for the enemy to find an alternative to this vital lifeline, which would be less vulnerable to USAF/VNAF bombings. This explained why he turned toward Cambodia, or more particularly, toward its seaport of Kompong Som. It was a most propitious time for the enemy's diplomatic maneuvers. Since Sihanouk had repudiated U.S. aid, communist countries, and especially Red China were rushing in to fill this void. It became just a matter of increasing the volume of aid shipments to Cambodia, then routing the surplus to NVA/VC forces; the process passed almost undetected. This alternate route was deemed even more reliable because it was not exposed to the risks of U.S. bombings.

In the meantime, Sihanouk seemed to have serious doubts about the viability of Cambodia and his regime. On the one hand he was harassed by unending border violations, the result of the pursuit of Communist forces from South Vietnam into Cambodia; on the other hand, he was worried by the subversive maneuvers of the NVA/VC and the local Khmer Communists. He launched therefore "an appeal for the recognition and respect of Cambodia's territorial integrity within its present boundaries." To this appeal, only Nguyen Huu Tho, president of the NLF, and Pham Van Dong, North Vietnam's prime minister responded favorably by their letters of 6 and 8 June 1967 respectively. The U.S. took nearly two years to respond, until 15 April 1969. All this resulted in a further consolidation of relations between Cambodia and the enemy which prompted Sihanouk on 13 June 1969 to extend formal recognition to the Provisional Revolutionary Government (PRG) of South Vietnam, created just 12 days earlier.

The first formal cooperation agreement between Cambodia and the PRG was concluded soon after Nguyen Tan Phat, PRG prime minister, paid a 6-day official visit to Phnom Penh on 29 June 1969. Designated "Trade and Payment Agreement," it was signed in Phnom Penh on 25

September 1969. Thus were formalized the illegal activities that Prince Sihanouk had already authorized for several years. The seaport of Kompong Som was now wide open to receive shipments of supplies intended for NVA/VC troops. These supplies were subsequently moved by truck to their destinations via Route 4. Unloading and transportation operations were the exclusive activities of a certain Hak Ly who owned about 200 cargo trucks. From Kompong Som to Kompong Speu or Phnom Penh, the cargos were carried on trucks rented by Hak Ly. Then from these places to final destination, the transportation was provided by Hak Ly's own trucks, which usually unloaded at Snoul and Mimot.

To rid himself of troublesome witnesses, Sihanouk ordered a black-listing of undesirable foreign correspondents, especially those of the free world. Finally, citing financial difficulties and criticizing its inactivity, Sihanouk terminated the mandate of the International Control Commission (ICC) on 6 October 1969. On his official request, all members of this international organization left Cambodia by the end of the year.

Thus it was accomplished that the Communists, by painstaking preparation, took advantage of the political uncertainties in that part of the world, and of the dilemma of Sihanouk. What was the attitude of the Cambodian people toward this political change by Sihanouk? Generally speaking, there were two contrasting schools of thought: the corrupt, who were partisan and enthusiastic; and the uncorrupt, who were disquieted. The first category consisted of courtiers and businessmen to whom this new kind of business had brought substantial and significant profits. The second category was mostly made up of intellectuals who found this new game risky. While the dissidents did not wholly approve of Sihanouk, with regard to his cooperation with North Vietnam and the Viet Cong, their manifestations were not vocal either, and one might think that they were indifferent. But on examination it could be seen that their silence was justified by the facts described below.

In the first place, Cambodia was the least endowed country in terms of materiel assets and particularly military equipment, as compared to its eastern or western neighbors. This was perhaps a result of its desire to stay away from either sphere of influence. Because of its neutral stance, Cambodia did not have much attraction for rich and powerful countries, especially since its only resources came from agricultural products. Elsewhere in the world, industrial powers seemed always attracted by countries with rich underground resources. Cambodia, therefore, had been forsaken for a long time; it was almost completely ignored.

Although Cambodia had received some foreign aid from certain friendly countries of the west since 1954, this aid was only dispensed at a trickling rate and after lengthy and complicated procedures. With the exception of rubber production, a French concession which was rather obsolescent, industry was non-existent, being at the level of handicraft and cottage enterprise.

From his relations with the Communists, Sihanouk was therefore able to obtain at least something with which to equip his country, such as the Khmer-Russian Hospital, the Institute of Technology, cement, paper, glass and plywood production plants and some military equipment as well. With regard to military aid, Cambodia usually received a quota which was alloted in each cargo shipment unloaded at Kompong Som.

All this largely explained the passivity and silence of dissident intellectuals.

Khmer Communist Political Origins

After the event of 18 March, Prince Sihanouk took refuge in Peking, where his activities led to the creation of FUNK (*Front Uni National du Kampuchea*) and the formation of GRUNK (*Government Royal d'Union National du Kampuchea*) as well as the Indochina summit meeting in Canton in April 1970.[1] For the pro-communist Khmer, these events offered them the opportunity to pursue their goals more actively and more openly. With the

---

[1] FUNK, Front of National Union of Kampuchea. GRUNK, Royal Government of National Union of Kampuchea. Kampuchea is a French rendering of an ancient name for Cambodia. The acronyms FUNK and GRUNK will be used throughout this monograph to designate these two entities.

help of the NVA/VC they were able to extend their influence and to develop rapidly, both politically and militarily.

The political movement of the Khmer pro-Communists passed through several stages, marked by parallel transformations:

1. 1945-1954. During this period, there was development of the movement of Khmer Issarak in Cambodia, the Lao-Issarak in Laos and the Viet Minh in Vietnam, movements all affiliated with the Indochinese Communist Party, directed by Ho Chi Minh.

2. 1950. This year marked the beginning of the disintegration of the Khmer Issarak movement as certain of the leaders rallied to Prince Sihanouk, then King of Cambodia. Certain other elements of the Khmer Issarak, however, remained true to their communist ideology, and under the leadership of Son Ngoc Minh, then in North Vietnam, went underground and continued their activities in Cambodia.

3. 1951 saw the dissolution of the Khmer Issarak movement and the formation of the "Prachea Chon Party" or Party of the People.[2]

4. In 1954, at the time of the conclusion of the Geneva Accords in 1954, it was the Prachea Chon Party that decided to send some 5,000 communist sympathizers to North Vietnam for political indoctrination and military training.

---

[2] According to the article by R. P. Paringaux, published 31 March 1978 by the French newspaper Le Monde (weekly selection) this movement took the name of *Parti Revolutionnaire du Peuple Cambodgien* (Revolutionary Party of the Cambodian People).

5. In 1960, the Prachea Chon Party changed its name to "Workers Party" and constituted a central committee for the party at the conclusion of its first plenary session.[3]

6. The second plenary session of the Worker's Party in 1963 continued in effect the decisions taken during the first plenary session in 1960.

7. In 1965, Son Ngoc Minh decided to profit from the difficult relations between the U.S. and Cambodia, following rupture of diplomatic relations in May of that year, by bringing about the return to Cambodia of a certain number of the Khmer Viet Minh who had been trained and indoctrinated in Hanoi. This corresponded with the sharp increase in Communist subversive activity noted during that period. These activities were brutally repressed by Prince Sihanouk, and this repression, carried out systematically, forced several dozen of these Khmer Communists and their sympathizers to go underground.

8. In 1966, the principal red leaders, Khieu Sampaan, Hu Nim and Hou Yuon, disappeared from Phnom Penh; they had been involved, with the help of the Khmer Viet Minh cadres from Hanoi, in carrying out subversive activities in Prey Veng and Kompong Cham. During the same year, there was a proposal to change the name of the Workers Party to "Communist Party of Kampuchea" and to adopt the basic political line

---

[3] In order to better understand this evolution, note the following footnote to the article by Mr. Parengaux already cited:

> "According to Radio Phnom Penh of 20 March 1978, Mr. Pol Pot told a group of Yugoslavia journalists that he had become the secretary of the Khmer Communist Party par interim in 1962, after" ...the secretary had been assassinated by the enemy: and that he had been confirmed in the position of secretary by the second party congress in 1963. Mr. Pol Pot added that he belonged to the anti-French underground from 1953 to 1954. Furthermore, according to official statements in Phnom Penh, the Khmer Communist Party was founded not in 1961, but on 30 September 1960.

of the Marxists-Leninists.[4] These proposals were destined to be approved during the 3d Plenary Assembly which would take place before 1970.

A study of the enemy would be incomplete without analysis of the various groups or tendencies among the enemy shortly after March 18, 1970.

Within the FUNK there existed three such tendencies:

1. Those Khmer Communists and Khmer Viet Minh who had gone underground before March 18, 1970, and who were decided on a war of long duration. This extremist group opposed the nomination of Sihanouk as President of FUNK and also opposed to the continued practice of Buddhism.

2. The group known as the *Khmer Romdas*, who were loyal to Sihanouk.

3. A moderate group within the Khmer revolutionary movement directed by intellectuals under the leadership of Khieu Samphan, Hu Nim, and Hou Yuon.

There was little harmony among the three tendencies, especially as it concerned political tactics. The Khmer Rouge and the Khmer Viet Minh called for all-out war until final victory, and for absolute non-cooperation with Sihanouk and his partisans. Even though they were in agreement on this point, there was some misunderstanding between the two groups. In general, the Khmer Viet Minh had a superiority complex vis-a-vis the Khmer Rouge. The Khmer Viet Minh were proud to have been educated abroad in a socialist country, and they underestimated the purely local Khmer Rouge, and the strategic and tactical competence of the latter for making revolutionary war.

The Khmer revolutionaries of Khieu Samphan et al, for their part, sided with Sihanouk on strategy shortly after the creation of FUNK and GRUNK, and were given key posts in these two entities. Khieu Samphan, Hu Yuon, and Hu Nim expected to make use of Sihanouk as they had done

---

[4] Note how this contradicts the statements attributed to Pol Pot in the Le Monde article cited above.

before; they organized behind him, reinforced themselves, and even called for his return to power for a period of transition. This would have given them the time to prepare the final phase of their revolution, that is the overthrow of Sihanouk, and the taking of power by their party. One could notice that the first pro-Sihanouk movement created at the start of the conflict, lost its influence little by little, and was eclipsed by the progressive expansion of the Revolutionary Movement.

Khmer Communist Military Development

Before 18 March 1970, there were two general periods in the development of Khmer communist military units and institutions. Between 1945 and 1954, the presence of the Viet Minh in Cambodia contributed to the formation of an auxiliary Khmer-Viet Minh force estimated at several thousand. After the Geneva conference of 1954, this force was disbanded. One part, along with certain sympathizers, moved to Hanoi, while the rest either returned to a more or less normal life or went underground. Between 1965 and 1967, several dozen intellectuals, mostly teachers and discontented students from the Sihanoukist regime went underground. Together with former elements of the Khmer-Viet Minh, these intellectuals constituted an embryo force which began to confront the established order by force of arms. The zones of action of these elements were found in the provinces of Battambang, Kampot, Prey Veng and in the frontier zone from Kompong Cham to Kompong Thom.

The concept for the organization of Khmer Communist forces after 18 March 1970, was established at the Indochinese summit, held in Canton in April 1970. There plans were made for a force of 50,000 regulars, including three divisions, all to be equipped by Communist China. They would be modeled after the Viet Cong and the Pathet Lao as follows:

1. Popular forces and auto-defense groups at village *(Phum)* and city *(Khum)* levels.

2. Regular forces with a territorial mission, organized at the levels of county or district *(Srok)* and province *(Khet)*.

3. Regular forces, having no territorial responsibility, and functioning under the orders of the general military command. The above

forces were expected to undertake military tasks under the same conditions as units of the Viet Cong or Pathet Lao, with the support of North Vietnam.

In practice, the first FUNK units were made up of: ex-Khmer-Viet Minh elements; some who had been Khmer Rouge prior to 18 March 1970; and certain individuals who deserted the FANK and the Provincial Guard immediately following the 18th of March. Because these cadre were of uneven military capability, the VC/NVA established special training centers for them and for new recruits, and located them throughout the regions they controlled in Cambodia and lower Laos. On leaving these training centers, the Khmer elements were incorporated into various VC/NVA units who trained them further in practical combat. As they became more accomplished, the Khmer elements participated more and more actively along side the VC/NVA in actions against the FANK. As the Khmer Communist infrastructure developed, autonomous FUNK units began to appear on the battlefield; these had been judged competent by the VC/NVA command and freed to operate more or less independently. The total strength of the FUNK was estimated at 12,000 to 15,000 by about the end of 1970; between 18 and 25,000 in November 1971; and between 35 and 40,000 in 1972.

The development of Khmer Communist forces took place in three discernible phases. 1970 to 1972 was a period of organization, recruitment and training, leading to the fielding of small units and cells acting in the capacity of auxiliaries to Vietnamese Communist units. The period from 1972 to mid-1974 saw the formation and deployment of the Khmer Rouge units of battalion and regimental size, cadred by VC/NVA personnel, and operating in their assigned sectors according to orders received from COSVN. The Khmer units received support (operational, logistic and politico/military) from regular VC/NVA units. During this same phase, specialized Khmer sabotage and suicide units were also trained and deployed. The final phase, from mid-1974 to 1975 saw the appearance of Khmer Rouge Divisions. Each of the divisions and regiments was assigned to zones and sectors corresponding essentially to the Military Regions and Military Sub-divisions, of the Khmer Republic.

Considering the phases discussed above, it was to be expected that the major Communist military activities in Cambodia would be carried out initially by the VC/NVA using their central military command activity, COSVN, which was actually located in Cambodia, in the eastern part of Kratie Province. From the outset of hostilities, the following major Vietnamese Communist units were identified:

1. The 1st NVA Division, operating in the area south and southeast of Phnom Penh.

2. The 5th, 7th, and 9th NVA Divisions, located east of the Mekong, in areas north and east known as their sanctuaries. Note that the 9th Division often placed its units west of the Mekong for certain periods.

3. An additional division of VC/NVA forces, called the C40 Division, operating in the area north and northwest of the Tonle Sap Lake.

4. A large base known as the B3 Base, established in the tri-border region of Cambodia, Laos and Vietnam. *(Map 3)* The territory occupied by the Vietnamese units at the start of hostilities in Cambodia was turned over for administrative purposes to FUNK authorities, who, with the help of VC/NVA regional units designated FUNK regional units to ensure their defense and to see to the organization of the population. During this first phase, from March 1970 to 1972, an increase in the strength and proficiency of the FUNK forces was apparent. However, their actions were still limited, even incoherent, due probably to the absence of a military high command and an overall strategy. During this same period, specialized training centers were opened in various parts of Cambodia (Kompong Thom, Kompong Speu, Siem Reap, Kompong Cham, Kratie and Kampot) with a view toward perfecting the specialized training of the elements of FUNK. The year 1972 thus marked the beginning of the so-called "Khmerization" of the war in Cambodia.

Throughout the war, the Khmer Communist struggle was as much political as military. Among the various Khmer communist units the leaders struggled to gain influence among themselves and among the masses of the population located in the zones under their control. In this regard, despite a strong position among the key posts of FUNK, the Sihanoukist persuasion was distinctly under-represented in the lower echelons, where

Map 3 — FANK Information as to Deployment of VC/NVA in Cambodia, 1970

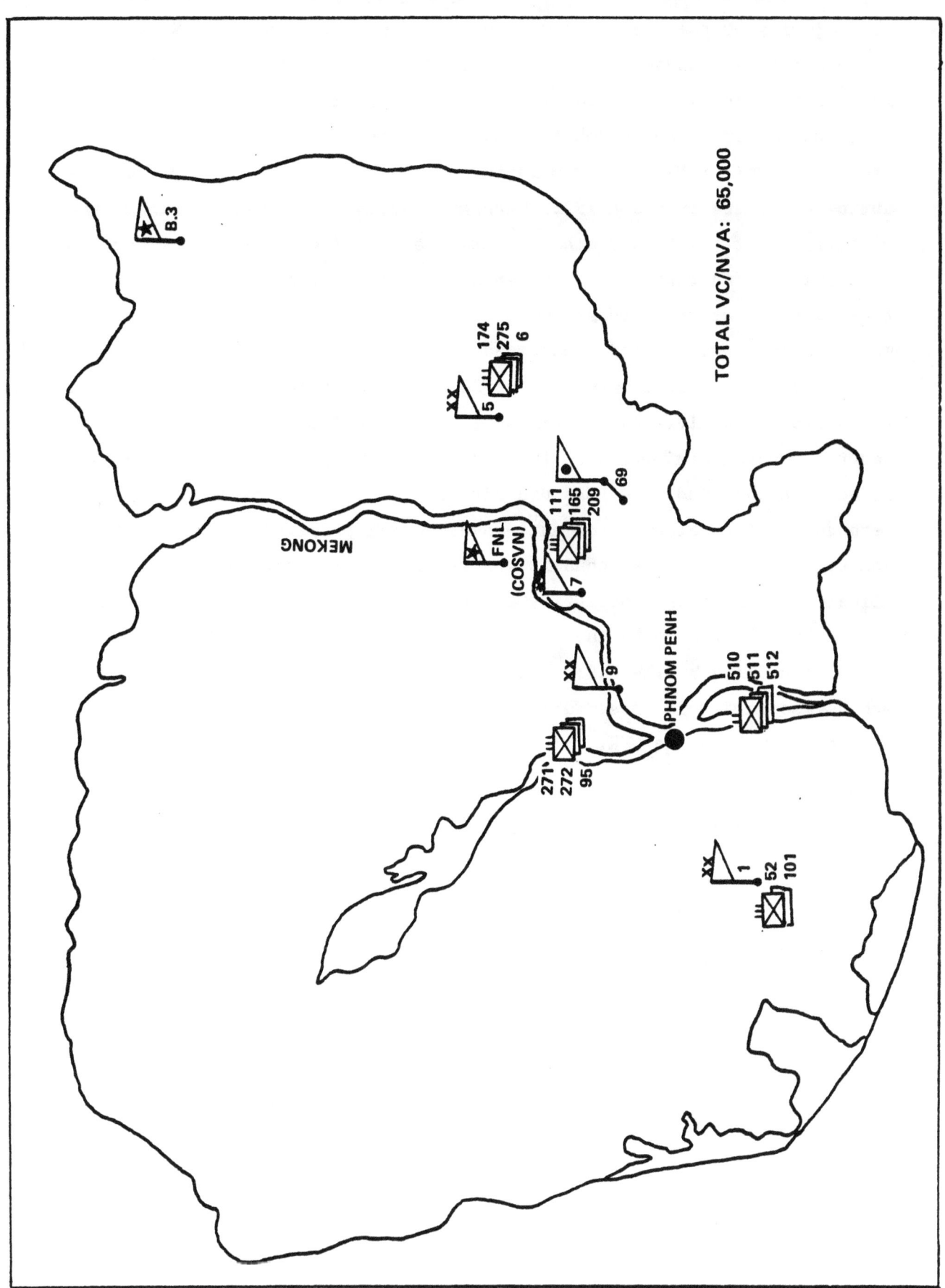

the majority of the positions were occupied by Khmer from the Khmer Rouge-North Vietnamese persuasion. For their part, Khmer revolutionaries, who had previously called for strategic and tactical cooperation with Sihanouk, actively undertook the task of unifying these dissident factions within FUNK. Their efforts seem to have made progress, because during the years 1974 and 1975 there was observed the disappearance from circulation of tracts and other printed matter originated by the various factions, and in their place the appearance of a single overall FUNK line, both in written and spoken propaganda, a development which became more and more intense and widespread.

Against the Government of the Khmer Republic (GKR), then in power, the political activities of FUNK were aimed particularly at bringing about a gradual diminution in the support of the population for the GKR. To achieve this end, the FUNK did not hesitate to use the following methods: the development of anti-governmental propaganda, both written and spoken; cutting the economic supply routes in order to create a climate of crisis and insecurity and to provoke divisions in the population, as manifested by the exodus from communist control toward the zones controlled by the GKR; carrying out of acts of sabotage, terrorism and assassination in those zones where the majority of the population remained loyal to the GKR.

Destruction in Tonle Bet (on Mekong Opposite Kompong Cham)
Following Communist Attacks in April 1970.
Photographed in November 1970

CHAPTER III

The Armed Forces of the Khmer Republic

Origins

Prior to the political event of March 1970, the Royal Khmer Armed Forces (Forces Armées Royales Khmères—FARK) were just a small military organization whose strength did not even reach the authorized ceiling of 35,000 men. They were distributed among three services—the Royal Khmer Army, the Royal Khmer Air Force, and the Royal Khmer Navy—all under the command of a Commander-in-Chief.

The following review shows that at that time the FARK were insignificant as compared to NVA and VC forces, and there were several reasons for this.

Prior to the Geneva Accords of 1954, Cambodia received military aid from France. During that period, therefore, the FARK were equipped with French materiel. The French also provided training for all FARK cadres, most of whom were even sent to France for advanced course. In addition, under the guidance of French advisers, the FARK were structurally similar to a miniature French Army. France, which at that time had just emerged from the First Indochina war, did not have enough resources to make the FARK a strong and modern military force. This French policy was also partly justified by the fact that according to the 1954 Geneva Accords Cambodia was not supposed to make war. The FARK were thus organized and equipped somewhat in a pre-WWII style, a condition which obtained as late as 1954.

Then came the U.S. and its more diversified aid, which included military assistance. The FARK were now subjected to transformation because, with new American equipment, the Command attempted to change the organization of the armed forces. Unfortunately, the quantity of equipment provided by the U.S. was not enough to allow the modernization of the FARK. And when Sihanouk renounced U.S. aid in November 1963, the FARK found themselves midway toward modernization. It was then that there surfaced the first difficulties resulting from the disparity of equipment and material in use -- French and American.

After the rupture of relations with the U.S., the only countries that gave Cambodia military assistance were France (which continued to dispense it at a trickle) and, especially, those of the Communist bloc, first the Soviet Union and then China. The net result of this new assistance was a further aggravation of the existing difficulties, for the FARK now had to contend with three different types of materiel and equipment: French, American, and Communist. It goes without saying that the FARK encountered no end of problems. The divergence of its materiel affected the training of combat and technical personnel, maintenance, and especially the supply of spare parts and ammunition.

All this explained why the FARK were never able to achieve the standardization of their units in order to become a strong and modern military force. Consequently, the primary mission of the FARK remained just territorial -- hence static -- defense. The Royal Khmer Army, which was the largest of the three services in terms of personnel and materiel, was thus assigned this responsibility.

The Army consisted of some 30 infantry battalions, 13-15 separate infantry companies, support battalions (signal, transportation, engineer), one armored reconnaissance regiment (1st ARR), one field artillery battery, and one anti-air artillery battery. All these infantry and support units were under the control of the FARK General Staff whose chief was the Commander-in-Chief. As to technical services such as Medical, Ordnance, Quartermaster, Signal, they were the responsibility of the Service Directorates which came under the Ministry of National Defense. Army units were deployed throughout the country with major concentrations in the northeast (Ratanakiri Province) and around Phnom Penh. *(Map 4)*

General reserve forces consisted only of two light infantry battalions and the combat support battalions (signal, engineer, armor, artillery).

Map 4 — Locations of Principal FARK Ground Units Prior to 18 March 1970

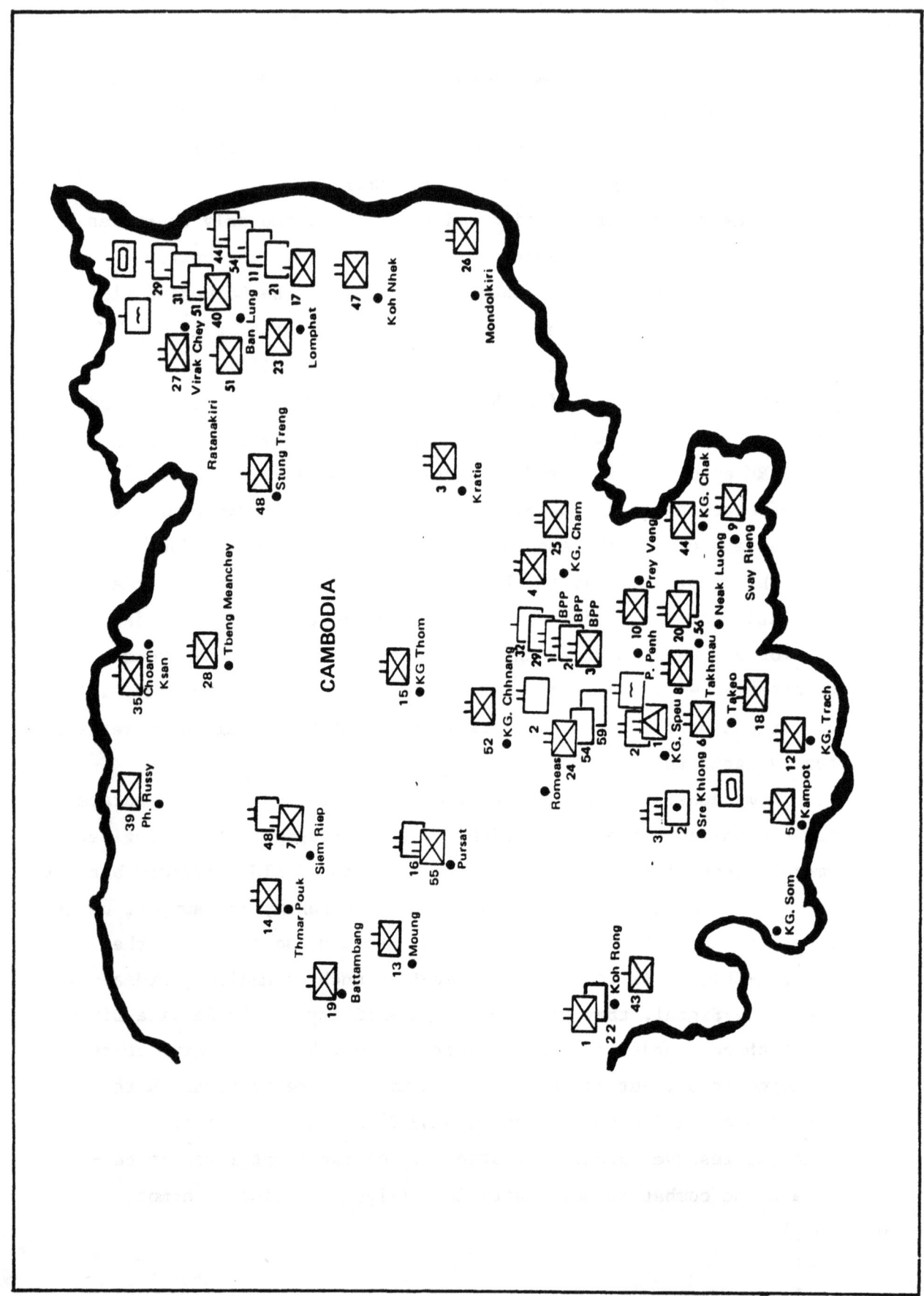

The Royal Air Force had a strength of 1,250 men, composed in great majority of flight crews (pilots, flight engineers, radio operators and flight mechanics) and aviation technicians. Its only airbase at Pochentong was placed under the control of the Commander-in-Chief. Because of its low strength and limited flying assets, the Air Force was far from being able to accomplish its primary mission which was to defend the national airspace. Although there were several airstrips other than Pochentong, they were only used temporarily as emergency landing strips and never as secondary airbases. Therefore, the Air Force was merely considered a combat support arm which provided air transport services to infantry units and occasionally close air support to combat operations.

The Royal Khmer Navy, whose strength was similar to that of the Air Force, had a river base at Chruoy Chang War (Phnom Penh) and a naval base at Ream. As was the case with the Air Force, the Navy did not have very great capability. There was one marine company in the Navy. Most naval activity was confined to the Bassac River, the Mekong, and the Tonle Sap in the vicinity of the Great Lake. As far as naval missions on the high sea were concerned, the Navy was capable only of routine coastal patrols.

Practically speaking, the FARK never had a corps of reserve units as in other armies. Starting about 1955, training was begun of reserve officers from among those high-ranking government officials who volunteered to take a course of basic instruction at the Military Academy or Officer school. This school was established in Phnom Penh after the French had accorded the Khmer a certain autonomy, an initial step prior to granting full independence. Instruction at the school was provided by French military personnel. Because of political considerations at the time, there was adopted for the first Khmer reserve officers an accelerated course of practical and theoretical instruction lasting one year. During the period of peace, from 1954 to 1969, this course was extended in length to two years. This was followed by the initiation of training of non-commissioned officers of the reserves, recruited this time from among the mid-level government officials; this course lasted only about six months.

For lack of a precise plan for the development of the armed forces, the reserve officers and non-commissioned officers were simply incorporated into the corps of active duty officers and non-commissioned officers. They were needed for expansion and to take the place of departing French cadre, as was the case of certain reserve officers in the territorial commands. Furthermore, certain civil servants were given military rank without having ever received military training of any sort; also their military grade was based on their civil rank. For example, the governor of a province or the president of a tribunal could become a Lt. Colonel or Colonel. This was done in a number of cases in order that the entire FARK might be Khmerized by the time of Cambodian independence.

Thus, a number of reserve cadre were trained, but there were no reserve units. Many of the reserve cadre, after their short periods of instruction, simply remained in the active armed forces and never returned to their civilian positions in the government.

As the number of reserve cadre grew, the FARK command became more aware of the lack of reserve units; in other words, the need for some mission for the newly trained reserve cadre. From this came the idea to institute compulsory military service for all Khmer of age for such service. Several laws were issued, and several groups of young people were trained in haste; but no reserve units were ever organized and, as in the case of the reserve officers and noncommissioned officers, the newly-trained recruits were used for fillers in the active units. By this time a number of the active forces were reaching the end of their periods of service or were ready for retirement. Now these errors were seen and understood by those in command, and several measures were adopted to fill this gap. Unfortunately, they met insurmountable obstacles, economic and financial, to mention only two. Cambodia could not afford to have a truly modern or "de luxe" armed force. This was the expression used over and over again by Prince Sihanouk, when addressing the nation, he launched for the first time the idea of the ". . . participation of the armed forces in the economic life of the country. . ." an idea called to mind by the picture Sihanouk formed of the "Grand Army" of Red China during his visits to that country. The general slogan under which the FARK developed was thus," as for the economy, Cambodia will aid itself."

With this changed situation, the impetus of the FARK toward orthodox military capability was essentially halted, and their efforts were devoted almost one hundred percent to the economy. FARK participated actively in the construction of roads, dykes, dams, etc., and the entire administrative and territorial organization of the country, neglecting for the most part military instruction and training. With the mission of FARK thus divided, their value as a defense force was reduced little by little. A battalion or company having a mission of territorial security in the region of the South Vietnam border (Moudolkiri, Ratanakiri, Svay Rieng Provinces, for example) would continue to be devoted to road work and building of model villages rather than looking after the security of the frontier. It was not surprising during this period (1963-1969), described as the time of "The Great Economic Leap of Cambodia," to note the increase of VC/NVA infiltration into the frontier zones of Cambodia and, equally, the construction of Communist base areas to support their war in South Vietnam. Much of the equipment of the FARK was also used to support projects in the economic sector. All vehicles and mechanical equipment received through U.S. and French military assistance were rapidly worn out, and no solution to the problem of their replacement could be found. The same can be said for the condition of materiel in the Navy and Air Force. I remember that in 1963, just prior to the Khmer rejection of U.S. military aid, the French Military Attache and the Chief, U.S. MAAG, Phnom Penh, called on me for the express purpose of registering their dismay and disapproval at the misuse of the equipment which their countries had granted to the FARK.

We have seen how and under what conditions the FARK were conceived, organized, and developed. On the eve of Cambodia's entry into the Indochina conflict, the FARK were armed and equipped in a haphazard way. Training to prepare them for their task had not been pursued. Their cadres (especially the noncommissioned officers) had grown older and older, and the same was true for the private soldiers. In a word, the

FARK of 1970 were a sad lot compared to the VC/NVA, and their first combat against the latter staggered the FARK units despite their real determination to fight to safeguard their country.

The Initial Expansion After March 18, 1970

The sudden attacks launched by the VC/NVA on 29 March 1970 profoundly shocked the units of the FANK (*Forces Armées Nationales Khmères*) involved and dispersed them to the point that by early May 1970 the Cambodian provinces along the RVN border were practically occupied by Vietnamese Communist forces.[1]

In these very first hours, the Salvation Government (*Gouvernement de Sauvetage*) led by General Lon Nol called on the entire population -- from whatever sector -- to organize itself for resistance under the direction of the military command in order to meet the aggression. This was the beginning of the general mobilization of the country to fight a new war of independence. The slogan "National Resistance" was adopted, and it must be admitted that there was great enthusiasm, particularly among the students, teachers, and certain intellectual circles for the abolition of the monarchial regime and for its replacement by a republican regime. The appeal by the Lon Nol government did not go unheeded; groups of young men and women volunteered to serve in the armed forces. Faced with this situation, the FANK high command, having named Lon Nol chief, assumed the heavy responsibility of preparing for the expansion of the FANK to

---

[1] The two acronyms used in this monograph to designate the Cambodian armed forces are based on both Cambodian usage and U.S. reporting practices. FARK stands for <u>Forces Armées Royales Khmères</u>, the official French name for Khmer forces during the Sihanouk period. FANK stands for <u>Forces Armées Nationales Khmères</u>, the official French name used by the Cambodians after 18 March 1970. It was standard U.S. reporting procedure, both before and after the departure of Sihanouk, to use FARK or FANK; no acronym based on an English translation (as in the case of RVNAF for Vietnamese forces) was ever developed to refer to the entire armed forces of Cambodia.

make it capable of carrying out the mission of defending the country. In the following paragraphs are described the initial decisions taken as the result of numerous meetings.

In those areas still under the control of the Khmer government, the military and civil authorities were required to recount and verify the number of persons volunteering for military service, to house them, and to begin their military instruction immediately. At the same time, all available civil and military resources available locally were to be used to establish and equip temporary centers of instruction. Also, the personnel of units overrun during the first VC/NVA attacks and who had been able to reach friendly lines were either regrouped for reconditioning or were used as cadre for the training centers. At the same time, the units of the Provincial Guard (an arm of the National Police and under the direct orders of the various provincial governors) were disbanded and their personnel and equipment spread throughout the FANK. This was no simple operation since many of the Provincial Guard units were known to be pro-Sihanouk. Nevertheless, the transformation of these police into military personnel happily took place without any particular incident. Everywhere, there were efforts to create recruiting stations to serve the volunteers, the majority of whom were at this time drawn from the ranks of high school and university students.

The FANK high command was surprised not only by the outbreak of war but it was surprised—even submerged—by the number of problems it had to face in the organization of the national defense. At the same time that the general enthusiasm was growing, the checks and defeats being suffered by certain FANK units increased to the point that by the month of May 1970 the north and northeast part of Cambodia (the provinces of Stung Treng, Ratanakiri, Kratie, and Mondolkiri) found themselves isolated and beyond the effective control of the FANK high command.

The training centers were directed to cut the period of recruit training by 50 percent as a way of accelerating the formation of new units. Another problem concerned equipment and arms for the new soldiers; what stocks were available in unit supply rooms were quickly expended and without concern for uniformity. In a single combat unit were to be seen an entire range of individual and crew-served weapons. The resupply and logistical support of FANK units as a whole became more burdensome and insoluble as the war developed.

There was another way in which the number of FANK units was increased. This was by means of incorporating directly into the FANK the armed villager forces, which had been in existence since the early days of Sihanouk's patriotic struggle for Cambodian independence from the French (1949-1953).[2] They had received very little military training because they were essentially the village populations and their principal mission was the defense of their own villages or districts. They were poorly armed with outmoded U.S., French, and English rifles which were not only ready for salvage but for which ammunition was no longer being produced. A third way in which the creation of new units was accelerated was by recalling the reservists to active duty who had not had the opportunity to remain in service after their initial training. It should be noted in passing that during peacetime these reservists, officers, and noncommissioned officers were never called to undergo periods of active duty for training. This situation, which was due to budgetary restrictions or the higher priority of the reservist's government service, caused a degradation of their military effectiveness.

In spite of the many problems encountered, during the first year of the war FANK made progress both in increases in strength and in the honing of its combat skills. Still, the capabilities of the VC/NVA were such that it was not unusual to see one of these new units (company or battalion), made up of 50 percent career cadre and 50 percent young recruits, completely decimated in its first engagement with the enemy. Further, there is no shame in admitting that during the period some of the original FARK units, which had earlier against the Vietminh acquired reputations as the most effective in FANK, were overrun or heavily damaged in their first encounters with the enemy of 1970-1971. The 3d FARK Battalion at Kratie, the 1st FARK Battalion at Takeo, and the 9th FARK Battalion at Svay Rieng are examples. All of this

---

[2]In French: *Forces Vives* or *Forces des villageois armées*.
In Khmer: *Chivapol*.

demonstrated the lack of training at every level and the poverty of logistic support.

As part of general mobilization, there was in each military region and military subdivision a recruiting station and a training center. Thus, there were created, day by day, new battalions, regiments, and brigades. The new recruits were given training in individual weapons and tactics for several weeks. The units departed for the battlefront in old requisitioned civilian trucks. In those days they were referred to as "24 hour soldiers."

There was a fourth way in which the strength of FANK was swelled. It was the practice of "unit doubling," whereby one-half the strength (officer and enlisted) was taken to form the framework of a new unit.[3] The majority of the personnel of these units were hastily trained recruits. The decentralization of recruiting and the practice of doubling units in the ways described above did result in the organization of new units to support the military regions and military subdivisions which were directly menaced by Communist attacks. And while they were counted as successes by the FANK high command in those early days, the policies which led to their deployment could not avoid results which became more and more unfortunate for the FANK as time passed. These new units were routed, overrun, or completely destroyed by the enemy. The large number of new units not only posed problems of combat effectiveness but greatly taxed the logistic and financial resources of the government.

In step with the increase in strength in the three services of FANK, there appeared the practice of rapid promotion of officers and noncommissioned officers to the point of provoking more and more profound feelings of jealousy within the armed forces; and this says nothing of the inevitable and increasingly serious drain on the budget resulting therefrom. It can be said, however, that the Navy and the Air Force were less affected by these bastardized recruiting practices, as these two services were made up of greater numbers of technicians than the

---

[3]In French: *l'Opération de Doublement des Unités.*

ground forces. Nevertheless, their morale was not helped by seeing their Army friends the recipients of unjustifiably rapid promotions. The unfortunate consequences of all these early policies were not lost on the high-ranking military and civilian members of the government and the FANK high command. They made manifest their disapproval and tried more than once to guide military policy back to a more professional basis. Unfortunately, they met with little success.

At the same time that the general reorganization of FANK structure was taking place—and always according to the concepts of General Lon Nol—there was carried out the organization of certain paramilitary units. The mission of these units was to ensure the defense of certain sensitive and strategic points designated by FANK. They were composed for the most part of students, civil servants, and local inhabitants who were not in the armed forces. Employed in this way, they would free the FANK from the static defense mission, ensure rear area security, and protect against an enemy fifth column. It must be granted that the appearance of this defense system, together with the surge of national awakening, gained for Cambodia both the admiration and the sympathy of foreign observers in general; but to the eyes of professional military observers, foreign and Khmer, the difficulties of all sorts which beset the FANK every day were more than clear.

Starting with 35,000, the FANK was expanded to 110,000 by June 1970, a level which was practicable and controllable. For his part, the initial force structure of 210,000 sought by General Lon Nol would have 200,000 for the Army and the remainder divided between the Navy and the Air Force. And he leaned on his own people in the General Staff and in the Military Regions to see that this higher level was reached by August 1970. Speaking now of the ground forces only, there would be two principal forces: the FANK General Reserve and the Territorial Forces. The latter were under the direct command of the military region commanders. At the same time, there were several changes to the organization of units; battalions were grouped into regiments; then the regiment was abolished in favor of a brigade consisting of several battalions. By 1 May 1970, twelve infantry brigades had been activated and deployed as follows: *(Map 5)*

- 1st Inf. Brigade: headquartered in Phnom Penh and constituting the general reserve.

- 2d Inf. Brigade: based in Kompong Cham and the main force unit of the 1st MR.

- 3d Inf. Brigade: activated in the 2d MR and based in the Kompong Som area.

- 4th Inf. Brigade: activated in Prey Veng (MR-1). This brigade was assigned the mission of defending the special zone of the Mekong River. It operated in the areas of Prey Veng and Neak Luong.

- 5th Inf. Brigade: composed basically of Muslim Khmers and intended for future deployment in the north. Located in Phnom Penh, it served as a reserve unit.

- 6th Inf. Brigade: also composed basically of Muslim Khmers. Its units operated in the Kampot area (MR-2) and in Kompong Cham (MR-1).

- 8th Inf. Brigade: composed of volunteers from the provinces of Takeo and Kandal. It was based in the border area of Takeo and Chau Doc (MR-2).

- 10th Inf. Brigade: activated in Siem Reap, then deployed to Kompong Thom (MR-4). Its units were stationed in Oudar Meachchey.

- 11th Inf. Brigade: activated with units stationed in Takeo (MR-2) and reinforced with volunteers from Kandal and Takeo. It defended Takeo and Route No. 5.

- 12th Inf. Brigade: activated exclusively with volunteers from Battambang and Siem Reap (MR-4). It defended Siem Riep.

- 13th Inf. Brigade: activated at Kompong Speu (MR-2) during this period, this brigade participated in the operation for the defense of Takeo-Angtasom. Later, it was redeployed permanently to Kompong Speu for the defense and protection of Route No. 4.

- 14th Inf. Brigade: based at Tram Khnar (MR-2) along with elements of the antiaircraft artillery half-brigade. This brigade had been reconstituted after its defeat by enemy forces from Phuoc Long.

Map 5 — Locations of Principal FANK Infantry Units on 1 May 1970

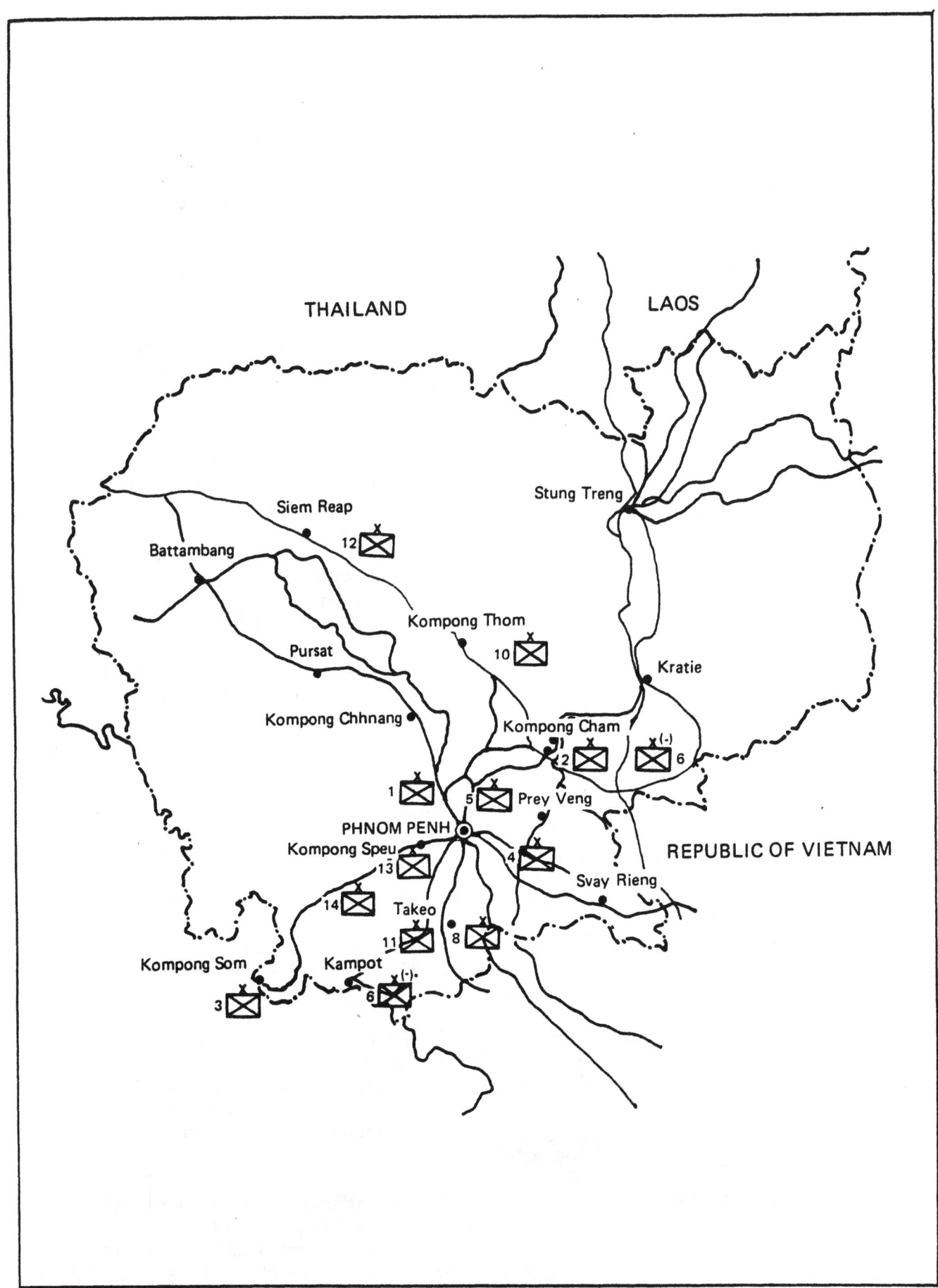

From a military point of view -- and I do not speak here of political considerations -- one can criticize General Lon Nol, Commander-in-Chief and Chief of the General Staff, FANK (later Marshal of the Khmer Armed Forces, and President of the Khmer Republic). The problem was his fairyland ambition to see the FANK transformed overnight into a grand armed force made in the image of the RVNAF or even the U.S. forces, bypassing all of the fundamental principles of development and operation which animated those great institutions. This ambition was particularly apparent when, in 1971, General Lon Nol did not hesitate to present to the U.S., through CINCPAC, a plan for the development of the FANK which envisaged an eventual total strength of 600,000 for the three services. In addition, there was a request for assistance in equipping an additional 53,000 so-called paramilitary forces.

During the period 1970-1971, there was a distinct difference in outlook between the level of decision-makers on the one hand and that of implementers of decisions on the other. The decision-makers operated in what can best be described as a dream world where plans were based on unreality or interpretations of history. The implementers were guided by the facts of the world as it was. The decision-makers were General Lon Nol, his younger brother Lon Non, and a small inner circle of military personnel and civilian advisors. In the second group were found most of FANK, the civil servants, many private citizens, and members of the political parties in opposition to the party of Lon Nol. This second category saw themselves removed from key posts in the government or given foreign diplomatic assignments. There was general agreement as to the depth of this divergence and the resulting consequences for the war effort of the Khmer Republic.

The FANK was severely criticized, not only at home but by foreign observers as well, particularly those of the friendly countries giving miliary and political aid to Cambodia. It must be acknowledged without shame that during the war period there existed a class of Cambodians who exploited the situation, who pursued their personal interests without concern for the ill effects procured by their acts. The FANK suffered not only from losses at the hands of the enemy but from the system of "stealing" personnel spaces or the use of "phantom" personnel in certain units, producing an effect on the capability of the FANK not unlike that of inflation or lack of productivity on an economy.[4]

Military Organization

During the time of Sihanouk, the FARK General Staff was under the command and control of the Supreme Commander of the armed forces and the Chief of State, with Sihanouk holding both titles. Under the General Staff were most of the personnel and operational units of the FARK. This situation was complicated by the fact that the Ministry of National Defense, where the technical and administrative services of the FARK were located, was a part of the Government subject, in theory, to the Prime Minister and was not under the control of the General Staff. Differences in point of view between the Minister of National Defense and the Chief of the General Staff were the order of the day. At the time of Sihanouk's departure, Lt. General Lon Nol was Chief of the General Staff, and the developmental needs of the FANK presented the high command with the problem of carrying out a complete reorganization of a system which had long since reached the limits of its capacity. A new concept was needed and without delay.

In my position as Deputy Chief of the General Staff during this period, I repeatedly suggested a reorganization of our armed forces in accordance with current thinking in other countries. But it was not until March 1975 that Lon Nol, by now convinced but still not happy, gave his consent to the idea. The command arrangements of the RVNAF were used as a point of departure, and a profound reorganization of the levels of Ministry of National Defense and General Staff was carried out. The title of Supreme Commander was abolished, and from that time forward the Chief of General Staff of FANK reported to the Government and no longer to the President of the Republic. *(Chart 1)*

---

[4] In **French:** *Voler les effectifs or l'Effectif fantôme.*

Chart 1 — FANK General Staff Organization After 1972

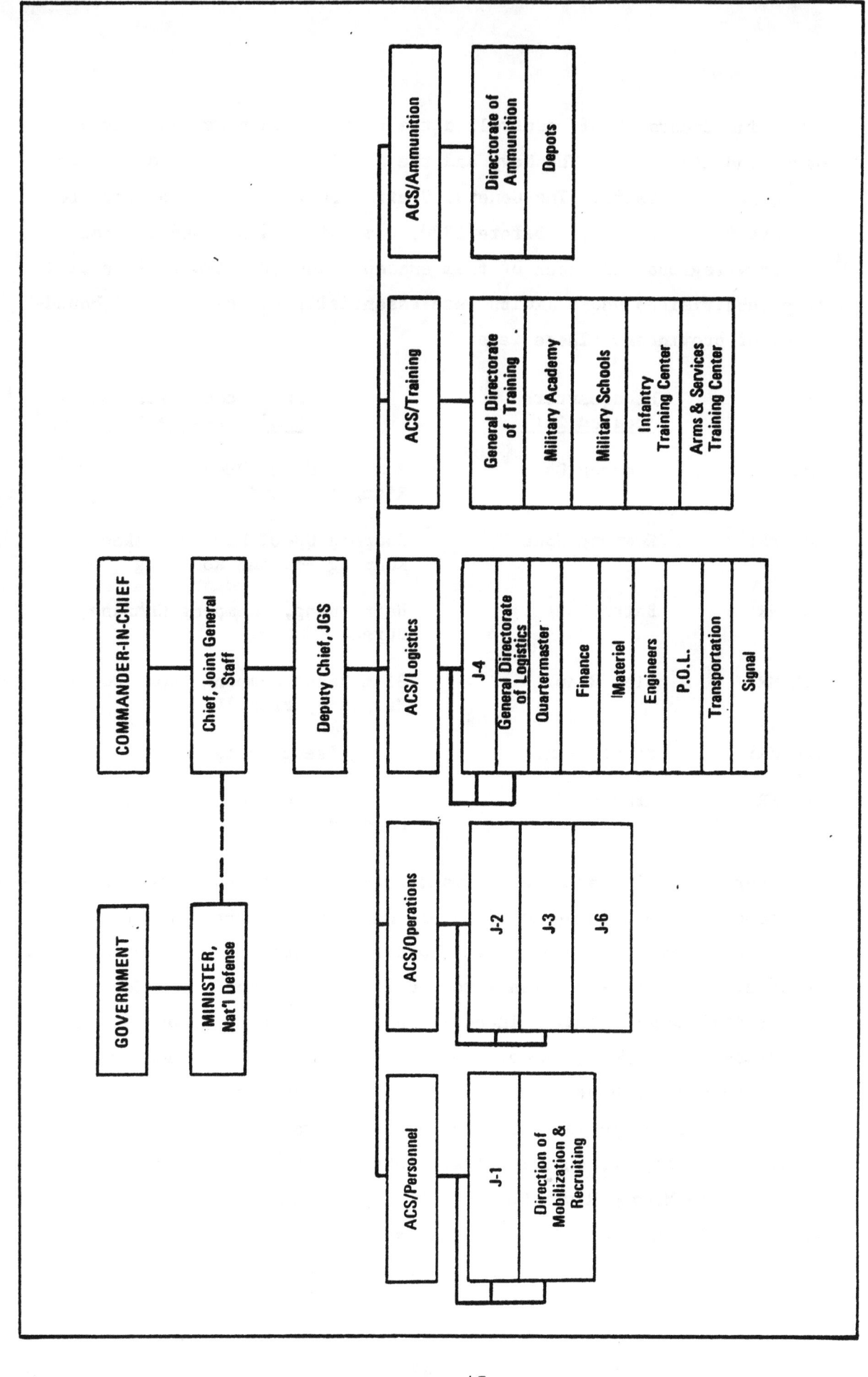

The General Staff controlled the three armed services: Army, Navy, and Air Force. The Navy and the Air Force had their own general headquarters (staff). The General Staff itself served as headquarters and staff for the Army. Before 1970, Cambodia was divided into six military regions (MR) each of them encompassing from two to five military subdivisions whose limits were essentially the territorial boundaries of provinces. These were:

	Headquarters located in:	Provinces Making up Military Region
1st MR:	Kompong Cham	Kompong Cham, Prey Veng, Svay Rieng and Kandal
2d MR:	Kompong Speu	Kompong Speu, Kampot, Takeo, Kompong Som and Koh Kong
3d MR:	Battambang	Battambang, Kompong Chhnang, Pursat
4th MR:	Siem Reap	Siem Reap, Kompong Thom, Oddar Meanchay, Preah Vihear
5th MR:	Stung Treng	Stung Treng, Ratanakiri
6th MR:	Kratie	(created in 1969) Kratie, Mondolkiri

In general, the MR commander commanded the infantry battalions and combat support companies deployed in his MR. As to technical service detachments, which were under the control of their parent Service Directorates, they were subordinate to the Military Region commander for operational control only. In addition to the FARK units and service detachments, the MR commander could in case of need also employ Royal Police forces which were subordinate to the local province governor. There was also a special zone around the capital having the status of a military region, and shortly after the start of the war a special defense zone for the Mekong River between the capital and the RVN border was established. *(Map 6)* By 1973, the exigencies of combat led to the creation of three additional MRs, some of which had operational zones

Map 6 – The Military Regions of the Khmer Armed Forces in 1971

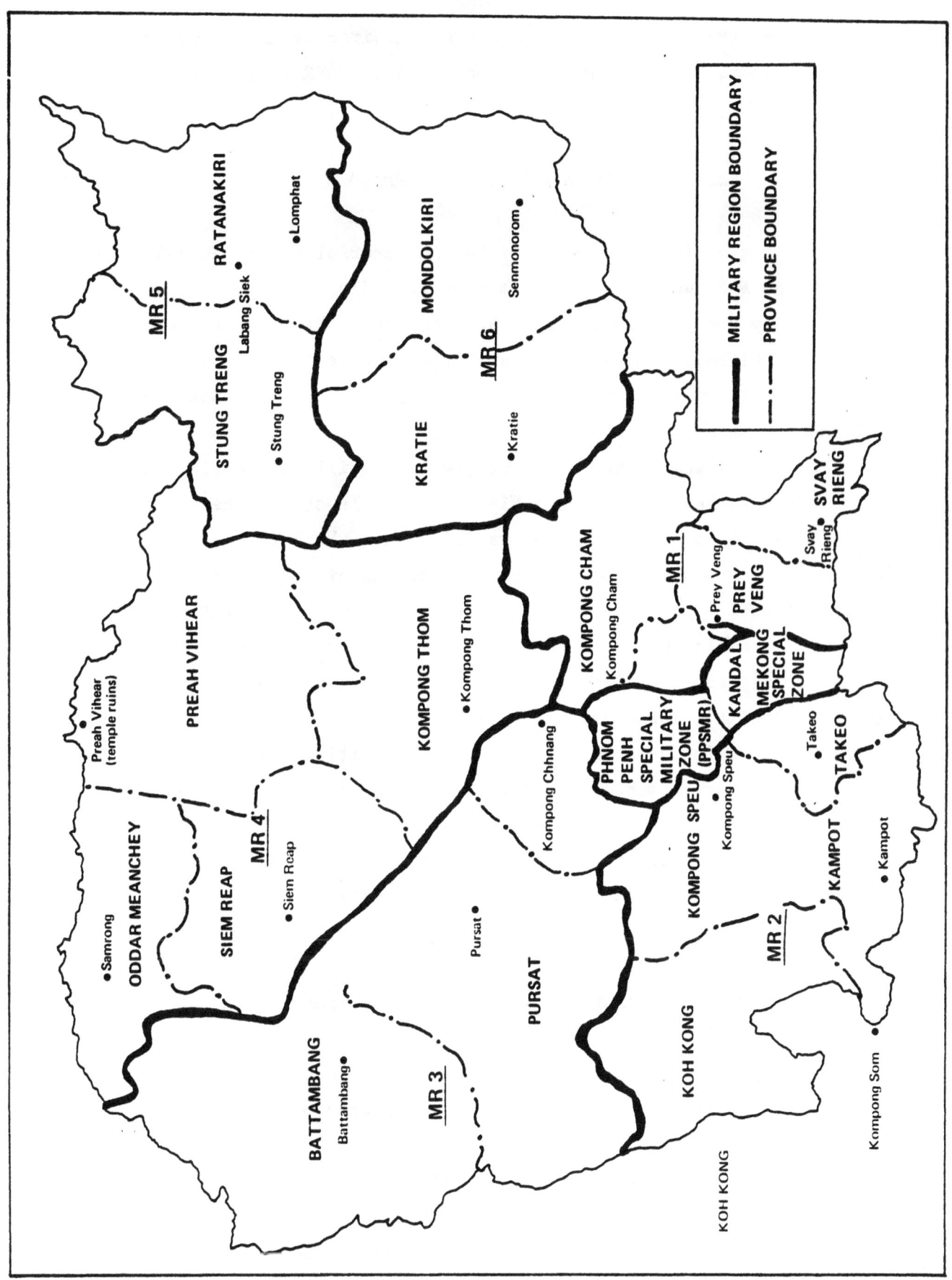

independent of the MR commander and operating directly under the control of the high command. The subordination of major FANK units after 1972 is shown on *(Chart 2)*.

The U.S. Military Assistance Program

Without question, improvements in the material and financial situations of the FANK were due to the aid of friendly countries, of which I mention only the program of the U.S., the nation known as the great supporter of Cambodia during the hostilities in the same way that the great Communist China and its allies supported the cause of Sihanouk's GRUNK and the Khmer Rouge.

The U.S. military assistance program was initially carried out through the intermediary of South Vietnam or at least via that country. Proof of this is to be seen in the rapidity with which the special forces of Khmer Krom personnel were sent to the aid of their compatriots, then in difficulty on all fronts; and note that they were sent at the same time as the launching of the RVNAF/U.S. incursion into Cambodia, intended to destroy the VC/NVA sanctuaries, and described as an operation which would relieve the enemy pressure on that part of Cambodia. Early aid was provided for or arranged through the Politico/Military Section of the U.S. Embassy which, according to my knowledge, was always in direct contact with COMUSMACV. For purposes of intelligence exchange and operational coordination, the FANK established a liaison officer at the RVNAF JGS; as time went on, the duties of this liaison officer were extended to include the monitoring of instruction given to FANK personnel in the RVNAF and U.S. training centers in RVN.

Until the establishment of the Military Equipment Delivery Team, Cambodia (MEDTC) in the U.S. Embassy in Phnom Penh in 1971, there existed no real plans for U.S. military aid inasmuch as the U.S. Government and Congress were surprised by the abrupt change in the policies of the Cambodian government, following the events of 18 March 1970. Under those circumstances the first military aid, following President Nixon's decision to help Cambodia, were South Vietnamese air shipments of old model weapons, U.S. M-1 Garand, etc., and ammunition, doubtless no longer needed by the

Chart 2 — FANK Organization After 1972

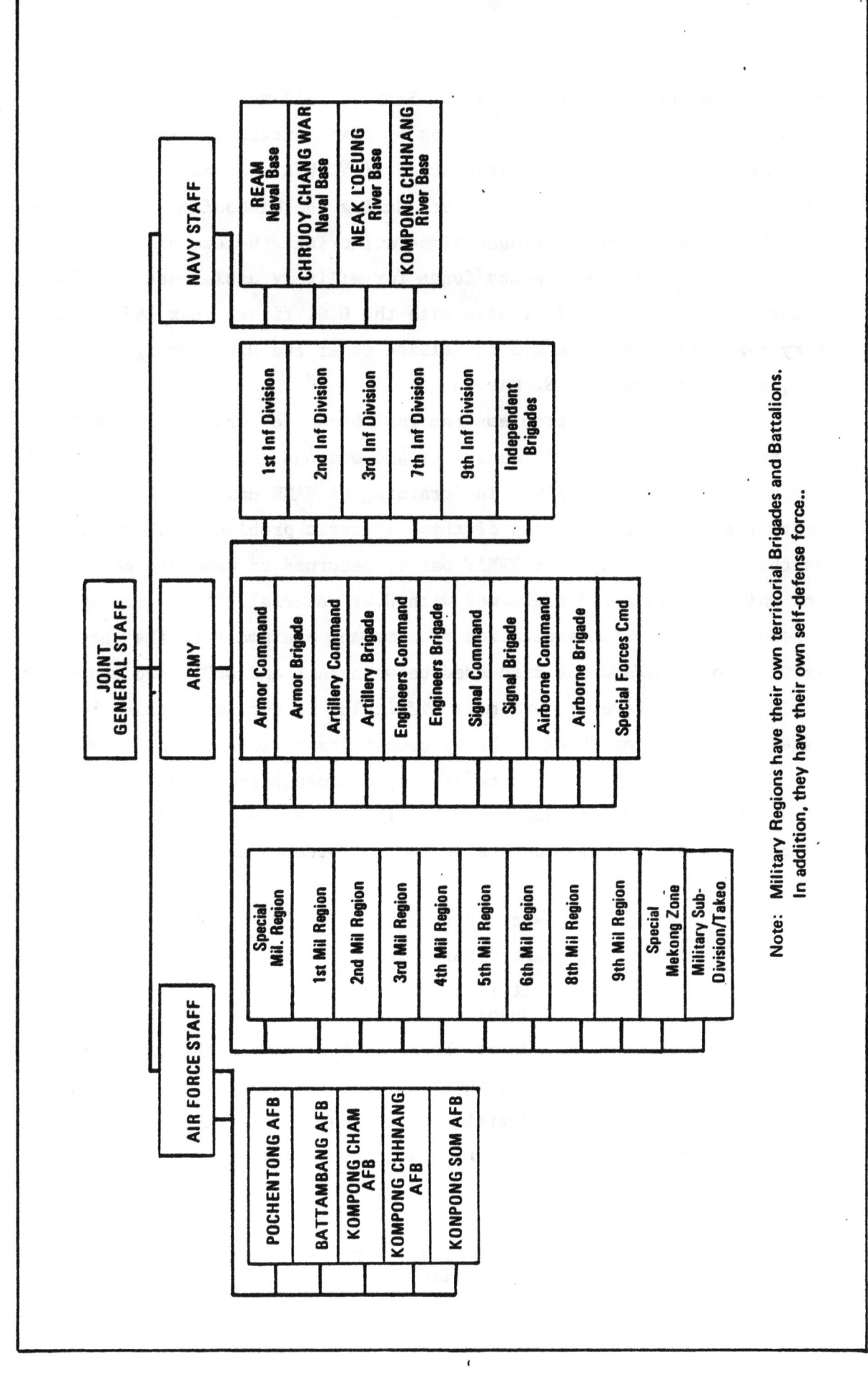

Note: Military Regions have their own territorial Brigades and Battalions. In addition, they have their own self-defense force.

RVNAF following its modernization. Similar old model U.S. weapons and ammunition were brought in from Laos by Khmer aircraft. These initial shipments were followed by plane loads of VC/NVA weapons and ammunition captured by the RVNAF and U.S., both during the Cambodian Incursion and in RVN. In addition, President Nixon authorized the use of some $10,000,000 of his contingency funds for military assistance to FANK prior to 1 July 1970. Beginning with the U.S. fiscal year 1971, military assistance for FANK was formalized under the U.S. Foreign Assistance Act, becoming regular U.S. MAP.[5]

One of the first problems the FANK began to work on with MEDTC was the great disparity in equipment and weapons and the attendant problem of ammunition resupply. The training of FANK units in RVN was another step toward solution of these logistic problems. These units, whether trained at U.S. or RVNAF bases, returned to Cambodia completely and uniformly equipped and armed with U.S. materiel. A program and schedule for the standardization of arms and equipment in the three services of the FANK was discussed between FANK and MEDTC and was adopted. Implementation, however, was made difficult, if not impossible, by the necessity to replenish early heavy combat losses in certain units.

During July 1972, a force structure coordinating committee, made up of members from FANK and the U.S. Military Equipment Delivery Team, Cambodia (MEDTC), agreed on the following force structure for FANK ground units:

Infantry Brigades	32
Infantry Battalions:	202
Territorial Infantry Companies:	465

Within the above totals, 128 of the battalions formed the maneuver elements for the 32 brigades, of which 20 were independent and 12 were organized into 4 separate divisions with appropriate supporting arms, i.e., a 155-mm battery and an armored cavalry squadron. Each of the

---

[5] For a more detailed discussion of the origins of U.S. Military Assistance for FANK, see the appendix by Colonel H.O. Amos in The Cambodian Incursion, this series.

brigades was to have an organic 105-mm howitzer battery. In addition, a separate artillery and armored brigade rounded out the combat elements of the force structure. The bulk of the army's 202,000-man slice of the MAP-approved FANK force structure of 220,000 personnel was located within the above units.

While there was agreement that the headquarters above the battalion would be the brigade, FANK continued, after July 1972, to employ a variety of higher headquarters (regiments, groups, brigades, half-brigades, brigade groups) to control these battalions. MEDTC and the U.S. Embassy considered both the variety of headquarters and the FANK practice of continuing to add battalions to the force structure for which there was no equipment to be unwise. Thus, in December 1972, three directives were issued by FANK to bring the FANK ground units more in line with the agreed force structure. The first limited FANK strength for 1973 to 250,000, suspended individual unit recruitment programs, and directed a manpower reapportionment. The second promulgated a standard TO&E for both intervention and territorial battalions. The third specifically spelled out how manpower was to be reapportioned and abolished all regiments, "brigade group" headquarters and numerous ineffectual battalions.

The administration of the U.S. MAP for Cambodia was affected in a significant way by certain provisions of the U.S. military assistance legislation, which applied specifically to Cambodia. In January 1971, the Cooper-Church amendment prohibited the assignment of U.S. advisors to the FANK. The Symington-Case amendment, passed in February 1972, ordered that the total number of official U.S. personnel in Cambodia—military and civilian—should not exceed 200. In addition, there could be not to exceed 85 third-country nationals (TCN) present in Cambodia who were being paid directly or indirectly from U.S. MAP funds. It should be noted that the ceiling for both official U.S. personnel and TCNs included not only those permanently assigned but those on TDY as well. In late 1972, the military activities at the U.S. Embassy in Phnom Penh were allocated personnel as follows:

	Cambodia	Saigon
MEDTC	74	10
DAO	17	
Military Communications Facility	5	
Vinnel Corp. Contract	40	

In addition to the Vinnell Corporation contract, other TCN spaces were used to fill contracts with Air America, Bell Aircraft Company, AVCO-Lycoming Aircraft, and Helio Aircraft Corporation.

The interface between the U.S. MILSTRIP system and the FANK logistic system was the FANK Foreign Assistance Office (FAO) in Phnom Penh. To accomplish the actual handling of materiel and its distribution to the three services, two warehouse operations were established, one in Phnom Penh and the other at Kompong Som. Some of the TCN personnel were assigned to the FAO and to the warehouses, where they monitored title transfer of equipment and worked to familiarize FANK personnel with the MILSTRIP system. Prior to the signing of the Paris Peace Accords in 1973, the majority of MAP cargo arriving by sealift was processed and transshipped using the facilities at Newport, RVN. Likewise, retrograde cargo was processed through the same port. Airlift of general cargo was through the 8th Aerial Port at Tan Son Nhut, RVN. By March 1973, all logistic support activities for Cambodia MAP had been forced out of RVN by the provisions of the Paris Peace Accords and had been relocated to Thailand. MEDTC personnel previously located in Saigon were relocated to Camp Samae San, Thailand, and designated the Joint Liaison Office. Transshipping activities for MAP materiel arriving by sea were established at the port of Sattahip, Thailand, while aerial deliveries were usually by C-130 aircraft from Utapao, Thailand, to Phnom Penh. The Paris Peace Accords did not affect the supply of bulk POL to Cambodia through RVN, which continued to originate at Nha Be or Vung Tau, RVN, for movement to Phnom Penh via the Mekong.

Approximate dollar amounts in millions for MAP Cambodia were:

FY71	FY72	FY73	FY74	FY75
180	220	131	414	254

The greatest single-item expenditure was always for ammunition. In FY72, ammunition costs comprised about 37 percent of MAP funds; in FY73, ammunition costs had risen to 65 percent of MAP funds and to 87 percent in FY74. In Appendix C are shown densities of major U.S.-furnished equipment.

The Khmer Krom Units

"Khmer Krom" is a term used to designate ethnic Cambodians living in communities in certain provinces of South Vietnam (Chau Doc and Vinh Binh primarily) as Vietnamese citizens or Cambodians born in Vietnam. During the 1963-65 period, U.S. Special Forces in South Vietnam expanded their Civilian Irregular Defense Group (CIDG), an indigenous paramilitary force composed mostly of Montagnards serving under U.S. control, by recruiting ethnic Cambodians to form additional light guerrilla companies. These "Khmer Krom" units were primarily deployed at border CIDG camps in the RVN's MR-3 and MR-4.

In the absence of documents, I cannot say whether the deployment to Cambodia of these Khmer Krom forces was carried out pursuant to a bilateral agreement, that is an agreement between the U.S. and Cambodia, or in accordance with a "tripartite" agreement between the U.S., Cambodia, and the RVN. What we knew at the time was that these "Special Forces" were under direct U.S. command in South Vietnam. In various ways the arrival of the Khmer Krom battalions was greeted with popular enthusiasm, while for the FANK authorities their arrival gave immediate help in reinforcing the combat units. Later there was a problem about how to integrate them into the FANK and to decide what rank their cadre would be given. A total of some 4,000 organized into eight battalions, were deployed to Cambodia during 1970.

Concerning the use of these units in combat, there were, without question, some problems at the start. These resulted from their need to adapt to the FANK system of command, to acquaint themselves with the Cambodian outlook, and the problems of their integration into the body of Khmer military institutions. The high command would have preferred to spread the personnel of the Khmer Krom units from South Vietnam -- that is those already trained by the U.S. Special Forces -- out among all FANK units. This was not possible because of problems of command. The final solution was to group the Khmer Krom personnel into separate units with their own Khmer Krom cadre.

Whatever the administrative problems may have been, I must pay homage, here and now, to the Khmer Krom units who fought so effectively by the side of their Cambodian brothers against the VC/NVA Communists. Theirs was a spirit of great determination and a willingness to make the supreme sacrifice. According to information I have since received, these Khmer Krom units returned to South Vietnam after the fall of Cambodia on 17 April 1975. There, they continue the fight against the Communists with the few means at their disposal in order to regain the South Vietnam lands of their families and ancestors.

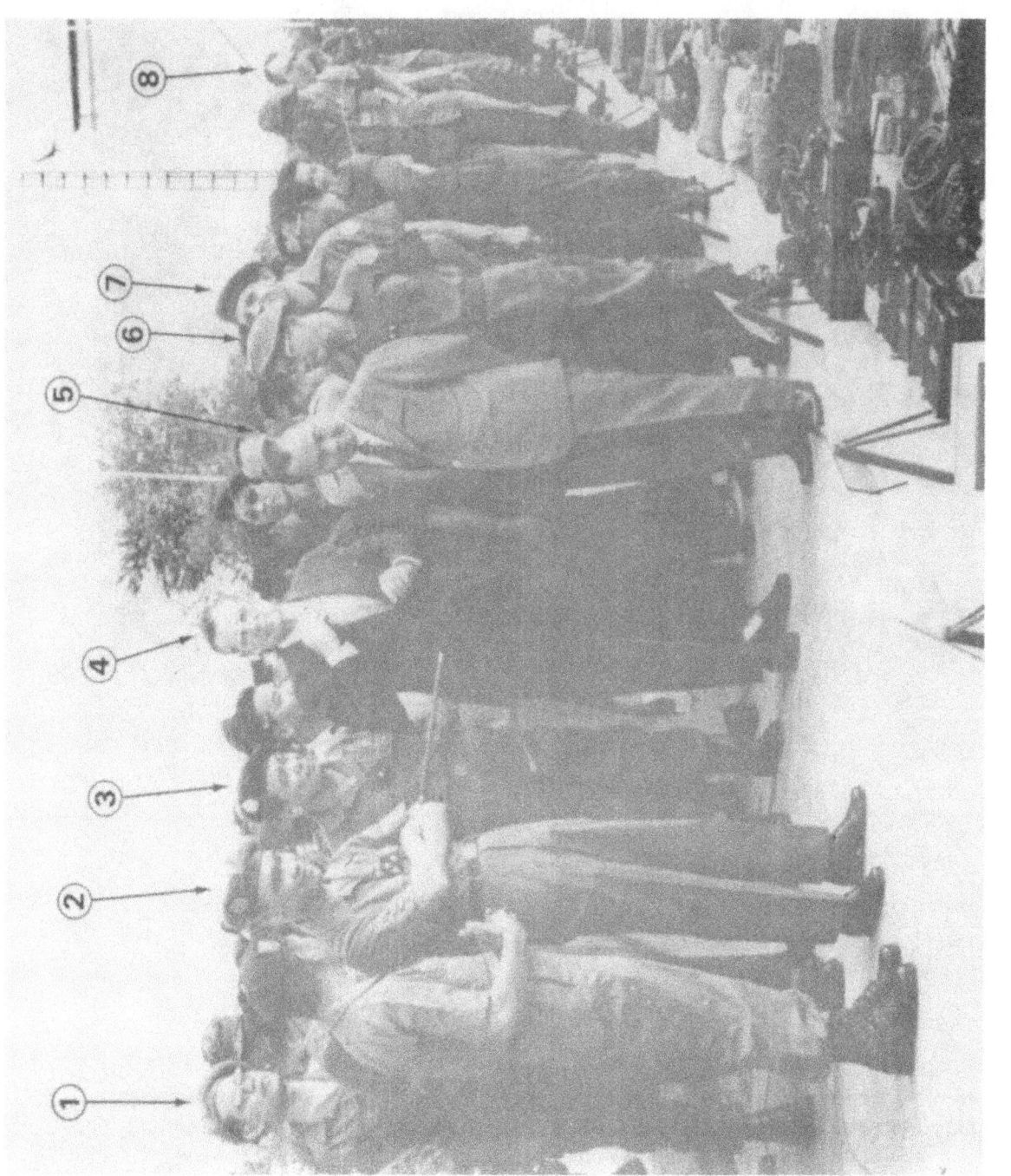

Ceremony at Phnom Penh in 1971 to Mark Return on FANK Special Forces Detachments from Training in Thailand. Identified are: (1) Maj. Gen. Fan Muong; (2) Lt. Gen. Sirik Matak; (3) Brig. Gen. Hou Hang Sin; (4) U.S. Ambassador E.C. Swamk; (5) Thai Ambassador to the Khmer Republic; (6) Maj. Gen. Sak Sutsakhan; (7) Maj. Gen. Pok Sam An; (8) Mr. J.F. Ladd, Politico/Military Counselor at the U.S. Embassy, Phnom Penh

Khmer Krom Unit, Newly Arrived from South Vietnam and Armed
with the U.S. M-16 Rifle, Salutes 1st Military Region Commander
During a Visit to Tonle Bet, November 1970

CHAPTER IV

The First Two Years of the War

The Initial Communist Attacks

An unsuccessful attempt to deal with the NVA/VC had been made on 24 May 1969 when Prime Minister Lon Nol met officially for the first time with North Vietnam's representative, Nguyen Thuong, and the NLF delegate, Nguyen Van Hieu. The purpose of this meeting was to request the NVA/VC to desist from committing violations against Cambodian territory, violations which were frequent and becoming more and more serious. No positive result was obtained from this meeting; the enemy simply ignored Cambodia's request.

Since NVA/VC forces continued to exert pressure on the local Khmer population, the inhabitants of Svay Rieng began in early March 1970 to manifest their dissatisfaction toward the intruders. These popular manifestations met with retaliations from the enemy and resulted in casualties. This in turn provoked a widespread feeling of discontent among the population which culminated in destructive rampages against the North Vietnamese and PRG embassies in Phnom Penh on 11 and 12 March 1970.

Amidst the gravity of this explosive situation, which pitted the Khmer population against the NVA/VC, the Cambodian government, by a diplomatic note of the Ministry of Foreign Affairs, formally requested the NVA/VC to withdraw all of their troops from Cambodian territory. The deadline set was dusk 15 March 1970.

Once more, the NVA/VC did nothing to comply with the Cambodian request. NVA/VC representatives were therefore invited to participate in a working session with staff members of the Khmer Ministry of Foreign Affairs on 16 March 1970. Nothing positive was achieved, however. The

NVA/VC representatives not only cited reasons of their own for non-compliance with the Cambodian request; they also asked in return that their governments be paid for damages caused to their embassies. Thus ended the working session which was also the last meeting between the Cambodian government and the NVA/VC.

On 25 March 1970, however, the Polish Embassy sent a memorandum to the Cambodian Ministry of Foreign Affairs informing the latter among other things, of the availability of good office's concerning the evacuation of all North Vietnamese and PRG embassy personnel. On 27 March 1970, all North Vietnamese and PRG embassy personnel took off by ICC aircraft for Hanoi. This departure marked the end of diplomatic relations between Cambodia and North Vietnam and the PRG.

Well before the enemy launched attacks against Cambodia, he had initiated deceptive maneuvers aimed at creating a feeling of insecurity and internal crisis. This was to divide governmental forces in the first place, and then to isolate the government from popular support; finally it would lead both domestic and world opinion to believe that the war in Cambodia had been staged by Sihanouk followers against the new regime—in other words, that this war was only a civil war.

All of this deception was but common Communist fare to those who were familiar with Communist strategy in Asia. However, to those ill-informed of this Communist practice, as was the case with several foreign observers, the enemy bait was palatable and for a certain time, questions arose as to whether or not Cambodian protests against the armed and overt aggression by NVA/VC forces were in fact justified. How perfect the Communist screenplay was!

In fact, under the pretext of helping Sihanouk return to power, an eventuality rather warmly welcomed by the majority of illiterate (ill-informed common people who lived far from the nation's capital) the enemy was able to incite the civilian population to demonstrate against the legal government. On 26 March 1970, several bloody demonstrations erupted in the city of Kompong Cham; these were quelled only by the intervention of Khmer troops.

On 27 March 1970, a second demonstration, more violent still, took place in Kompong Cham; but this time the army was forced to open fire.

In Takeo, similar demonstrations also compelled the Khmer army to intervene. The same thing happened to the inhabitants of Prey Veng who were stopped by Khmer troops only 15 kilometers from Phnom Penh.

The question on the minds of many people at that time was whether or not these demonstrations had been organized by Sihanouk followers. To clarify the question, I think we should point out the fact that in its interventions, the Khmer forces had detained several NVA/VC cadre among the demonstrators; there was no doubt that it was they who had orchestrated the entire show. We may deduct with reasonable certainty that these cadres were members of the Vietnamese communist infrastructure because all of these demonstrations were staged in provinces adjacent to NVA/VC sanctuaries.

Following this stage play, the NVA/VC suddenly began on 29 March 1970 their overt aggression against Cambodia. These enemy forces were known to be NVA/VC regular units whose total strength was estimated at between 45,000 and 60,000. Meanwhile, the defending forces, our FANK, numbered merely 35,000.

It was a very sudden and widespread attack conducted along the eastern and southeastern boundaries and coming from the sanctuary areas. The suddenness of these attacks did not cause much of a surprise to the FANK command because it had expected them all along. But the time available for defense preparations was so short (just two days, from 27 to 29 March) that many isolated and weakly manned outposts succumbed under the violence of the first enemy assaults. From the very first days, therefore, the FANK was driven back by the enemy push. In rapid succession, the following towns and cities fell into enemy hands:

In MR-1: Snoul, Chup, Mimot, Krek, Saang, Koh Tham

In MR-2: Kompong Trach

In MR-5: Stung Treng (which had been heavily threatened)

In MR-6: Mondulkiri, Kratie City

In addition, other important towns were attacked. *(Map 7)* The FANK units in Ratanakiri were cut off from Phnom Penh by the enemy capture of Stung Treng and Kratie.

During the month of August 1970, the situation stabilized a little but the enemy did not relent in his push. The FANK were found then holding

Map 7 — Initial Communist Attacks, March - April 1970

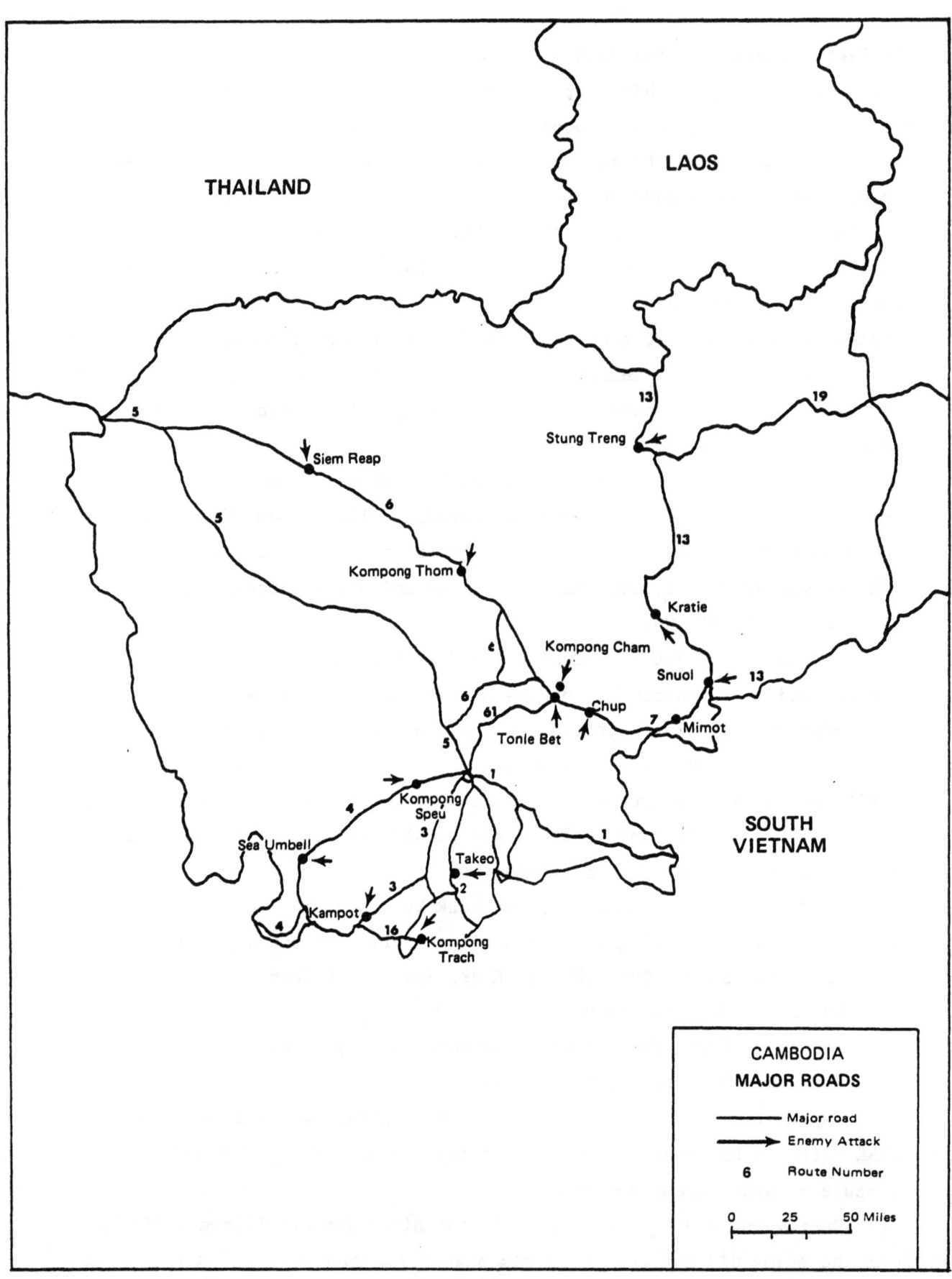

a shrinking area which extended on both sides of the Bassac River and the Tonle Sap Great Lake from the northwest to the southeast. *(Map 8)*

The Evacuation of the Ratanakiri Garrison

It is necessary to go back to 1969 in order to explain how it was that such a large portion of the FARK combat elements were in the relative isolation of Ratanakiri Province at the time of the Communist attacks. By 1969 the VC/NVA presence in that region was beginning to exert pressure on Khmer authorities and the local populations. Responding to this situation, the FARK high command launched OPERATION TEST VC/NVA in November 1969 in order to determine the size of the VC/NVA forces and to fix the extent of their bases and sanctuaries. *(Map 9)* It made use of the best of the FARK units at the time, and I was placed in command. We were organized as follows:

    Colonel Sak Sutsakhan, Commander

    Colonel Pok Sam An, Chief of Staff

    Colonel Lay Chhay, Director of Materiel

    Lt. Colonel Chhuon Chhum, Commander 5th Military Region and Commander GT #1

    Lt. Colonel Um Savuth, Commander GT #2

    Lt. Colonel Hong Yung, Commander Sub Region Ratanakiri and Commander GT #3

    Major Dien Del, Commander GT #4 Reserve and Support Troops

I remained in command in Ratanakiri until 11 March 1970, when I was called to Phnom Penh. During my stay there, a number of operations were launched against enemy base areas in the vicinity of Bokeo, Lomphat, Siem Pang, all in Ratanakiri Province. There was little success, however, because the VC/NVA units were under orders at that time, and for political reasons, to refuse direct combat with the FARK. They were content to leave the fighting for the moment to their auxiliary troops, the dissident *Khmer Loeu*[1]. These auxiliaries were used either to slow

---

[1] Literally, "Upper Khmer." Unlike the Khmer Krom or "Lower Khmer," so called because of their habitat in the lower Mekong valley, the Khmer Loeu are not ethic Khmer. The term was developed during the Sihanouk era to facilitate the integration into Khmer society of the non-Khmer hill tribes living in northeast Cambodia. The Khmer Loeu were actually members of the same tribes found in the uplands of Vietnam, the Jarai, for example.

Map 8 — FANK - Held Areas in Cambodia in August 1970

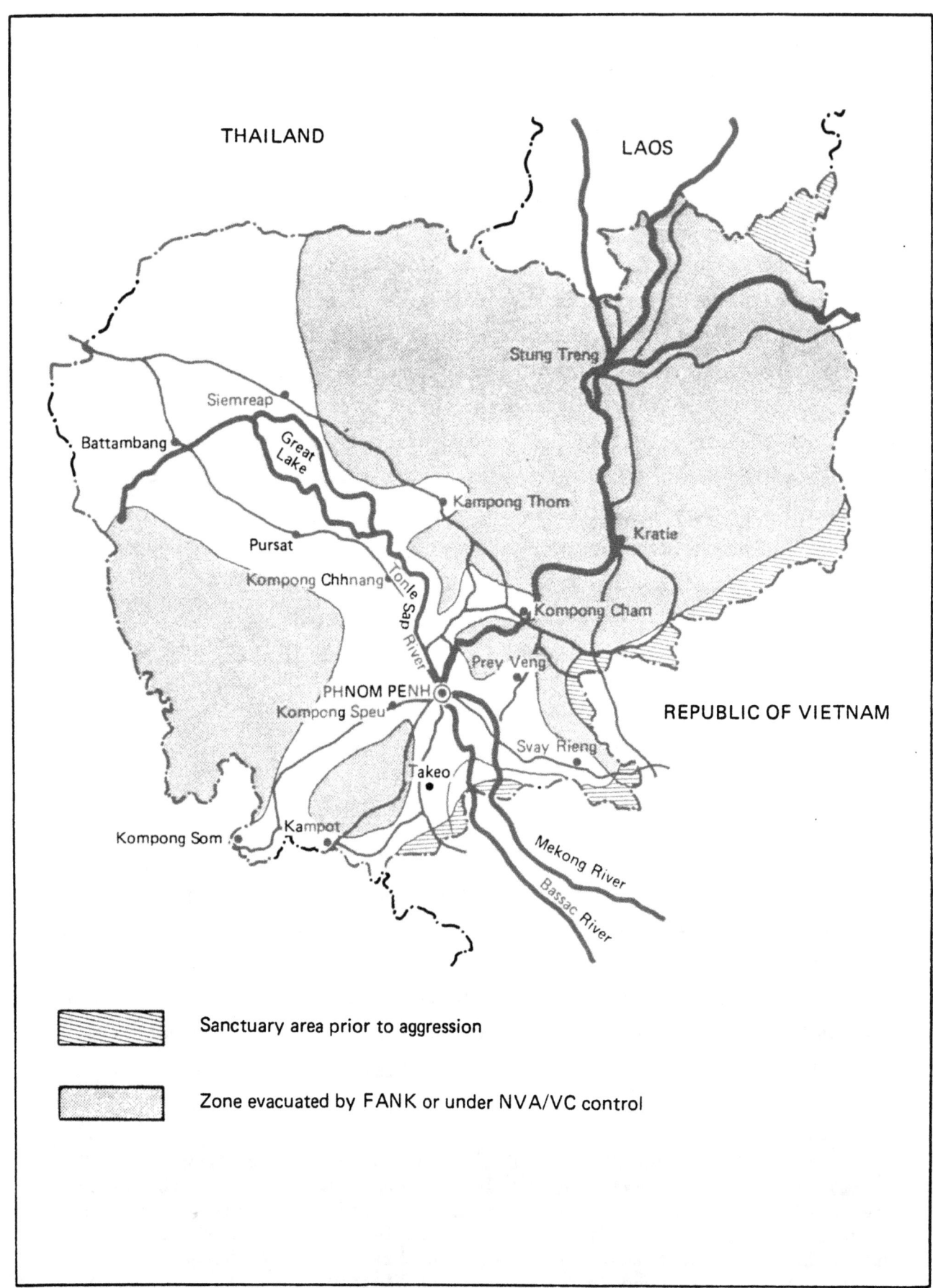

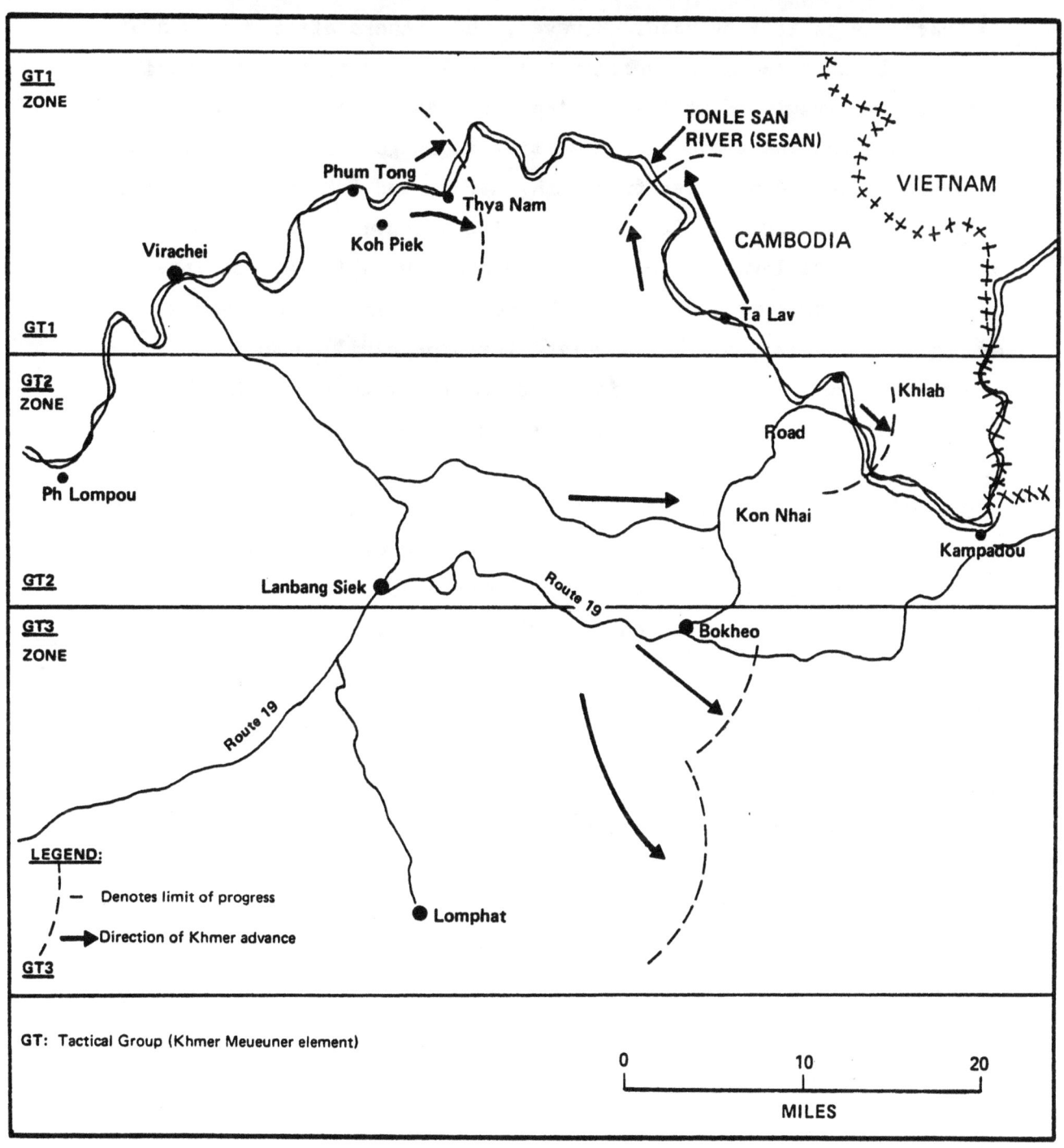

the advance of FARK units or to divert them from the main centers of VC/NVA strength. However, the operations did permit the FARK to conclude that the VC/NVA presence on Cambodian soil was becoming greater and greater and moving toward the interior of the country.

Shortly before the 29th of March, the high command recalled two infantry battalions and one engineer battalion; these units were able to reach the capital by road. However, the attacks after the 29th of March isolated this major concentration of FARK units in Ratanakiri, and those in Kratie as well. The important question of how to evacuate these units was the subject of a meeting in Saigon in April 1970, and attended by representatives from FANK, RVNAF, and U.S. MACV, and presided over by General Abrams. On the Khmer side we gave our agreement in principle to the launching of such an operation, which was of interest to us in that some of our units might be saved for use in other areas of combat. We asked at the same time that the civil authorities and their families in the area be included in the evacuation. At the meeting it was decided that HQ MACV would take the lead in organizing and executing the evacuation, ensuring thereby the availability of both U.S. and RVNAF assets dedicated to the operation. On the FANK side we did not interest ourselves in the details, but in order to facilitate cooperation, particularly concerning the evacuation, the FANK established a liaison detachment in Saigon, directed by Brigadier General Pok Sam An, to stay in touch with U.S. and RVNAF authorities in Saigon, and the RVNAF II Corps commander. Pok Sam An also handled the liaison with Brigadier General Neak Sam, Commander, FANK 5th Military Region to designate and move FANK units toward a protected assembly point at Bokeo in preparation for the move. The evacuation itself was carried out according to plan; however, several of the units at great distance from the assembly point (Stung Treng, Sumpang, Voeun Sai, etc.) did not get out. They were either overrun in their locations or ambushed and destroyed en route to Bokeo.[2]

---

[2] For a description of the operation as carried out by the RVNAF and the part played by the U.S. Embassy in Phnom Penh, see Tran Dinh Tho, *The Cambodian Incursion*, this series.

It must be pointed out that this evacuation applied only to our forces in Ratanakiri. There was no similar opportunity to save the smaller garrisons in Mondolkiri and Kratie Provinces.

FANK Strategy

By about May 1970, following the initial enemy attacks, it was clear that the capital of Phnom Penh was in effect surrounded on three sides by territory in the hands of the enemy. Only the corridor along Route 5, running to Battambang and Thailand, was still under our control. Even the fall of Phnom Penh seemed possible. However, the U.S./RVNAF cross-border operations, and the combined FANK/RVNAF operations during May and June lead to a period of stability by the month of July. The enemy appeared to pause to recondition his units and receive reinforcements. The initial strategic concept developed for defense of the Khmer Republic took this situation into account. *(Map 10)* It was keyed to a line (A-B) running generally along Routes 6 and 7. The line came to be known as the Lon Nol line, and the strategy was to be executed in three phases:

1. Phase I: Survive south of the line
2. Phase II: Consolidate all territory south of the line
3. Phase III: Regain lost territory north of the line

As the war progressed, it was necessary to revise strategic priorities in order to meet the increasingly critical enemy threats to Cambodia. By late 1972, it was generally accepted that while trying to keep Route 5 open to Battambang, and Route 6 and Route 7 open to Kompong Cham, the priority of effort should go to the highly populated regions near and south of the capital, the area south of line C-D-E.

Returning to the period July-August 1970, there were a number of factors in addition to the lull in enemy activity which prompted the FANK to consider offensive action against the enemy for the first time. There was the acceleration of the formation of combat units, the reorganization of FANK, and the receipt of U.S. military aid. There was a need to regain the confidence of the public in the FANK and to raise the morale of the troops, themselves greatly shocked by the defeats of

Map 10 — FANK Strategic Concepts for Defense of the Khmer Republic

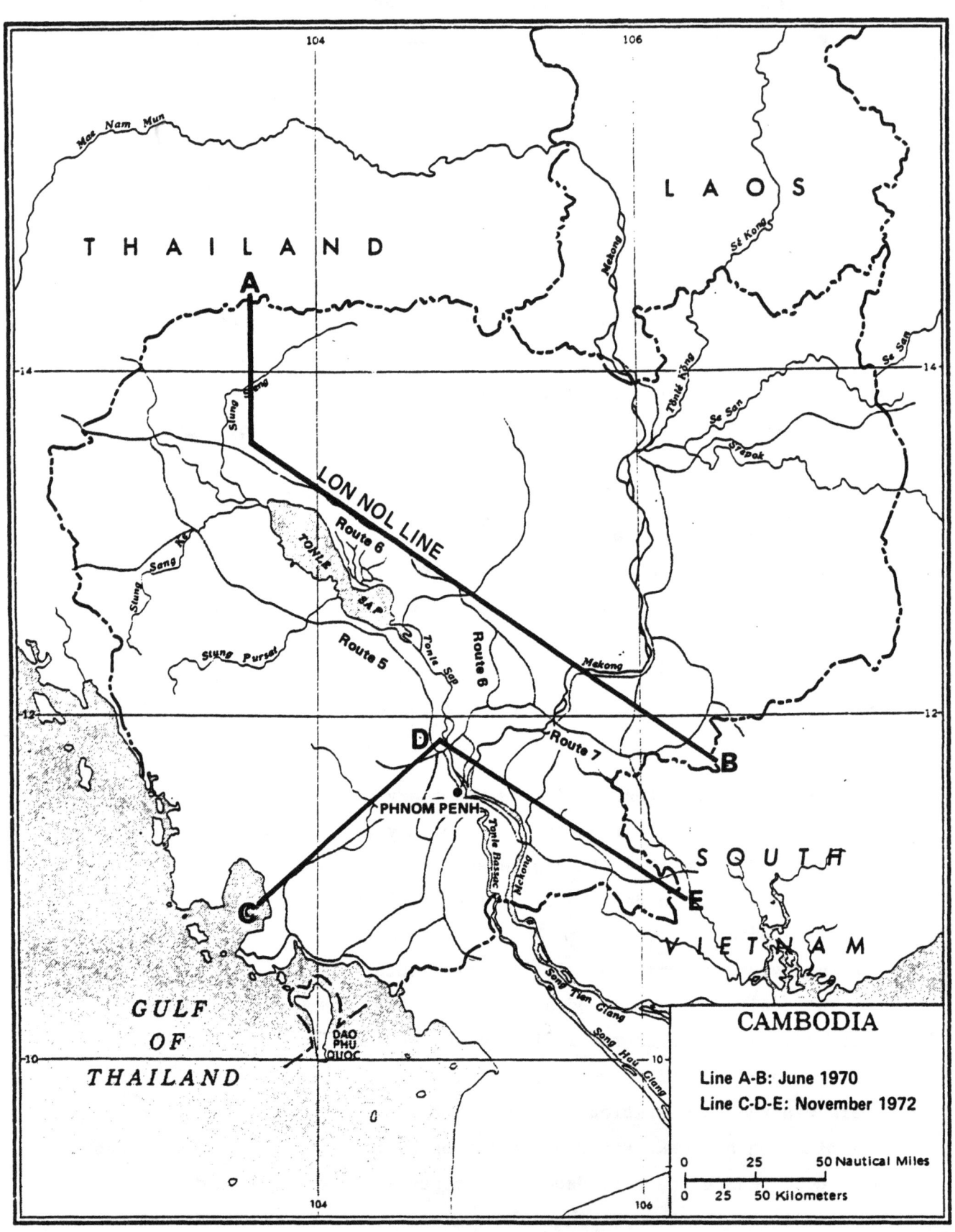

the early days of the struggle. Another important consideration was
the desire to retake areas rich in rice and fish which had fallen under
enemy control. The economic situation had deteriorated rapidly, and
there was no longer sufficient rice-growing area under friendly control,
and what was needed was to bring some of this rich land back under FANK
control without delay. This would not only ensure more adequate rice
stocks, it would also provide places to settle the growing numbers of
refugees, by then streaming from the areas of communist control toward
the population centers, and whose care and feeding constituted an
increasingly heavy burden for the government. The FANK initiatives in
1970 and 1971 which responded to these circumstances were primarily the
operations known as CHENLA I and II, which I now discuss.

CHENLA I

The initial zone of operation for OPERATION CHENLA I was the
triangle formed by the three villages Skoun - Kompong Thmar - Troeung
the base of which was Route 7 connecting Skoun and Kompong Cham.
(Map 11) Skoun had been repeatedly attacked during the initial fighting
and had changed hands often. Just prior to this operation, it was
under FANK control, and was developed as an advanced logistic base for
CHENLA I, and for operations around Kompong Cham. All of the high command were in agreement that the final objective of CHENLA I should be
Kompong Thmar, assuming that the U.S./RVNAF air support which we expected
to have at FANK disposal would be able to neutralize a large part of
the enemy combat power. The final objective of Kompong Thmar was to
be achieved in three phases; however, any advance beyond the Phase One
objective of Tang Kauk would depend on the enemy situation.

Some ten to twelve of the best FANK infantry battalions, with
artillery and armor support were chosen for the operation, and all were
placed under the command of Brigadier General Um Savuth. The operation
was launched in late August 1970, and went entirely according to plan.
Tang Kauk was retaken in early September without great difficulty and
to the surprise of the enemy. This initial success was followed by a
period of calm during which the civil and military authorities worked

Map 11 – OPERATION CHENLA I and Area of Operations

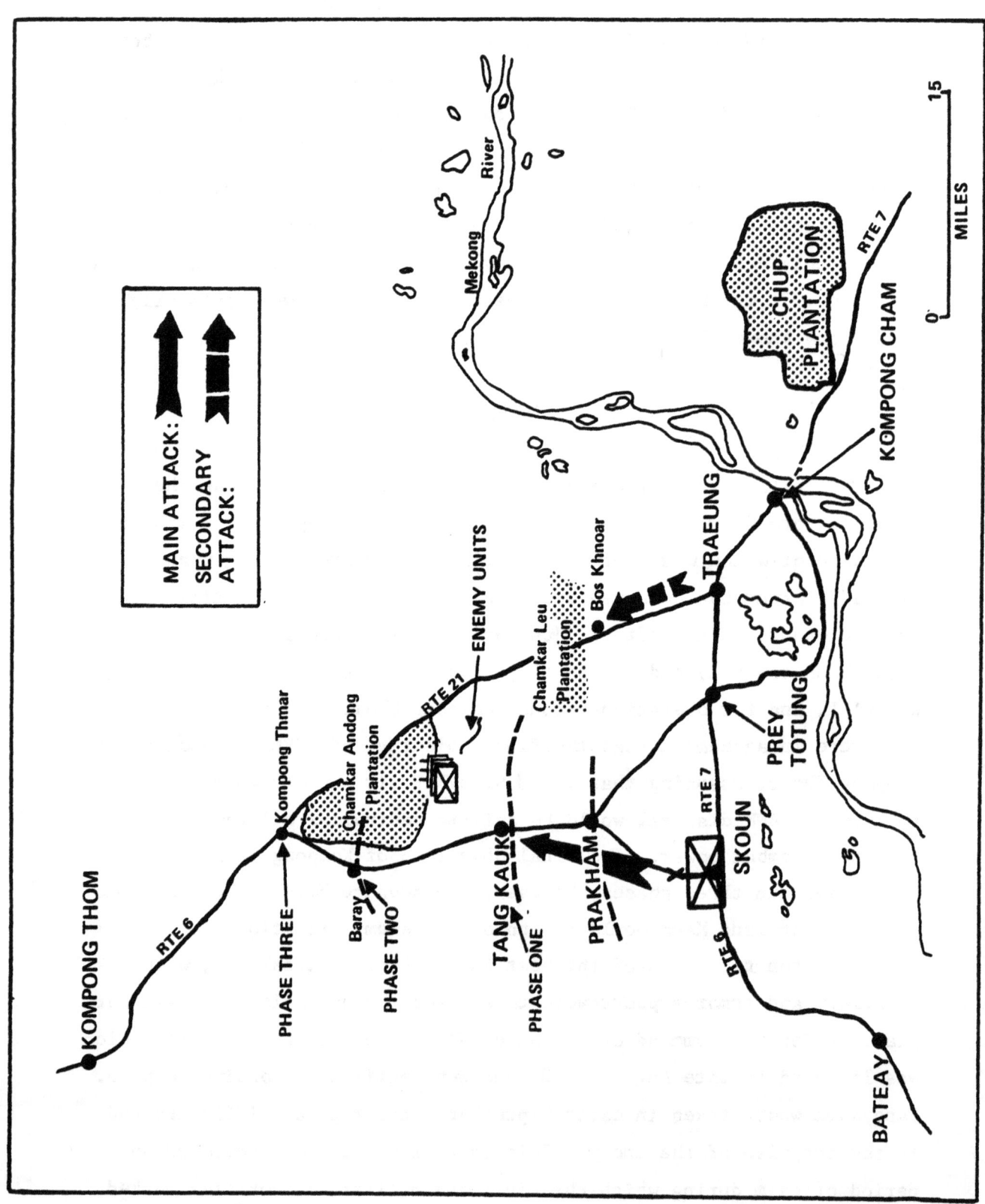

to revitalize the civilian communities around and south of Tang Kauk. Special efforts were made to resettle refugees, and to provide for their protection by the establishment of self-defense units, made up of local inhabitants, and cadred by active-duty personnel.

In conjunction with the main advance north along Route 6 from Skoun, there was a secondary attack from Traung to Bos Khnaor. Pressure from units of the 9th NVA Division located in the rubber plantations east of Route 6 prevented advance of the CHENLA I column beyond Tang Kauk during 1970.

While there was a general slowing of enemy attacks throughout the northern parts of the country following the recapture of Tang Kauk, the areas east of the Mekong, around Kompong Cham, and south of Phnom Penh were scenes of significant enemy initiative in November and December 1970. The enemy reaction to CHENLA I was not directed at the column itself; rather VC/NVA elements carried out a series of attacks against FANK posts along Route 7, between Prey Totung and Kompong Cham, which had the effect of cutting the Route 7 LOC to Kompong Cham. When it appeared in December that the enemy was preparing for a major attack on Kompong Cham, the RVNAF conducted an airmobile operation into the airfield in Kompong Cham. Several days of FANK/RVNAF operations to the north and west produced little contact with the enemy but permitted the FANK to reopen Route 7. FANK units received help from RVNAF units east of the Mekong, and there was a major combined operation to reopen Route 4 by clearing enemy units from the Pich Nil Pass.[3] It should be noted that the enemy carried out these operations while at the same time appearing to displace many of his major units toward his front in South Vietnam.

But for the high command the most remarkable and also the most depressing enemy action came in January 1971, when a group of perhaps

---

[3] For descriptions of the two operations at Kompong Cham and Pich Nil Pass, see Tran Dinh Tho, op cit.

100 VC/NVA commandos mounted a spectacular attack on the Khmer Air Force base at Pochentong airfield west of Phnom Penh. Carried out during the night of 21-22 January, it destroyed practically all of the aircraft, including all of the MIG fighters. The attack on the air base was accompanied by attacks on villages located to the west and northwest of Pochentong. In this situation it was necessary for the high command to withdraw some of the units from the CHENLA column at Tang Kauk to reinforce the outskirts of the capital. On 5 February, the "State of Emergency" was extended for another six months. General Lon Nol spent the entire day of 8 February at the National Assembly, answering the questions of the legislators concerning the attack on the air base and the defense of the country in general. That night he suffered a stroke which left him partially paralized and incapacitated. The following day the government announced that Lon Nol was incapacitated, and on 14 February he was evacuated by U.S. military aircraft to Tripler General Hospital in Honolulu for treatment.

CHENLA II

Lon Nol returned to Phnom Penh on 12 April 1971, after making good progress during his hospitalization. As he became active in military matters again, there was concern for regaining the initiative, and a desire to return the enemy's "blow for blow", to take "eye for eye" and "tooth for tooth". A reactivation of the operation on Route 6, stalled since October 1970, and to be known as CHENLA II was decided on. It would also serve the purposes of Lon Nol's program of general mobilization of the population *(Mobilization Générale)* by returning additional civilians to friendly control. The concept this time called for reopening Route 6 all the way to Kompong Thom. *(Map 12)* The garrison in this provincial capital had been isolated from all land contact with the remainder of the country for almost a year; further it was at the center of another very rich rice-producing area. The relative calm in the year previous had permitted the build-up of large stocks of rice which could only be utilized in the remainder of the country if Route 6 were opened again to friendly truck traffic.

Map 12 – Concept for OPERATION CHENLA II and Area of Operations

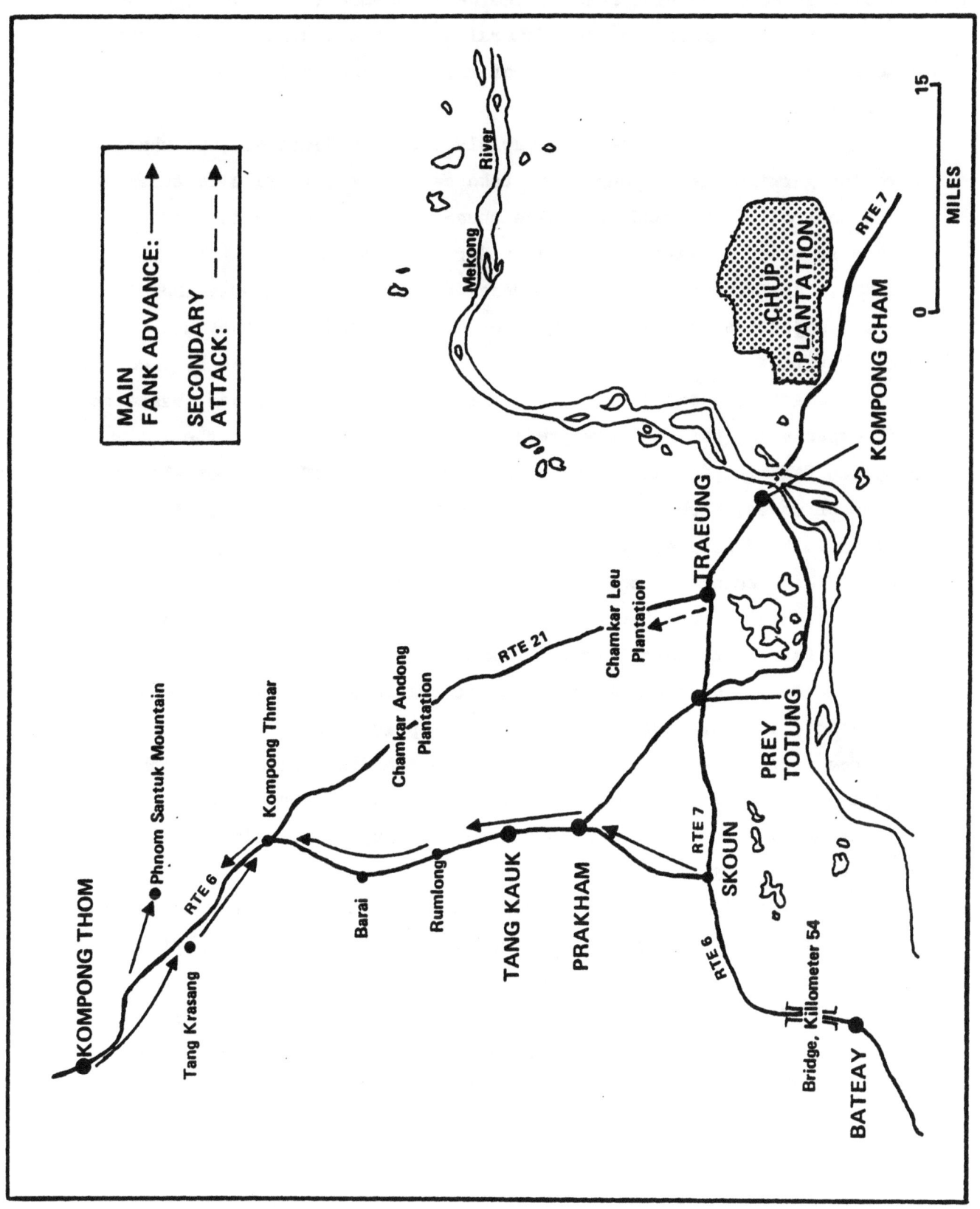

At this point I leave the narration of events in order to discuss the divergence of opinion between the decision-makers in the high command and the technicians of the General Staff concerning the operational concept for CHENLA II. The extent of this divergence is summarized in the following two points of view:

1. Lon Nol saw the need to rapidly liberate Route 6, join hands with the garrison at Kompong Thom, take certain key terrain features which controlled the road, organize these, and to operate from these points in order to extend the area under FANK control.

2. The technicians of the General Staff did not dispute the overall objective of the operation Lon Nol proposed that they accomplish; what they took issue with was the way the operation would be carried out, given the actual enemy situation in the operational area, and, based on FANK experience, the entirely predictable enemy reaction to the proposed FANK initiative. The General Staff favored, first of all, a series of moves which would lead or draw the enemy into areas where they could be destroyed by air or ground action; this would take into account the presence of enemy sanctuaries and command posts in the Chamker Andong rubber plantation. The rapidity with which Lon Nol would hurl the FANK units north along Route 6 would leave them highly vulnerable to fragmentation by flank attack and afterwards easy prey for the enemy. The technicians were guided as well by the principle of economy of force; for some time it had been the same units which did most of the fighting on the various battlefields. The same units would have to be used again for CHENLA II. They were understrength, lacking in certain skills, and required refitting.

Thus, the elaboration of concept into operational plan went forward with great difficulty, given these different points of view. But as always the final decision being with Lon Nol, the difficult birth of the CHENLA II plan was, in the end, carried out over the objections of these technicians who, for their part, watched with sinking hearts the launching of this operation on 20 August 1971.

The first phase of the operation involved some hard fighting, but was a great success for the FANK. Again, the enemy was surprised. Prakham was retaken on the first day. By 24 August, FANK units were attacking north of Rumlong and were able to retake Barai on 26 August. The recapture of Kompong Thmar on 1 September was followed by a period of rest and consolidation of the liberated zones south of Kompong Thmar. On 2 September, one brigade of the 5th Brigade Group attacked south from Kompong Thom along Route 6 and east toward Phnom Santuk. There was heavy fighting in these areas, and Tang Krasang was taken on 20 September. On 5 October FANK units advancing from north and south met in the vicinity of Kompong Thmar. On the same day, three brigades were committed to the capture of the key terrain of Phnom Santuk mountain from the south. The 8th Brigade was moved by helicopter to a position from which it could attack southeast. The fighting was intense, including hand-to-hand combat, as the enemy had time to prepare his defensive positions following FANK capture of Kompong Thmar. Phnom Santuk was taken, however, and on 25 October 1971, the first phase of CHENLA II was declared officially at an end. Marshal Lon Nol marked the junction of FANK units on Route 6 with an "Order of the Day", dated 5 October, and there were numerous religious and military ceremonies on 25 and 26 October to mark the victory.

The enemy gave our units little time to savor their accomplishments, however. Barely hours into the second phase of the operation, the enemy inflicted on the FANK the greatest catastrope of the war, up to that time. On the night of 26 - 27 October 1971, enemy units, attacking out of the Chamkar Andong rubber plantation, launched a general assault on our positions along Route 6, particularly that portion between Tang Kauk and Rumlong. *(Map 13)* I quote here extracts from the after-action report of Brigadier General Hou Hang Sin, commander of the operation, which indicate the circumstances and the conditions of the combat of the two sides.

> On the night of 26 - 27 October 1971, the 9th NVA Division, reinforced by the 205th and 207th regional regiments, launched a general attack against our static defense positions. About 0100, the enemy attacked in force the FANK 376th Battalion, located on Route 6 at WV115640, one km north of Rumlong. This greatly understrength unit was completely overrun at a single blow; about 20 were able to make their way to Barai, and some others got to Rumlong.

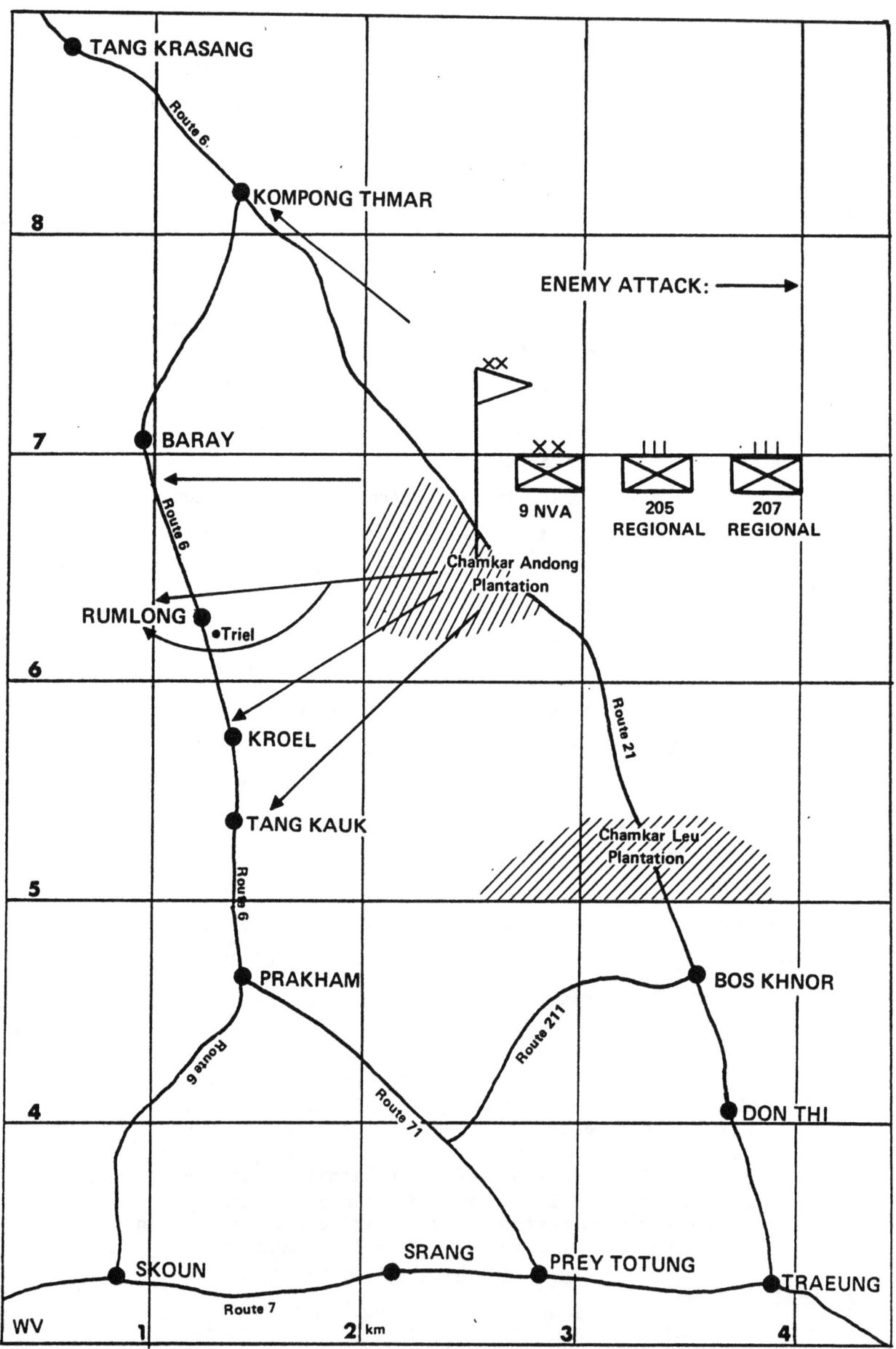

Map 13 — Enemy Attacks Against OPERATION CHENLA II Column, 26-31 October 1971.

Simultaneously with the above attack, the enemy was able to encircle and isolate Rumlong, held by the 14th FANK Battalion and the CP of 46th Infantry Brigade, reinforced by a platoon of 105-mm artillery. The bridge at Spean Dek at Kilometer Mark 54, Route 6 was blown by the enemy on the same night.

The 211th FANK Battalion at Damrei Slap (WU 134592) was heavily attacked on the night of 28 October 1971 by enemy units using toxic gas shells. The majority of the FANK were overcome by the gas and retreated to Kreul.

The 118th FANK Battalion at Kreul, after having suffered successive enemy attacks, retreated to Tang Kauk on 29 October 1971, in company with the 211th Battalion.

After having sustained successive attacks on 28 and 29 October, the 61st Infantry Brigade (composed of the 63d and 425th Battalions) located at Kiri Andeth (WU 157642) was ordered to withdraw to Treal, at that time held by the 22d Battalion.

Having also been attacked at the same time as the 211th Battalion, the 377th Battalion, at Neak Veang (WU 127608) retreated in turn on the night of 31 October to Tang Kauk.

During this critical period from 27 to 31 October 1971, our side suffered numerous dead, wounded, and missing, both military and their families.

From 28 to 31 October, the FANK counter attacks by two brigades to break the line of enemy resistance on Route 6 between Phum Svay and Rumlong did not produce the results hoped for. The combat was very difficult; at times our units arrived just at the line of the enemy, only to have to withdraw because of losses. The following day the same terrain had to be retaken. We were on very unfavorable terrain; there was water everywhere, in the rice fields, and bordering Route 6 north of Rumlong. During the first five days of the counter-attack, our air support was, for a variety of reasons, insufficient.

The troops were by this time very tired. Many of the cadre had been killed or wounded. The average FANK losses were estimated at 100 personnel put out of action per day. In spite of this, we tried to carry on; and orders were given to all those who continued to fight bravely to try to break through. But

we were not able to succeed, due to difficulties
on the battle field, irregular arrival of resupply,
the air drops being intended one day for the counterattacking force, and the next day for the garrisons
at Rumlong and Treal, which were surrounded. During
this effort, our air support was reported to have
strafed our own units, at the time in the process of
infiltrating toward Rumlong. We do not know who
called for this strike, but the incident led to the
discouragement of our troops in their efforts to
relieve Rumlong. In order to accelerate resupply,
an air strip for light aircraft was established
north of Barai, and put into service on 25 November
1971. We were not sufficiently mobile, due to insufficient helicopters and armor, which could have
permitted us to move in force from one point to
another.

In contrast, the enemy, expert in this type of
warfare, dug deep trenches in which their drugged and
chained soldiers waited to strike us, all of which
was synchronized with the fire of heavy weapons located
in the Chamkar Andong Plantation, and directed by
observers located everywhere. We found it impossible
to carry out effective counter-battery fire, due to
lack of sufficient weapons.

In order to strike the enemy a heavy blow,
we were able to obtain B-52 strikes in the Chamkar
Andong area on the 1st and the 14th of November.
We asked for additional strikes, but did not receive
them.

We see, therefore that during a period of only 15 days, the counterattacks of the VC/NVA caused such heavy losses in men and materiel as to completely demoralize the FANK units participating in the operation. I remember traveling to Skoun during that critical period in order to see first-hand the condition of the troops who retreated toward that base; it was not surprising to find the young soldiers and cadre sleeping, a sign of their loss of all sense of combat responsibility. One could say that they were all pursued by the spectre of war ... reinforced in their minds, no doubt, by the spectacular atrocities and other horror which they had witnessed. Many waited for medical evacuation and air support to arrive from on high, which never arrived.

Certainly one cannot completely blame the high command insofar as reinforcements and resupply were concerned. At the same time that operation CHENLA II was in progress there were other places in the country where actions of the enemy required the attention of the FANK. It was a situation where everyone seemed to be trying to cover himself. In these circumstances Marshal Lon Nol presided at a conference on 14 November 1971 which was attended by the senior commanders of CHENLA II. In the course of this meeting, important modifications were made to the initial plan of operation, now more urgent in view of the heavy enemy action to the west of Phnom Penh along Route 4.

Another problem was that the CHENLA II column had been cut into several sections and all that they could do was to use their own means to escape from the grip of the VC/NVA. There was insufficient logistical support and what there was did not arrive in time. The large bridge on Route 6 southwest of Skoun (Kilometer Mark 54) had been blown; thus the logistic base for the operation which had been established in Skoun could not be resupplied except by aerial transport.

During the entire month of November and until 3 December 1971, the final date of operation CHENLA II, there were bloody combat actions the entire length of Route 6 from Prakham to Phnom Santuk. Several of our units took heavy losses, some of them simply vanishing into the countryside, and others fighting courageously to regain friendly lines as best they could. The commander of the operation was no longer in control of the situation and seemed to adopt the solution of "every man for himself". Marshal Lon Nol, with the officers of the general staff, traveled to the CHENLA II front on 30 November 1971 in order to survey the situation as it actually was. Faced with the sad spectacle caused by the collapse of his troops Lon Nol could do nothing more than to conclude the tragic story of operation CHENLA II. In this operation FANK lost some of its best units of infantry as well as a good part of its armor and a great deal of transport, both military and civil. There was never an exact count, but the estimate was on the order of ten battalions of personnel and equipment lost plus the equipment of an additional ten battalions.

Cooperation and Coordination with the RVNAF and the U.S.

In early April 1970, General Lon Nol twice received very discreet, night visits by Nguyen Cao Ky, South Vietnam's Vice President. Though highly secret, these visits nevertheless can be seen as the first steps toward reestablishing diplomatic relations between South Vietnam and Cambodia on the one hand, and toward the initiation of military cooperation and assistance in the face of a common enemy on the other. It is not known exactly how the first of these visits was arranged. Very few people in Phnom Penh knew of them, and they were attended on the Khmer side by General Lon Nol and Prince Sirik Matak only. It is considered possible, however, that General Lon Nol's younger brother Lon Non played a part in the arrangements. Soon after the 18th of March, and before the reestablishment of formal diplomatic relations between the two countries, Lon Non was authorized to enter into liaison with South Vietnamese officials and with Son Ngoc Thanh, the anti-Sihanouk Khmer leader then living in South Vietnam. It is possible that the idea for such a meeting was discussed between Lon Non and Son Ngoc Thanh, and then presented to General Ky by one or the other.[4]

In conjunction with these activities, President Nixon also issued a warning to the enemy when, announcing the next increment of U.S. troop withdrawal from South Vietnam, he referred to the enemy's escalation in Laos and Cambodia and declared on 20 April 1970:

> "The enemy would be taking grave risks if they attempted to use American withdrawals to jeopardize remaining U.S. forces in Vietnam by increased military action in Vietnam, in Cambodia, or in Laos; if they were to do so I shall not hesitate to take strong and effective measures to deal with that situation."

---

[4] At the same time as these contacts, the Cambodian government was also approached by other countries of the Free World, first Thailand, then the Republic of China (Taiwan), followed by South Korea shortly after. All offered to help in some way.

Ten days after issuing this warning, President Nixon announced on 30 April 1970 that U.S. forces, in cooperation with the Republic of Vietnam Armed Forces (RVNAF) were going to launch immediate attacks to destroy enemy sanctuaries along the Khmer-Vietnamese border.

Toward the end of April 1970, simultaneously with an increase in military personnel attached to the U.S. Embassy in Phnom Penh, contacts between the FANK General Staff and the JGS, RVNAF, as well as MACV, became more regular and increasingly solid, even though diplomatic relations were not established between Phnom Penh and Saigon until a month later, on 27 May 1970.

At the same time, the FANK Command authorized the assignment of one RVNAF liaison officer to each Subdivision commander in the 1st and 2d Military Regions. The purpose of this arrangement was to exchange information and coordinate fire support.

In May 1970, a RVN delegation headed by Vice President Nguyen Cao Ky, and including the GVN Minister of Defense, made an official visit to Phnom Penh. At the end of this visit, an agreement was concluded which created a 15-km deep zone on each side of the Cambodian-South Vietnamese border, in which Khmer and Vietnamese military authorities at the Province and District level could operate freely without prior clearance from either government. It was further understood that operations which might require a deeper penetration into Cambodia would be the object of special government agreement. However, the FANK never had the opportunity to make use of this agreement.

In the same spirit of cooperation, the Cambodian government also authorized South Vietnam to establish an operational base at Neak Luong, on the Mekong. This base even received a visit by President Nguyen Van Thieu in June 1970. During this visit, President Thieu met for the first time with H. E. Cheng Heng, then Cambodia's Chief of State, who was accompanied by General Lon Nol and Prince Sisowath Sirik Matak.

During the period of cross-broder operations conducted by U.S./RVN forces, very little was known by the FANK General Staff except for the fact that these operations were designed to destroy NVA/VC sanctuaries and COSVN headquarters in Cambodia. To my knowledge, only General Lon Nol had been informed to some extent of U.S. intentions concerning these operations. As to the FANK General Staff, the information it obtained was general and sketchy. It only knew that U.S. and RVN forces had been authorized to conduct a military operation across the Cambodian-South Vietnamese border during the period May-June 1970. The FANK had no detail whatsoever concerning the plans of this operation; it did not even know the size of forces committed. This lack of information extended equally to the results of these operations. No details of the results were ever communicated to the Cambodian government.

Nevertheless, the ties between the military authorities of Cambodia, South Vietnam, and the U.S. were becoming closer. These were strengthened by instituting regular Tripartite meetings, initially at MACV headquarters or the JGS in Saigon. Here FANK, RVNAF and MACV delegations met each month. Because of its lack of facilities and material resources, the FANK General Staff was not able to host tripartite meetings until 1972. The objectives of these tripartite meetings were to: (1) exchange information concerning South Vietnam, Cambodia and a part of Laos; (2) study and plan for current military operations which were to be conducted either by Khmer forces alone or by combined forces (FANK-RVNAF) with U.S. air support; (3) study and plan for logistic support, and; (4) study and plan for the training of Khmer military personnel.

In 1970, a liaison office was established by the RVNAF in Phnom Penh, following a parallel agreement to install a similar office by the FANK in Saigon.

As far as air support was concerned, cooperation was equally close. The Khmer Air Force, for example, installed an Air Support Coordination Detachment at Headquarters, U.S. 7th Air Force in Saigon, another at Tan Chau to accompany river convoys, and a detachment of observer-interpreters at Bien Hoa. In return, the Vietnam Air Force also installed an Air Support Coordination Detachment in Phnom Penh which dealt directly with the FANK General Staff in matters concerning air support. During this period of cooperation, the majority of daylight air support missions, especially reconnaissance support missions, were provided by the U.S. 7th Air Force and the VNAF, both of which also flew night support missions that only they could provide. As to the Khmer Air Force, it was responsible for transport missions within Cambodia and close air support in medium-scale operations.

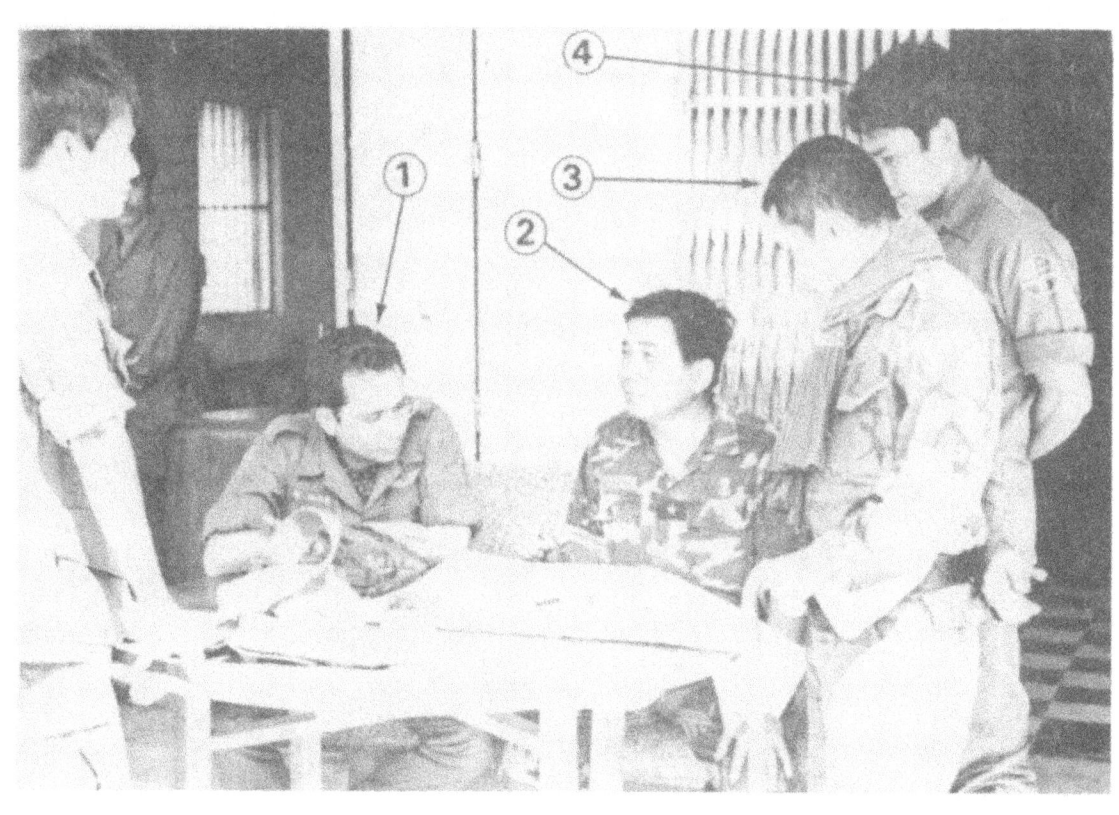

A Planning Session for OPERATION CHENLA II
Identified are: (1) Brig. Gen. So Sato; (2) Brig. Gen. Hou Hang Sin;
(3) Brig. Gen. Um Savuth; (4) Brig. Gen. It Sung

Brigadier General Fan Muong, Commander 1st Military Region,
Inspects a Squad in Kompong Cham Armed with the U.S. M-1 Carbine,
November 1970

FANK Recruits Move to the OPERATION CHENLA I Area on a Requisitioned Civilian Truck, Armed with the Communist Assault Rifle, AK-47; November 1970

CHAPTER V

The Politico/Military Situation in Cambodia, 1972-1974

The Political Situation

Before discussing the political situation itself, it is well to recall to mind the following dates and periods: 9 October 1970, date of the proclamation which transformed the Kingdom of Cambodia into the Khmer Republic; June to December 1971, the period during which the text of the constitution of the Khmer Republic was written; 10 March 1972, the date on which Mr. Cheng Heng, the Chief of State of Cambodia since the removal of Prince Sihanouk, resigned and transferred his powers to Marshal Lon Nol (the honor of "Marshal" was conferred on Lon Nol by the Khmer Parliament on 21 April 1971); 4 June 1972, the day on which Marshal Lon Nol was elected as the first President of the Khmer Republic after the text of the constitution had been adopted by a popular referendum on 30 April 1972.

The period from 1972 through 1974 saw both an intensification of military activities and internal political activities in Cambodia. If the efforts at fighting the war merited a certain amount of respect during those years, the internal political maneuvering diminished these accomplishments, while the enemy concerned himself with a struggle to the end on both the political and diplomatic fronts.

These internal political divergences grew not out of the proclamation of the Khmer Republic but rather during the time of the preparation and the putting into effect of the republican institutions themselves. With the promulgation of the constitution, the first signs of division were reflected in the political parties of which the three principal leaders of the events of 18 March 1970 (Lon Nol, Sirik Matak and In Tam) were also the founders. These three were never in agreement. Two principle tendencies appeared from this discord. The first took as fundamental, the need for a respect for and strict application of the rules and principles announced in the new republican constitution. The second, while not opposed to these principles nevertheless insisted that certain of them were inadequate for a country at war and should be temporarily suspended, such as the prohibition against the participation of military personnel in elections, that is, the holding of political office, as came to pass in the election for President and for members of legislature. The second group also favored limitations on the formation of political parties during the period of hostilities. By means of maneuvering which was more or less shady and calculated, the second tendency gave way to the first and thus, there were three political parties which came into being during the course of these troubled years. Marshal Lon Nol created his Socio-Republican Party backed by his young brother Lon Non, a Lieutenant Colonel in the FANK at the time; Lieutenant General Sirik Matak, who no longer exercised military command in view of his frequent use on political and diplomatic missions, formed and directed his Republican Party; Brigadier General In Tam, having both military and civil functions (President of the National Assembly on 18 March 1970 and Commander of the 1st Military Region at Kompong Cham and later Prime Minister and member of the High Political Council) was also the Director of the Democrat Party, having as his own strong right arm Mr. Chau Sau who in his turn became leader of the party after In Tam retired from the post, provoked doubtless by a difference of opinion between In Tam and Chau Sau.

The years from 1972 on saw for these political parties an intensification of their individual political campaigns among which the mass of the population, the armed forces, the religious leaders, the civil servants and the young students. All of these, who had already suffered greatly from the war, and from its propaganda campaigns now had to express their support for one or the other of the political parties, or even to submit to intimidation or to illegal force. The violent politics and criticisms which the political parties attempted to hurl more or less openly at each other only contributed to widen the gap between the governing group and those who were being governed.

The waves produced by all of those ardent political campaigns shook the foundations of the FANK, already severely hurt by the enemy; and, if the foundation of the Armed Forces was not completely destroyed during this unhappy period of struggle for internal influence this was thanks to the conduct of the majority of the senior military leaders who placed their noble mission of "defense of the country in danger" above all personal and political ambition and above all other temptation. Unfortunately, and it must be admitted without shame, there were minorities, both civil and military, who let themselves be carried along more or less voluntarily and with enthusiasm by these currents of political evasion without actually realizing that by these acts they served only the interest of the enemy. Disruptions of the political, social, and economic order manifested themselves among the mass of students and against the regime of Lon Nol, certain of which manifestations lead to tragedy and death both among the demonstrators and on the side of the government. There were the tragic instances of the death of the Minister of National Education, Mr. Keo Sang Kim, and a well-known teacher, Mrs. Thach Chea. Certain of the student leaders were arrested, imprisoned and then brought before a military court. At the same time as these crises were being encountered there were other unhappy situations which intruded themselves into the arena of military command, such as the almost total dissatisfaction among the FANK because of the stoppage or slowing of the payment of salaries, the lack of sufficient rice, the totally unfair and partial way in which decorations and promotions were passed out to military personnel in combat.

In short, the seeds of democratization which had been thrown into the wind with such goodwill by the Khmer leaders returned for the Khmer Republic nothing but a poor harvest. The divisions among the republican leadership was a worse situation and the personal conflict between the leaders was irreconcilable at a time when the enemy had succeeded in uniting all of its forces into a single solid front and was marching toward the wide-swinging gates of the country.

Enemy Strategy

During the years 1972 to 1974, the strategy practiced by the VC/NVA enemy in Cambodia was marked by a movement toward "Khmerization" of the war, that is to say, the relief by Khmer communists forces, called *Khmer Rouge*, of VC/NVA units which had operated in Cambodia since 1970. This program to pass the military task to the Khmer Communists units was in line with decisions adopted at the Indochina Summit Conference, to which I have already referred. Within the space of two years the VC/NVA succeeded in forming the basis for a Khmer Communist armed force. There were created battalions, regiments, and even the beginning of establishment of divisions, these later observed shortly before the fall of the country. Within this Khmer Communist force, composed for the most part of Khmer, there existed nevertheless certain important Vietnamese Communist cadre, such as political counselors.

The process of deploying the Khmer Communist units took place progressively on the various fronts in coordination with what appeared to be a general movement by regular VC/NVA units from the interior of Cambodia toward Vietnam. A good number of the battles of war involved Khmer Communist units in action against the FANK while the VC/NVA limited their action to providing the support of their weapon units. Certain specialized VC/NVA units acted in concert with the Khmer Rouge in order carry out commando raids against important military objectives, as well as to carry out acts of terrorism, particularly in the interior centers of friendly control. An example was the commando raid carried out on the night of 7 October 1972 against the armored vehicle park situated in the north section of Phnom Penh. Two others were the big battle around Kompong Cham in September 1973 and the bombardment by rockets of the southeast suburbs of the capital, the latter causing several deaths and wounded among the civil population and the burning of more than 200 homes.

In short, the major thrust of the enemy strategy was achieved by two routes: on the political side there was the almost complete transformation of the face of the war itself from one of aggression carried out by foreign forces to one of civil war between the Khmer Republic and the Khmer Communists. This political transformation was extremely valuable to the enemy in consolidating his position in international opinion. On the military side, beyond the sabotage of the morale of the FANK provoked by the increase in intensity and frequency of battle, the enemy succeeded by the middle of 1974 in isolating the capital of Phnom Penh from its contact with the various provincial capitals. Thus, the fragmentation of the mass of the FANK into similar groups, cut off from each other, resulted in their inability to provide mutual support and left them more and more to defend in their own zones.

General Mobilization --
The Plan for the Countryside

General Mobilization was declared on June 25, 1970, to be followed on 7 November by publication of the implementing directive for that law.

It should be remembered that since its independence Cambodia had never had any clear idea of what general mobilization would consist of in time of war. It was imagined that it would be taken care of by the various responsible officials of the Ministry of National Defense but it was overlooked or even treated with indifference due primarily to the great confidence which Cambodia had in its policies of neutrality and peace.

For a Cambodia at war it must be pointed out that the dominant figure in this sort of activity was none other than Marshal Lon Nol. When the law was first published it appeared that its application would be as straightforward as its application in other countries at war, simply the mobilization of all human resources, the mobilization of other resources such as industry, finance, property, private or semi-private and their placing at the disposal of the state so that each might contribute to the war. But great was the surprise even among the responsible civil and military officials and equally among foreign and diplomatic observers in the country.

For Cambodia the charter of its general mobilization was so broad and so complex that neither the decision-makers who were assigned to manage general mobilization or the lower ranking people who were charged with its execution were ever able to comprehend completely the complete sense of the program. If you analyze the various aspects at some depth it would seem that the general ideas for Cambodia's general mobilization were, in fact, excellent. The problem was that to make them work it would be necessary to carry out wide-spread instruction, education, and training among the mass of the population and to do this in time of peace.

It was with good reason that Marshal Lon Nol gave to this law the name of "The Chessboard of General Mobilization".[1] The law was, in fact, a sort of profound reform of Khmer institutions, touching all aspects of the organization of the state. For example, considering just the problem of defense, Cambodians would, according to this plan for general mobilization, be required to organize themselves hierarchically from bottom to top, beginning with groups of 10 houses. These groups of 10 would be grouped together by 50; groups of 50 would be called a sub-cluster; sub-clusters would form clusters of sub-sectors of defense; and several sub-sectors or clusters would constitute a sector of defense. A sector of defense would correspond essentially to a municipality or a province. If the concern was only for defense organization, it was not bad and could have been carried out rather easily. But in the course of its application the organization just for defense became more and more complicated by the interjection of general or extraneous ideas and by overloading the defense organization with additional missions such as the care of refugees and victims of war, the receipt of ralliers, the feeding of the population, instruction and social well being.

---

[1] In French: *L'Echiquier de la Mobilisation Générale.*

Marshal Lon Nol was personally very attached to this law; it was his masterpiece and he never informed himself of the difficulties and obstacles which presented themselves at every turn in our efforts to apply the law. His actions with respect to general mobilization were such as to create confusion both among the administrative authorities at various levels and between civil and military authorities. The confusion was less marked in those cases where the military chief exercised both civil administrative functions and his regular military responsibilities. On examination, it could be seen for example, that one person acting as chief of a group of 10 or a group of 50 houses would find himself the final authority in his group not only for matters of defense but for social well being, carrying out a census of refugees, collecting intelligence, feeding, and the distribution of food. And, to go further, this chief of group became himself a representative in his own sphere of various ministerial authorities in the central government. The decentralization and delegation of central powers to this extreme lead thus to the loss of authority on the part of the person responsible for general mobilization and it was unfortunately true that the chief of the Commissariat of General Mobilization did not know where to turn.

Day-by-day the events of war brought crisis after crisis to the social, economic, and political order and crisis after crisis in questions of defense, for which the responsible authorities sought always to place the blame on each other. It was not surprising that the post of Commissioner of General Mobilization changed hands frequently, passing from military to civilian incumbent and vice versa.

I remember how Marshal Lon Nol worked day and night for months to put his own ideas on general mobilization into the law. From my own knowledge I have the impression that Lon Nol's ideas were inspired by his own experiences while he was Royal Delegate for the province of Battambang during the "Crusade for Independence" of Prince Sihanouk in 1952, 1953. During this period he was the founder of the armed villagers of *chivapols* which I have mentioned earlier, in Chapter III.

It is recalled that the mission of these armed villagers was limited to the static defense of their village or to the participation in small combat actions in the rear areas or under the cover of regular units. Another source of inspiration for Lon Nol was doubtless the image he formed of the organization of the Chinese Communist communities and of their system of defense during his visit in the People's Republic of China. Finally, as soon as war itself came to Cambodia, the desires of Marshal Lon Nol were equally tempted by the mechanism of the pacification program which the South Vietnamese had organized in certain vital areas and called "strategic hamlets", these operating within the framework of a general regional defense plan. Another factor which should be mentioned as having had influence on Lon Nol's thinking was the doctrine of political warfare as developed by the Chinese on Taiwan, who were at that time considered expert in matters of anti-communist struggle. It seems to me therefore, that Marshal Lon Nol attempted to draw from all of these sources in the process of writing the law of general mobilization for Cambodia. All his efforts were devoted from the very first hours of the crisis to the establishment of the system. But unfortunately all of the problems, social attitudes, time required, the enemy, etc. all acted to prevent him from achieving his desire. Thus for this "General Mobilization" the chessboard was set out, the squares were drawn, certain pieces were set into place, but not all of them. The great handicap was that the game in all its aspects (art, rule, moves of the pieces) had to be played in the face of enemy action.

Condition of the FANK

We have seen in the preceeding chapters how the morale of the FANK became more and more beat down by the defeats of such battles as CHENLA II on Route 6. The enthusiasm on 18 March 1970 and its spirit of determination to struggle was no longer held to the same degree by the time of 1972 to 1974. The successes which FANK had had in certain battles and the incentives and decorations of individuals and certain units were not sufficient to reverse the tide of ever-lowered morale.

The deployment of hastily formed FANK units, trained in South Vietnam or in Thailand and newly armed and equipped, the great increase in the level of U.S. military and economic aid had seemed to give some general comfort and encouragement if only for a short time, in a climate greatly agitated by the opening of numerous military fronts and also by the jolts to political, economic, financial and social order. The intensification of combat and the losses suffered by FANK affected the recruitment campaign to the point that it became more and more difficult to organize new units.

In all three services of the FANK, there were complaints about the lack of means, about the bankruptcy of efforts to improve social conditions, and about the injustice of the system itself. Whether true or not, there was no lack in either camp -- friendly or enemy -- of those willing to exploit these complaints. The shortages of food, particularly rice, and its improper distribution, the ever decreasing results from recruitment, the prolonged use of the same units in combat without relief, all gave yet another blow to the morale of the FANK.

If these internal conditions, mentioned briefly above, were instrumental in destroying the morale of the FANK, it would be unjust on my part not to mention the various events on the international scene which also influenced in one way or another the general morale of Khmer troops. The signing of the cease-fire agreement in Paris in January 1973 by the U.S. and Hanoi, followed shortly by a series of declarations, about both the unilateral cease-fire which Lon Nol ordered the FANK to carry out, and the often repeated peace initiatives of the Khmer Republic during 1973 and 1974, plus the rumors of a cessation of U.S.-aid, rumors which were embellished by less than favorable comment on the Lon Nol government, all worked to lower the morale of military personnel. These factors provoked in a certain poorly-informed part of the FANK a sort of hypnotic spell which locked them into an attitude of opportunistic, day-to-day wait and see, hoping always for a well-deserved peace.

The End of U.S. Bombing

In January 1973 the world opinion acclaimed the signing of the Paris Accords on a cease-fire in South Vietnam. And Cambodian opinion prepared itself for the shock of surprise which might create a disagreeable military consequence. Among the many measures which followed from the new policy of the United States, the cessation of U.S. air support in the Khmer theatre of operations provoked different reactions among different groups, both within the nation and among foreigners, the majority of which predicted the immediate collapse of the FANK and therefore the fall of the regime.

On 15 August 1973, the U.S. announced officially the end of all its aerial operations in support of FANK combat operations; thus all of these responsibilities fell on the shoulders of the Khmer Air Force (KAF). We remember that the KAF was almost completely destroyed by the VC/NVA commando attack on the January 21 - 22 1971. Following 1971 and until 1973 the KAF was progressively reconstituted with U.S. aid. The formation and training of personnel and the deployment of aircraft was carried out in record time. It should be said that at the end of two years the KAF possessed a full, though on small scale, infrastructure, capable of inspiring confidence in their colleagues in the ground forces. The challenge for the KAF after 15 August 1973, therefore, was to provide the very large number of missions required to support military operations and also be available and prepared to support our civil sectors as required. Speaking only of military support, the KAF achieved brilliant results in the support of operations at Kampot and Prey Veng, at Lovek and at Kompong Thom, during which the T-28s were able to achieve a rate of 80 sorties per day, excluding missions of reconnaissance, liaison, and support of other fronts with the C-47s. As for the helicopters and transport aircraft, they were able to successfully transport three brigades of infantry in order to save the situation at Kampot City, at a time when a part of the city was already occupied by communist forces. In addition to this direct support of troops in combat both day and night, the KAF carried out a large number of transport missions for the benefit of the civil sector.

From the 15th of August 1973 forward, both foreign and Khmer observers witnessed the growing war between the Khmer themselves, that is between the FANK of the Khmer Republic and the forces of the Khmer Communists. The land, the high seas, the rivers and lakes, the skies clear and cloudy were all criss-crossed by ships, vehicles, and aircraft flying the emblem of the Republic as they went in search of the enemy prey. It was also the date when the FANK began to operate independently of all assistance from foreign forces and it was for that reason that the date of 15 August was chosen as Armed Forces Day for the FANK, an occasion which the Khmer Republic celebrated for the first and last time on 15 August 1974 before the esplanade of the sacred Stoupa of the Great Teacher Buddha Sakhyamoui.[2]

---

[2] The Stoupa Sakhyamoui is located in Phnom Penh, in a large open square in front of the railroad station. It is considered by the Khmer to contain a relic of Buddha.

Marshal Lon Nol, President of the Khmer Republic, April 1972

CHAPTER VI

Major Military Operations, 1972 through 1974

The three years of 1972 through 1974 were a period during which combat activity was more or less general throughout those portions of Cambodia which remained under friendly control at the end of 1970. *(Map 8)* It was also a period during which the overall initiative passed from the FANK to the VC/NVA and then to the Khmer Communist forces. As the initiative passed more and more firmly to the communist side, the FANK was concerned more and more with the defense of vital lines of communication, the population centers, and, finally and especially the capital of Phnom Penh itself. During this period the war became increasingly conventional in nature, with both sides learning to use increasingly sophisticated materiel and to deploy larger and more cohesive combat units, to the point that by the end of 1974 there were both FANK and Khmer Communist divisions in the field. The operations I have chosen to discuss in this chapter demonstrate these general trends. Once more I pay tribute to the valor and patriotism of the FANK as a whole. Despite all of the losses and difficulties, despite the ever-tightening circle, the forces of the Khmer Republic remained in the field to the end.

Following the high levels of combat activity that characterized the period of CHENLA II, the first three months of 1972 saw a decided lull in activity, as the VC/NVA carried out logistic activities in preparation for combat in SVN. During this three-month period, the FANK participated in operation PREK TA and ANGKOR CHEY. *(Map 14)* In eastern Kompong Cham Province, RVNAF withdrawal of its OPERATION TOAN THANG units prompted the FANK to withdraw the 22d Brigade from Krek on 10 January 1972, and redeploy it to the vicinity of Neak

Map 14 – Locations of FANK Operations ANGKOR CHEY and PREK TA

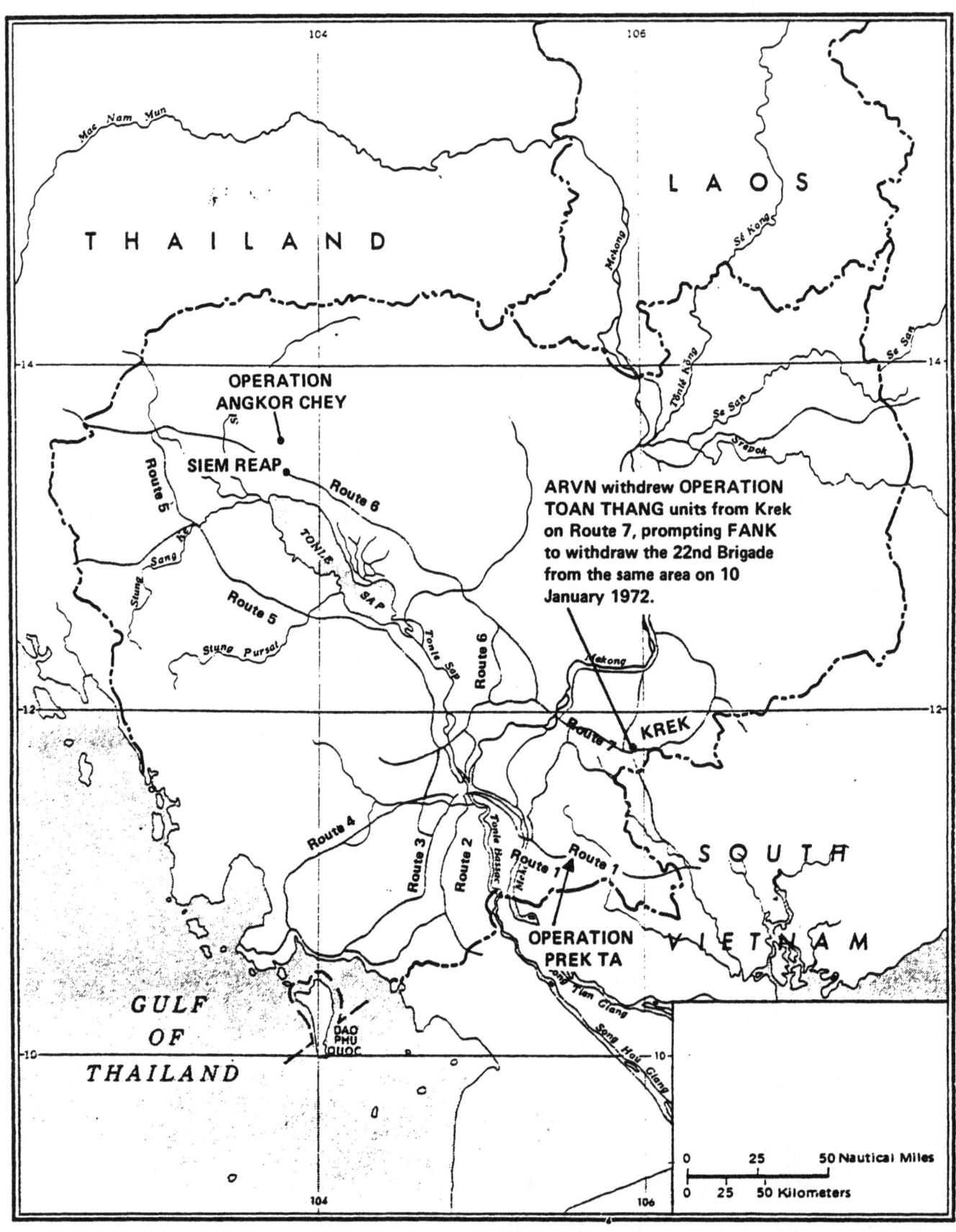

Luong. These withdrawals left this part of the province in enemy hands, and it was never again reoccupied by the FANK. Operation PREK TA, a combined FANK/ARVN operation involving 11 battalions, was launched on 10 January south of Route 1, between the Mekong and the RVN border. In Siem Reap Province, OPERATION ANGKOR CHEY was launched on 29 January with the objective of encircling the Ankor Wat/Angkor Thom temple complex and ruins, and interdicting the flow of enemy supplies into the Angkor area. The enemy had been able to create a sort of sanctuary there because of our hesitation to risk damaging these national treasures. Initially the operation was marked by small-scale skirmishes along Route 6, east and west of Siem Reap. On 21 February FANK units ran into stiff resistance as they tried to route the enemy from fortified positions along the southern periphery of the temple complex.

Operations in Military Regions 1 and 2, and Against Phnom Penh, March-June 1972

The three-month lull was broken on 20 March 1972 when the enemy directed attacks against Prey Veng City and Neak Luong. *(Map 15)* Friendly positions in and near Prey Veng City were subjected to heavy 60-mm, 82-mm mortar, 75-mm recoilless, and 120-mm rocket fire, followed by ground actions further south along Route 15 and approximately 20 km west of Prey Veng City. An allied POL and ammunition storage depot at Neak Luong was also destroyed by 122-mm rocket fire. Cumulative friendly casualties were 18 killed, 60 wounded, and ten missing, while enemy losses were 33 killed.

ARVN's operation TOAN THANG VIII, which began on 9 March north of Svay Rieng City, ended on 29 March with significant results. Enemy losses were reported as 764 killed (583 by air), 29 captured; 1,117 individual weapons and 37 crew served weapons captured. Additionally 871 tons rice, 49 tons salt, 73,000 meters of communication wire and 24,000 litres of gasoline were captured and other miscellaneous items destroyed. Friendly losses were nine killed and 67 wounded.

Map 15 — Areas of Operations, March - June 1972

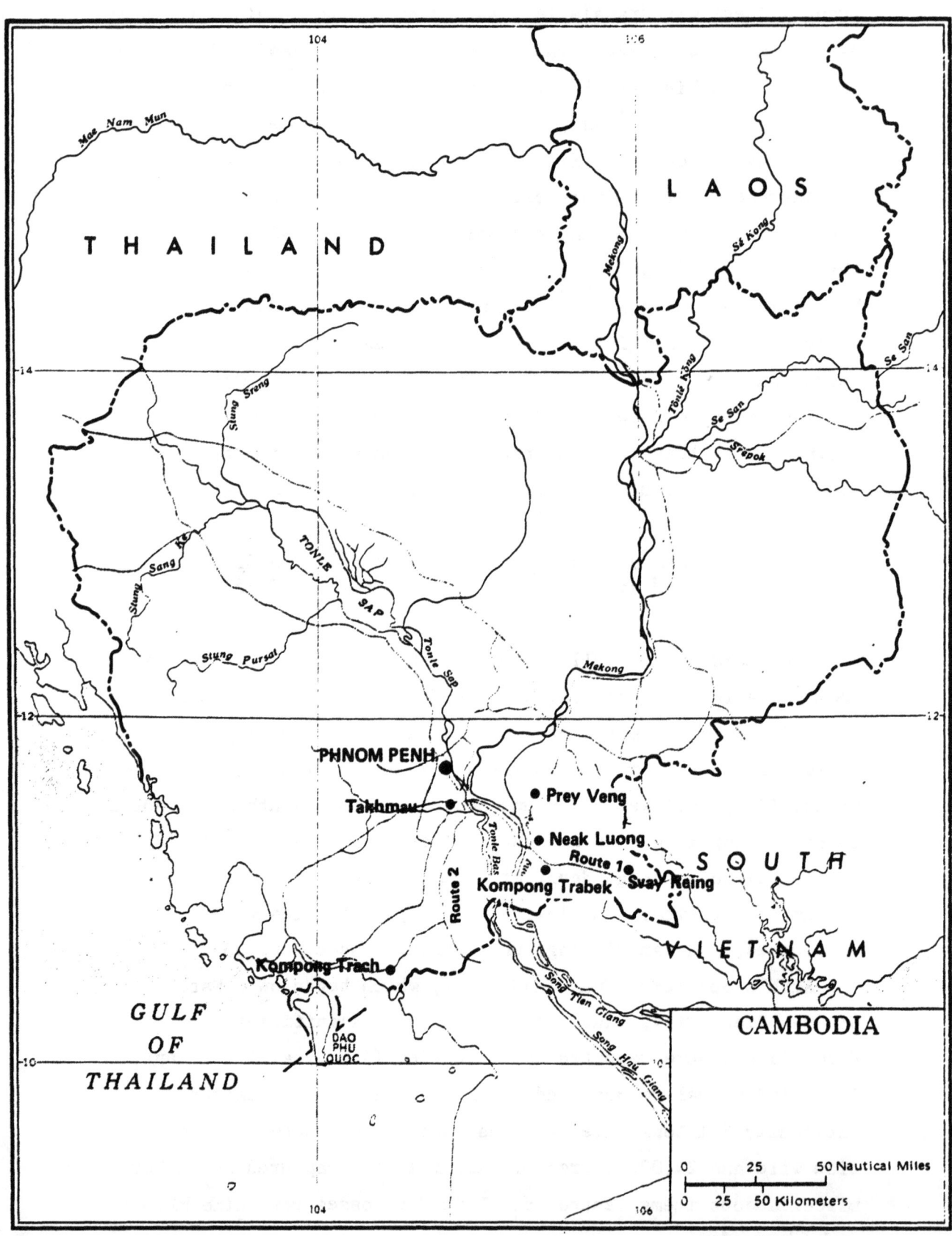

Combat action in Military Region 2 stepped up significantly on 23 March, following several months of only small scale enemy harassments. ARVN's 93d Ranger Battalion and 12th Armored Regiment were involved in several engagements in the vicinity of Kompong Trach, including at least three enemy ground assaults, while receiving over 500 rounds of mixed rocket and mortar fire from 23 to 31 March.

At the same time as the attacks at Prey Veng, the enemy launched what was to that date (March 20) its heaviest rocket and mortar attack against Phnom Penh. *(Map 16)* Seven separate areas within the city's west and northwest sector, as well as positions near Pochenton Airfield, received a total of about 200 rounds of 122-mm rocket fire and 75-mm recoilless rifle fire. The shellings, accompanied by a ground attack against the government's radio transmitting facility southwest of the city, left 102 friendly killed (mostly civilians), 208 wounded, and 400 families homeless; additionally, one light aircraft and more than 200 wooden homes were destroyed, while four small aircraft and the radio station were damaged. In response to the attack on Phnom Penh, several small-scale (two-four battalion) clearing operations were immediately launched by FANK on the capital's outer perimeter. Terrorist incidents also increased in the capital area. Grenade attacks against a military dependents' housing area on the 26th and against a bus carrying military personnel in Phnom Penh on the 28th left 11 persons dead and 66 others wounded.

Following the attacks of 21 March, the enemy conducted a series of terrorist and sabotage actions, mostly targeted against Cambodian shipping. On 23 March, a cargo vessel was sunk and another damaged on the Mekong near the Chruoy Chang War Naval Base. A few days later, two POL barges moored in the same area were damaged by floating mines. On the 24th, a span of the Chruoy Chang War Bridge was damaged when a vehicle containing an estimated 200 kilos of explosives was detonated at mid-point of the structure, killing four and wounding seven persons. The bridge was repaired with Bailey bridging and opened to traffic by the 27th.

About one month later, on 18-19 April, the enemy renewed attacks along Route 1 east of the Mekong. Within three days, a total of 22 government positions along the highway had been abandoned, leaving only

Map 16 – Points of Military Interest in Phnom Penh

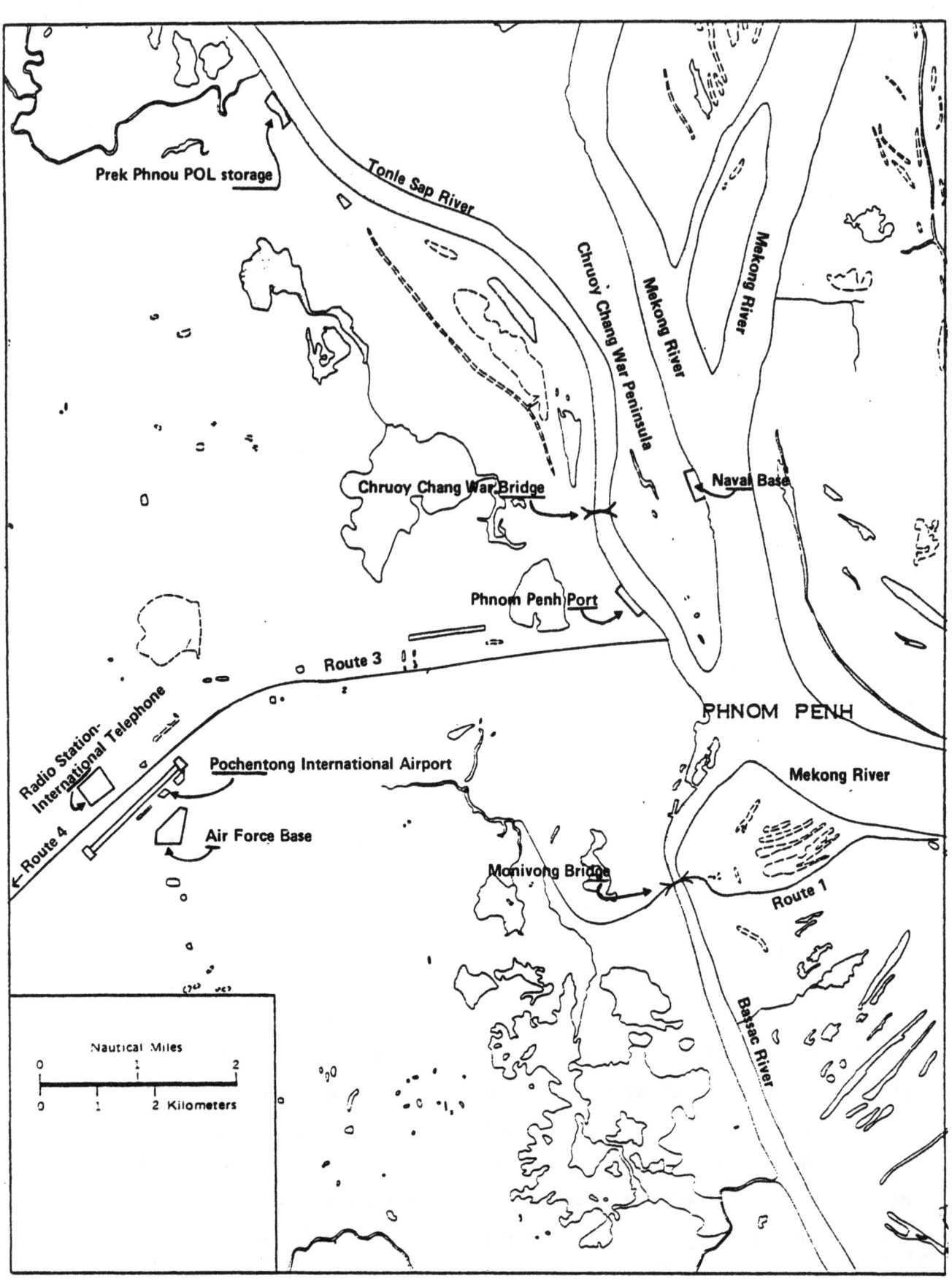

Neak Luong, Svay Rieng and Bavet Village (near the border) in friendly hands. In response to the attacks, Neak Luong and Svay Rieng were reinforced and a route-clearing operation was launched toward Kompong Trabek. However, FANK forces had made little headway in reopening the roadway by the end of April. Five FANK battalions were withdrawn from training in the RVN to augment forces which were stalled about 6 km west of Kompong Trabek. Five FANK battalions previously stationed along Route 1 were unlocated. In a related activity, Prey Veng City received 17 separate rocket, mortar and recoilless rifle fire attacks during the month; casualties were light and no significant damage reported. The city was isolated on 7 April by an estimated two-battalion enemy force located on Route 15 midway between Banam and Prey Veng City. Attempts to reopen the roadway were halted when the 23d Brigade (originally from Pursat) was redeployed to Neak Luong for use along Route 1. Two battalions of the 15th Brigade were subsequently assigned to Prey Veng City to augment the garrison there in anticipation of increased enemy pressure. In Military Region 2, FANK/RVNAF forces continued to engage what were probably elements of the 1st NVA Division in the vicinity of Kompong Trach. The town was surrounded by the enemy in mid-April, creating a serious situation which was eased only after RVNAF reinforcements from Ha Tien arrived on 24 April.

On 6 May, the Phnom Penh area received its second major attack by fire in less than two months. This time the city, Pochenton airfield, and Chruoy Chang War Naval Base received attacks by rocket, mortar, and recoilless rifle fire, killing 28 persons and wounding 96 others (2/3 civilians). An aircraft was destroyed and four other planes and several houses were damaged. Enemy sapper raids, estimated at battalion strength, were conducted in the city's southern environs against the Monivong Bridge, electric power station, and the Caltex storage facility. The attackers were repulsed after causing only light damage. The city was lightly shelled again on 9, 10, and 11 May. Beginning 26 May, Svay Rieng City was subjected to enemy attacks by fire and small-scale ground assaults, with no major casualties or damage reported. This increased action was probably designed to keep FANK confined to the city's defense, thereby facilitating a new logistic push by the enemy in southeast

Cambodia. ARVN Ranger units, supported by artillery and tactical air strikes, reported killing 180 enemy southwest of Kompong Trabek on 31 May, while suffering 6 killed and 33 wounded. In Military Region 2, enemy forces further expanded their control over key terrain in southern Kampot and Takeo Provinces. Following the capture of Kompong Trach on 30 April, the enemy advanced north on Route 16, forcing FANK to abandon five outposts and burning several towns in the wake of their attacks. RVNAF units continued to conduct cross-border operations in the area east of Kompong Trach in an effort to curb the flow of enemy supplies and reinforcements into the delta region of RVN.

The month of June 1972 was marked by an attack by fire on the Phnom Penh area—the third since March—and the ambush of two FANK battalions. Phnom Penh was shelled by 18 rounds of 122-mm rocket fire, impacting in the vicinity of the water works, railroad station, Ministry of National Defense and Pochentong airbase. Positions at Takhmau, 10 km south of Phnom Penh, received 100 rounds of 75-mm RR fire, followed by enemy ground attacks in the vicinity. Pochentong airfield was again hit on 11 June, this time by three 122-mm rockets, with no damage or casualties reported. Also three 107-mm rockets were fired from a Volkswagen Microbus against the Ministry of National Defense building on 5 June. The situation near Svay Rieng eased substantially during the month as enemy forces directed efforts towards RVN. Southeast of Neak Luong, two battalions of the 48th Khmer Krom Brigade were ambushed on 25 June in the most significant action along Route 1 since its closure on 18-19 April. Only 13 soldiers returned to friendly lines while approximately 600 others were officially unaccounted for. A joint ARVN/FANK operation to retake Route 1, and scheduled to be launched on 24-25 June, was subsequently delayed until 4 July.

FANK Efforts to Keep Lines of Communications Open, July-December 1972

During the first few days of July 1972, active military operations slowed markedly for the inauguration activities of President Lon Nol, and no enemy actions marred the 3-day holiday period. On 4 July, FANK launched OPERATION SORYA, a combined operation with ARVN, to seize Kompong Trabek; this was accomplished on 24 July. *(Map 17)* Five battalions of the 11th FANK Brigade Group and three battalions of the FANK 66th Brigade were left to hold FANK positions on Route 1, pending phase II of OPERATION SORYA, planned for late August. In Military Region 2, the enemy encircled Ang Tassom. *(Map 18)* Ang Tassom was relieved on 11 July while funeral services were being held at Phnom Penh for Brigadier General Kong Chhaith, Takeo Province Governor, killed while leading the earlier relief efforts. In Military Region 3, Khmer Communist activities were instrumental in closing Route 5 to rice convoy traffic for about two weeks.

The enemy reacted to FANK/ARVN successes at Kompong Trabek by attacking friendly positions on Route 1 on 6 August. These attacks were supported by enemy armor and left him in control of a 7-km section of Route 1, isolating five battalions of the FANK 11th Brigade Group west of Kompong Trabek. This was the first use of enemy armor in the Cambodia conflict. An NVA prisoner captured at Kompong Trabek stated that the tanks came from the Chup Plantation and were to return there after completing their mission in the Route 1 area. As of 24 August, a total of 31 armored vehicles had been destroyed or damaged. OPERATION SORYA II was launched on 11 August with the objective of clearing the road and relieving the five surrounded FANK battalions. After 10 days of artillery and air strikes on enemy strongholds along the highway, allied forces (ARVN from Neak Luong and RVN) succeeded in linking up with 11th Brigade Group elements. A FANK garrison was established at Kompong Trabek. However, there was no immediate plan to push eastward toward Svay Rieng. South Vietnamese forces assumed positions south of Route 1 along the RVN-Cambodia border, and Route 15 between Neak Luong and Prey Veng City was reopened by government forces on 13 August. A FANK helicopter carrying refugees was shot down on the 8th by a SA-7 missile, killing 14 people. In Siem Riep, FANK OPERATION ANGKOR CHEY was dealt a serious blow when elements of the 203d VC/KC Regiment recaptured Phnom Bakheng mountain a key terrain feature which had been in FANK hands since May 19 *(Map 19)* Enemy control of this high ground left the Siem Reap airfield exposed to

Map 17 — Objective Area, OPERATION SORYA, July — August 1972

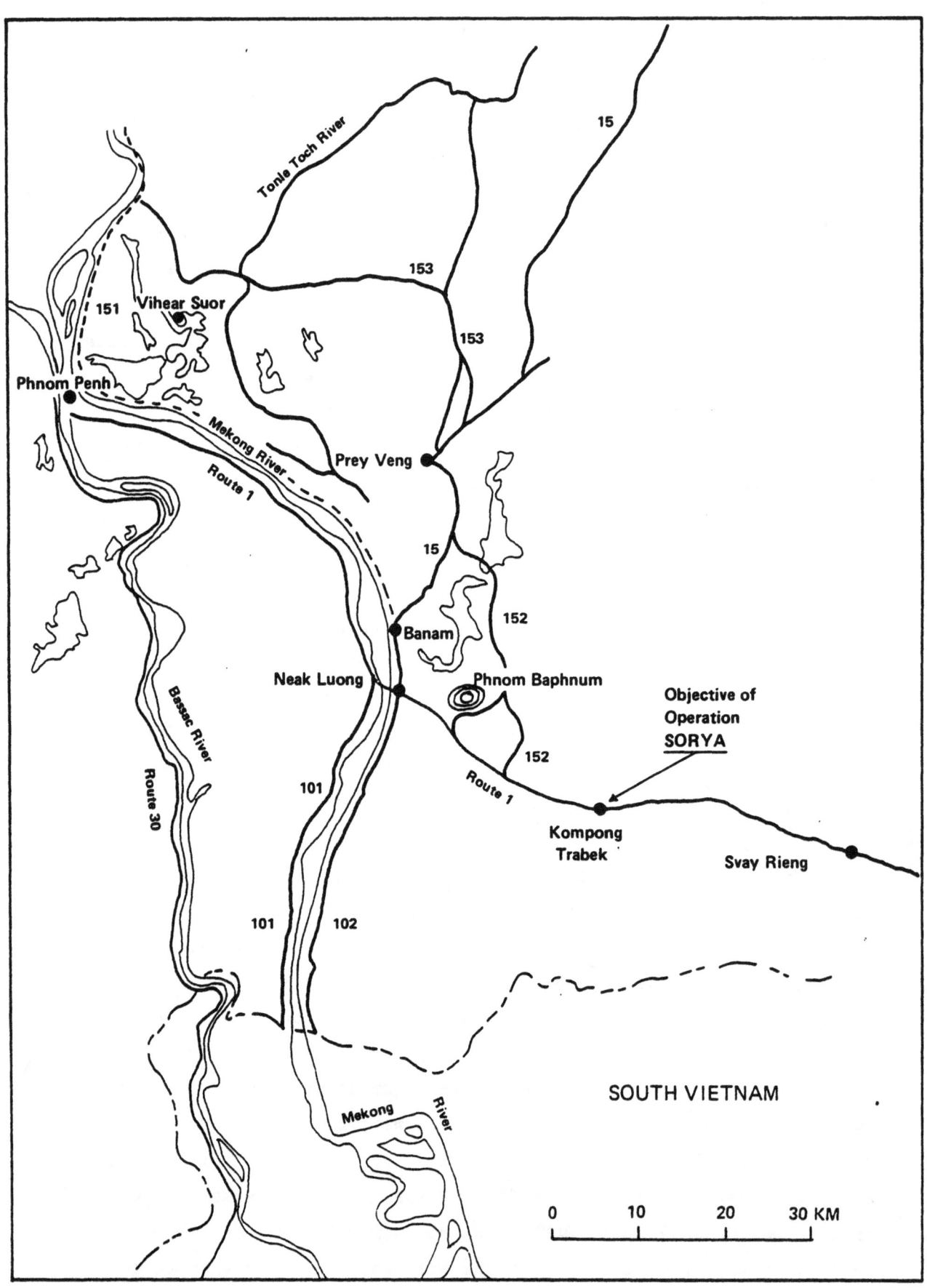

Map 18 — Area of Operation Along Route 2, July — December 1972

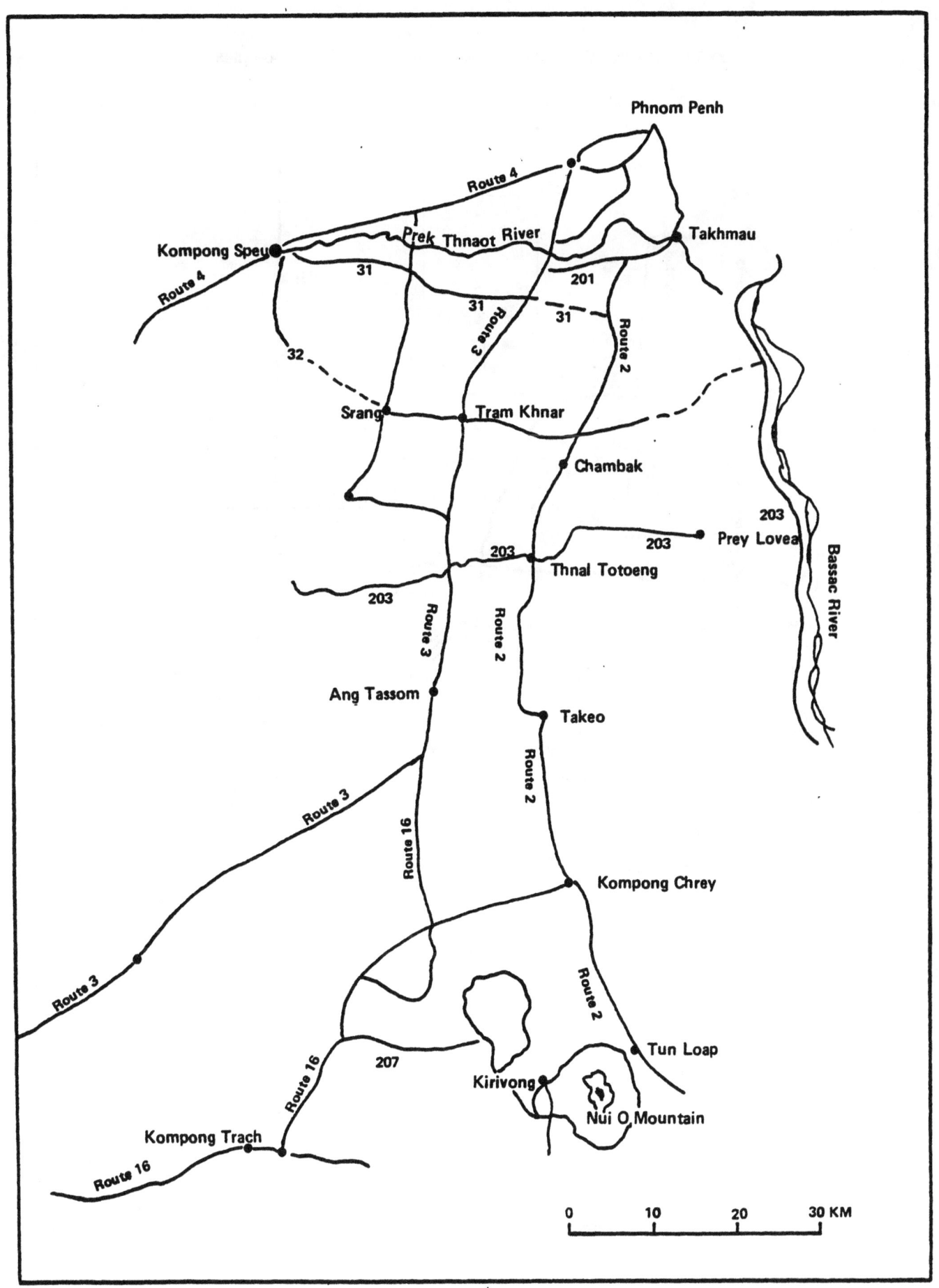

Map 19 — Angkor Wat/Angkor Thom Temple and Ruins Complex

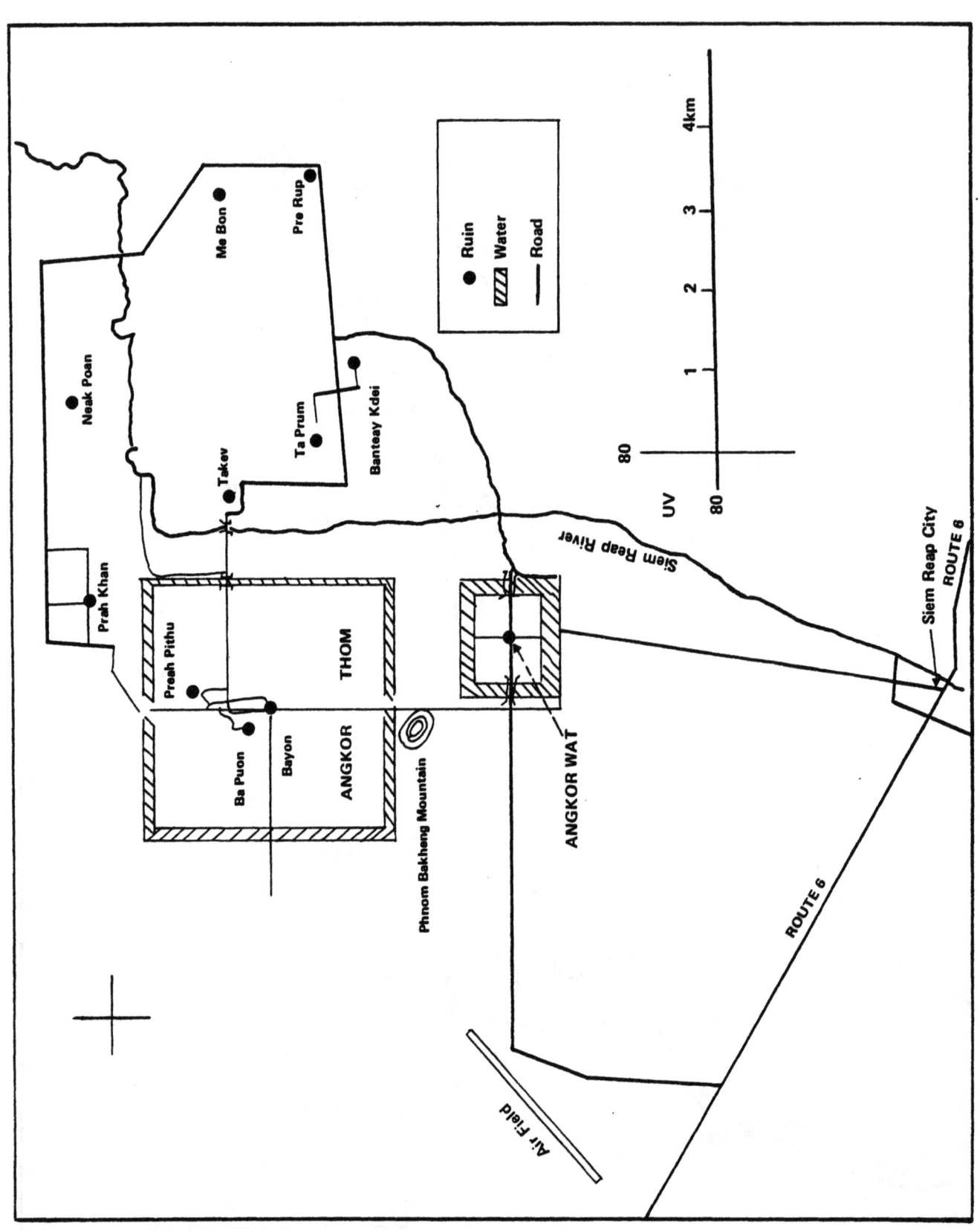

harassing fire and denied to friendly air operations. As a result, the FANK were forced to use the Tonle Sap Lake and the new airfield south of Siem Reap for supply deliveries.

After FANK's hard-won battle to relieve the garrison at Kompong Trabek in August, many of the FANK general reserve forces returned to Phnom Penh. The enemy then attacked Kompong Trabek in strength on 8 September, forcing three FANK battalions to evacuate to Neak Luong, with two 105-mm artillery pieces reported destroyed and two more captured. Three days later, the enemy attacked FANK territorial units on Phnom Baphnum, forcing a withdrawal from this important high ground north of Route 1. FANK reinforced with elements of Colonel Lon Non's 3d Brigade Group from Phnom Penh and after limited progress by the 3d Brigade Group, the enemy counterattacked in force on 16 September, using a riot control agent to disorganize the FANK forces. FANK managed to hold the southwest corner of the hill until 26 September, when it launched its own counterattack. The attack, relying on a frontal assault, bogged down quickly and FANK prepared for a new offensive after a realignment of troops. In Military Region 3, Route 5 remained closed during September despite the efforts of a FANK 17-battalion relief force. This interruption in the rice supply provoked a "rice crisis" in the capital and a two-day period (7 - 8 September) of rice looting and demonstrations in which FANK soldiers were involved. A number of stores were broken into and rice was taken or bought at low prices. The government acted decisively to reestablish order; leaves and passes for FANK personnel were cancelled; mixed patrols of FANK soldiers and MP's circulated in the city; announcements of extraordinary measures to solve the rice shortage were made. This was followed by the first rice shipments to Phnom Penh by air, and these stabilized the situation within 48 hours; Phnom Penh was essentially calm after 12 September. In the capital area, the Prek Phnou POL storage facility received 30 rounds of mixed 82-mm and 75-mm fire on 31 August. At the same time, enemy mortar and ground attacks against surprised FANK personnel guarding two brigades near Prek Phnou left 25 killed, 19 wounded and 6 missing. On 4 August, the cargo vessel *PACLOG DISPATCH* was sunk while at anchor in the Phnom Penh port. On 27 September, unknown terrorists attempted assassination of Mr. Enders, U.S. Chargé d'Affaires; approximately 15 kilos of plastic were exploded near his car as he exited Independence Circle on the way to the U.S. Embassy. Mr. Enders escaped unharmed, although his car was destroyed by the explosion and subsequent fire. A security outrider and a passing cyclist were killed.

On 7 October, an enemy sapper force of about 100 infiltrated into the northern part of Phnom Penh and attacked the Chruoy Chang War Bridge and the M-113 APC parking area near the west end of the same bridge. A large cut was blown in the bridge, sufficient to prevent its use for the time being, and a total of seven M-113 APCs were destroyed. The FANK reaction force killed 83 of the attacking force and prevented the sappers from carrying out what appeared to be intended attacks on the Prek Phnou POL facility and the main municipal electrical power plant on Chruoy Chang War Peninsula. Again on 30 October, the enemy launched a series of attacks by fire against sensitive installations in the capital area. Ammunition in a storage facility near Pochentong airfield was destroyed, and the Komboul radio station was heavily damaged by enemy indirect fire. In Military Region 2, elements of the 1st NVA Division put heavy pressure on FANK positions south of Takeo, systematically overrunning or forcing evacuation of Kirivong, Tun Loap, Nui O Mountain, Kompong Chrey, Lovea, and Koh Andet. ARVN initiated cross-border operations on 11 October to break up what they viewed as a prelude to an important infiltration of troops and supplies, but the intervention was too late to save the FANK positions. The commander of the 15th Brigade Group, which had been operating in the area, was seriously wounded and the Brigade Group ceased to exist as an effective unit. FANK presence returned to the area following successful ARVN operations. In Military Region 3, despite strenuous efforts by the FANK, a five-km section of Route 5 remained in enemy hands during October, denying it to the movement of rice into the capital.

During November, FANK gradually overcame enemy resistance on Route 5 and a total of five convoys were able to make the trip (Battambang-Phnom Penh) without incident. At Takeo, strong enemy pressure built up against the town early in the month; several positions on the outer defense belt fell between 5 and 8 November, thereby isolating Ang Tassom on Route 3 and Prey Sandek on Route 2. Nightly attacks by fire and probes against the town caused significant casualties among the civilian population. USAF units responded with daily air support as well as aerial resupply of ammunition. Beginning 16 November, the pressure on the town fell off gradually. Elements of three FANK battalions were helilifted into Takeo on KAF UH1s at intervals during the month and, on 30 November, FANK launched the first phase of an operation to clear the enemy from central Route 2.

During December, FANK units were able to open Route 4 after the enemy had closed it at the end of October. On Route 2, FANK units relieved the garrison at Prey Sandek on 4 December, breaking a six-week isolation. FANK engineers worked for several weeks to complete the repairs to Route 2, needed after the fighting on the road in October and November, and finished the task on 16 December. Repairs were also made on the roads from Takeo to Ang Tassom and to Prey Sandek, opening these villages to convoy resupply for the first time since October. FANK and ARVN forces then turned their attention to the last remaining section of Route 2 still under enemy control, the section from Prey Sandek to Tun Loap. In combined operations launched 21 December with an ARVN regiment, three Ranger battalions, armored cavalry support, and three FANK battalions and the Parachute brigade, the road was cleared by 23 December. Both FANK and ARVN Engineers began bridge reconstruction and road repair that day, while combat forces moved westward on 29 December to retake Kirivong. However, the major enemy offensive effort in December was directed against Kompong Thom, in Military Region 4, where an estimated 4,000-7,000 mixed KC and NVA troops attacked on 7 December. The 3,000-man FANK garrison suffered heavy losses in the first two days of fighting, giving up four defensive positions to the west and southwest of town, with over 400 listed as missing. USAF tactical air strikes helped to slow the offensive as FANK readjusted its defensive perimeter. FANK and USAF also reacted with aerial resupply of vitally needed ammunition. Enemy effort then shifted to light ground probes and nightly mortar attacks. FANK Hq began to reinforce Kompong Thom on 19 December with 12th Brigade troops from Siem Reap. 77th Brigade troops from Phnom Penh were staged out of Kompong Chhnang in a helicopter shuttle. The enemy made another drive on 23-24 December but the attack was driven off by a strong defense with major assistance from USAF strikes. On 27 December, FANK shifted to the counterattack, expanding the Kompong Thom perimeter to the west and southwest and permitting the farmers to harvest rice along Route 6. At the end of the month, enemy pressure continued at a reduced level. On the Mekong, most significant was the increase of frogman activity in Phnom Penh Port, resulting in the sinking of the cargo ship *Bright Star* on 7 December (with all cargo still on board) and a POL barge on 15 December. The sinking of the ship resulted in the commander of the Khmer Navy being charged with responsibility for port security. The enemy harassed two of three scheduled northbound Mekong River convoys during December.

The Enemy Dry-Season Offensive, January-July 1973

We had hoped that the cease-fire in South Vietnam would also bring peace to Cambodia, that the enemy would respect the FANK unilateral suspension of offensive operations order by Marshal Lon Nol, effective 29 January 1973. But this was not to be. While the VC/NVA activities in January were clearly directed toward the RVN, Khmer Communist units supported the VC/NVA with initiatives throughout Cambodia in January. The most continuous enemy pressure was exerted on Kompong Thom, but without success. The KC and VC/NVA initially achieved gains on Route 1 and along the Mekong south of Neak Luong. Poor performance by FANK territorial units along the Mekong was compensated for somewhat by rapid and effective operations by two brigades of the 2d Division and the Khmer Navy, where working together, they quickly regained the lost position. FANK kept all major LOCs open during the month except for a two-day period during which one Mekong convoy was delayed. A major FANK operation was the relief of the battalion-size outpost at Romeas, southwest of Kompong Chhnang. An unidentified enemy force estimated at 2-3 battalions, encircled the battalion outpost on 6 January. Casualties mounted steadily inside the camp from probes and shellings until 13 January when FANK committed some eleven battalions to the relief of the outpost. Two columns proceeding from Kompong Chhnang and Sala Lek Pram made slow progress against moderate resistance. Realizing relief would not arrive in time, FANK field commanders switched to an airmobile assault on 16 January. The 210 man force was intercepted and dispersed by the enemy prior to linkup with the camp. FANK then committed another 750 men by helicopter on 19 and 21 January, with the combined group reaching Romeas on 23 January. USAF tactical strikes and aerial delivery of ammunition played a vital role in the defense and linkup operation.

By early February, it was clear that the KC had no intention of accepting Lon Nol's call for a cease-fire. During February, KC units launched a major offensive along the Mekong and made secondary efforts on Routes 2 and 3 and at Kompong Thom. These initiatives appeared to be aimed at exploiting the unilateral suspension of offensive actions announced by President Lon Nol and the associated decrease in U.S. air operations in the Khmer Republic following 29 January. FANK reacted with effective U.S. air support, and contained the major enemy efforts. Active U.S. air support permitted the passage of two major convoys despite the presence of well over two KC regiments actively employed by the enemy on both banks of the Mekong. The major enemy effort of the month began 6 February with attacks on FANK positions in the Neak Luong-Banam-Prey Veng corridor. An early thrust made against Route 15 between Prey Veng and Banam was repulsed by units under control of the Prey Veng commander. The enemy then shifted his efforts southward between Banam and Neak Luong, seizing Banam itself on 10 February and cutting Route 15. FANK's counterattack was unproductive. Four battalions moved up Route 15 and halted in place two km outside Banam. Two battalions from the 78th Brigade, committed by MNK craft to the west and north of Banam, suffered heavy casualties from enemy fire. These battalions refused further combat and were returned to Phnom Penh. The 78th Brigade, to which these battalions belonged, was a rapidly assembled collection of companies, battalions and fillers, brought together for the newly created 2d Division. Enemy pressure against FANK positions along the east bank of the Mekong remained constant during the month.

As a result of this pressure a 13-km section of the river bank below Neak Luong was not under FANK control by the end of the month. Above Neak Luong, the river bank between parallels 50 and 56 remained under enemy control for the last three weeks of the month. *(Map 20)* Banam was retaken on 27 February by a volunteer force from the 43d Brigade, and the east bank was cleared by FANK on 29 February. USAF tactical sorties continued at a high level during February as a special USAF operation was mounted to break the enemy siege of Kompong Thom and to provide close air support for ground operations in the Route 15 and Routes 2 and 3 areas. Limited U.S. strategic air was used on pre-selected targets, generally in the Chup-Tapano Plantation area during one 24-hour period.

In March, the general military situation reached a critical stage for the FANK.[1] Enemy efforts continued at a high level throughout the country, directed primarily at the Takeo area and the Mekong-Route 1 corridor. Early in the month Prey Sandek, 9 km south of Takeo, was isolated. On 9-10 March, a two-company position east of Takeo was overrun, as were two positions on Route 2 north of Chambak. On 12 March, both Prey Sandek and Chambak were lost, and the three battalions at Chambak were dispersed. On 13 March, the 45th Brigade of the 7th Division was committed to attack east from Tram Khnar to retake Chambak and Samroang Yong. This mission was shared by elements of the 3d Division moving south along Route 2 from Phnom Penh. The 45th Brigade was stopped 6 km west of its objective with heavy casualties. On 16 March, Brigadier General Un Kauv, 7th Division commander took command of the operation and reinforced the 45th Brigade with the remaining elements of his division. His arrival, and four U.S. B-52 strikes, resulted in rapid progress against decreasing enemy resistance. The 7th Division reached Chambak on 18 March, followed by the 3d Division on 20 March, and the road was opened to Takeo on 23 March. On 31 March, the enemy renewed his offensive, this time against the 7th Division positions.

---

[1] The situation was further complicated by an attempt on the life of President Lon Nol, carried out by a former Khmer pilot on 17 March, when he appropriated a T-28 and dropped two bombs near the Presidential Palace.

Map 20 — Areas of the Mekong Controlled by the Enemy, February – April 1973

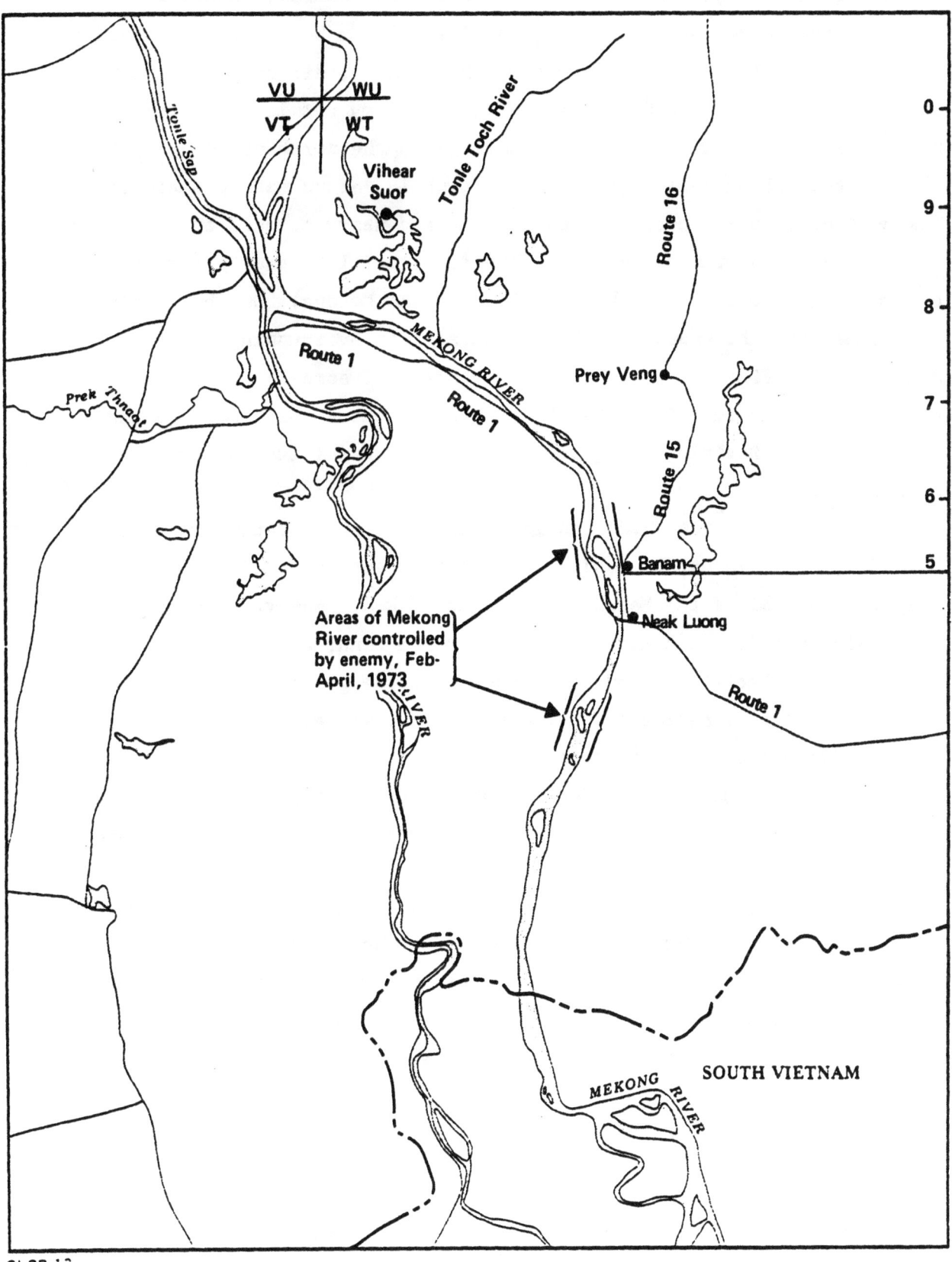

The enemy's action, primarily attacks by fire plus a costly ambush, led to the withdrawal of the 7th Division forces to Chambak; substantial materiel losses were incurred, including five 105-mm howitzers.[2] In spite of significant FANK reinforcements north of Takeo, air drops to isolated units and substantial U.S. air support, the enemy retained control of Route 2 south of Takeo and much of Route 2 to the north of Takeo City.

In the Mekong-Route 1 corridor, meanwhile, after safe passage of a Mekong convoy on 29 March, the enemy launched heavy attacks on both sides of the river, overrunning several FANK territorial company positions and controlling some 25 km of the east bank of the Mekong. On the west bank of the Mekong, the enemy was also successful in overrunning six FANK positions along Route 1, leaving him in control of some 25 km of Route 1 north of Neak Luong. On 31 March, Brigadier General Dien Del, Commander of the 2d FANK Division was given overall responsibility for the clearing of Route 1.

During April, the enemy continued the offensive actions in southern Cambodia, begun in March, making his greatest sustained effort to take complete control of the Mekong and capture Takeo. Enemy forces approached to within artillery and mortar range of Phnom Penh, where rationing of gasoline and electricity impressed many with the gravity of the situation. Several foreign embassies evacuated non-essential personnel and the U.S. Embassy evacuated its dependents. After initial FANK success in deploying troops along the Mekong corridor in early April, enemy forces again cut Route 1 and had occupied substantial portions of both banks of the Mekong at month's end. 3d Division elements were driven back north on Route 2 to positions north of Siem Reap/Kandal, some 10 km from the outskirts of Phnom Penh. After Siem Reap was retaken, it was inexplicably abandoned by these same elements under no enemy pressure, thus opening the southern flank of the capital's defense. The high command ordered the town retaken and after a delay of two days, Siem Reap was occupied, once again with no resistance. Takeo continued to hold against heavy enemy attacks by fire and ground pressure, thanks to a very heavy application of air power, re-

---

[2] The 7th Division was pulled off line on 1 April and replaced in Chambak by the 37th Brigade. On 2 April, the 37th Brigade was routed and Chambak fell, leaving an 11 km stretch of road between Chambak and Thnal Totung under enemy control.

inforcement by several battalions, and U.S. aerial resupply of ammunition. At southern Kampot Province, the sea resort of Kep fell on 16 April. At the beginning of April, FANK controlled only some 30 percent of the Mekong River bank. The last April convoy was delayed 12 days as FANK reinforced with elements of more than two brigades and then conducted clearing operations on the east and west banks. As the security situation improved in the Cambodian portions of the Mekong, it deteriorated in South Vietnam in the vicinity of Tan Chau. Because of heavy harassment in RVN, the convoy was only able to penetrate the border in two sections on successive days. The final section was only able to close Phnom Penh on 15 April. FANK maintained security of the Mekong through the passage of the next convoy on 24 April which again suffered heavy enemy attacks in the vicinity of the SVN border. Towards the end of the month, FANK gave up important portions on the east bank and Route 1 was closed again north of Neak Luong. In spite of a declining security situation on the Mekong, the Khmer Navy was able to transit at night one tug pulling an important ammunition barge. Enemy efforts against Mekong shipping during April resulted in the loss of one POL and one munitions barge, two cargo ships, and the damage of eight ships. The crew of one POL ship refused to sail and had to be replaced. Commodore Vong Sarendy, Commander Khmer Navy, was formally designated commander of the Mekong Special Zone.

The enemy offensive continued into May, but slowed at month's end, due in part to high levels of U.S. air support. On the Mekong, the enemy continued to control portions of both banks. Six merchant convoys (three each way) received 56 major hits, causing the loss of one ship.

Relatively speaking, the month of June began on a positive note for the FANK, a carry-over from May. Route 5, which had been closed for two months, was reopened on 5 June. A Mekong convoy arrived in Phnom Penh without serious harassment. This breathing spell did not last, however, as the enemy launched an offensive on Route 4 only 25 km from Phnom Penh. FANK committed four brigades (7, 13, 28, 43), supported by two squadrons of M-113s and some 12 105-mm howitzers. Both U.S. and Khmer air units provided air support as weather permitted, and FANK's superior numbers and firepower -- due to U.S. air support --

forced the enemy to withdraw. A FANK night attack against the remaining enemy position on 19 June permitted convoys to move on Route 4 the following day. Route 5 was reopened to traffic on 7 June, and three rice convoys reached Phnom Penh before the enemy closed the road again on 16 June.

Although the military situation continued to deteriorate in July, the FANK were able to survive another month of the enemy offensive which had begun six months previously. The enemy appeared to shift from his earlier strategy of attacking major LOCs to one of more direct assault on the capital. As the month began, there were three active combat areas in the region of Phnom Penh: *(Map 21)*

1. Route 2 and 3. Originally an adjunct to Route 4 operations in June, this LOC became a major combat area in July as the enemy offensive spread from Route 4 east into the near regions of the capital. Early in June, the 3d Division (-) had initiated sweep operations south of the Prek Thnaot River which threatened the east flank of the enemy's Route 4 attack. Reacting sharply to the threat, the enemy drove the 3d Division units back 5 kms to Route 3, with over 100 casualties. Following that, the 3d Division (-) held to the road in a basically defensive posture, conducting only shallow sweeps away from the LOC. Two key positions held by the Division fell in mid and late June. Counterattacks proved ineffective but served to prevent the enemy from penetrating Phnom Penh's inner defenses. On 6 July, the enemy captured the Kompong Tuol Bridge, a district headquarters, and neighboring town, following a sharp attack. Casualties in the FANK 3d Division were high, and increased further as the 43d Brigade, cut off south of the Prek Thnaot River, exfiltrated to the north following an unsuccessful FANK airmobile operation to relieve it six days later. The 3d Division could not hold against subsequent attacks and fell back another four kms. U.S. air support stabilized the situation and the commander of the 3d Division was replaced. Despite U.S. air support on a 24-hour basis, FANK was not able to push its defense line south to the Prek Thnaot River during July.

2. The Phnom Baset approach. This area, northwest of Phnom Penh, was controlled by the FANK 7th Division. Despite strong efforts by

Map 21 — Combat Areas Near Phnom Penh, July 1973

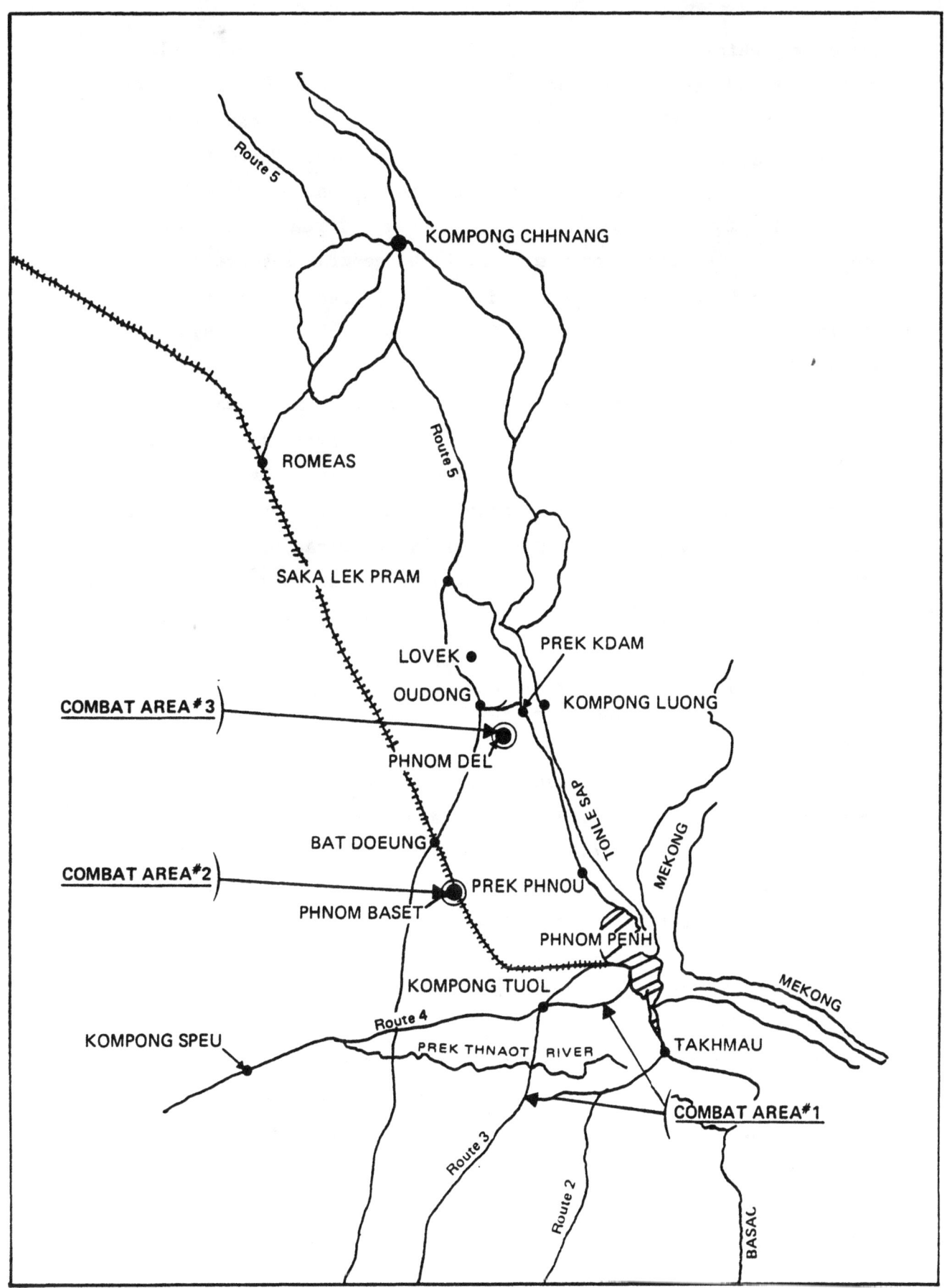

the enemy, which rendered ineffective the 72d Brigade (previously critically understrength), the 7th Division fought back aggressively and, in concert with U.S. air support, inflicted heavy casualties on the enemy and was in control by the end of July. Units from the 7th Division, as well as others from the Phnom Penh and 2d Military Region were committed hastily to counter enemy threats northwest of Pochentong during the prior week. With the general reserve fully committed, FANK was forced to withdraw sorely needed units from other battlefields, notably Route 3 and Phnom Baset, to counter this developing threat.

3. Phnom Del. The FANK were unable to hold on to its two remaining positions in the area north of the capital; they fell in quick succession on 6 and 9 July despite aerial resupply and reinforcement. The last chance to retain a friendly presence in this area disappeared when an airmobile operation by the Parachute Brigade was cancelled in order to send the parachutists to the more critical Route 3 area. On 13 July, the enemy captured the ferry site at Prek Kdam.

The First Months Without U.S. Air Support, August - December 1973

The enemy dry-season offensive against Phnom Penh came to an end in August and the capital area entered a period of lessened activity which lasted into December. The 3d Division reestablished control of the north bank of the Prek Thnaot River, and the 1st Division was able to clear Route 1 south to Neak Luong.

However, north of Phnom Penh there was heavy fighting in the Route 6, Route 7, Kompong Cham areas. *(Map 12)* With the fall of Tang Kouk, Skoun, Prey Totung and Traeung, FANK lost eight 105-mm howitzers, two mortars, large stocks of ammunition, three battalions and 19 territorial companies to the enemy. By 16 August the enemy was able to direct all his efforts to capturing the first provincial capital of the war, Kompong Cham; a series of shelling attacks, followed by strong ground attacks caused the FANK defense line around Kompong Cham to be steadily threatened along with the loss of full use of the airfield.

FANK reinforced initially with the 79th Brigade, two battalions of the Parachute Brigade, two battalions of the 5th Brigade, and an additional battery of four 105-mm howitzers. Efforts to restore or expand the perimeter were unsuccessful. The enemy's main effort to take the city came on 1 September with heavy mortar and 105-mm fire, and multiple ground attacks which penetrated the FANK defensive line to within 1 km of the city. FANK forces were able to stop the enemy's momentum and stabilize the situation on 2 September. The two remaining battalions of the 5th Brigade and the Parachute Brigade, two Special Forces Detachments, and 12 Navy craft were designated as additional reinforcements for Kompong Cham. Major General Sar Hor, the commander, was given authority to give up the airfield in order to defend the city proper. The situation continued to deteriorate despite the arrival of the remainder of the 5th Brigade. On 7 September, following the exfiltration of two Parachute Battalions from the airfield to the city, and the arrival of a 16-ship naval task force, FANK contained the enemy's advance and slowly began to push him back from within the city. The 80th Brigade arrived by navy convoy on 10 September and was immediately inserted south of the city behind the enemy. By 14 September the enemy had been cleared from the city; link-up was made between the 80th Brigade elements and city defense forces, the university area had been reoccupied, and FANK had gained offensive momentum which continued throughout the month. As FANK advanced and regained control of lost territory, enemy efforts diminished to attacks by fire and ground probes of friendly positions at the airfield. As the month ended, FANK reoccupied and controlled Wat Angkor Knong, the village of Boeng Kok, the textile factory, and were effecting linkup with friendly forces at the airfield. During the last week of September, approximately 100 Air Force personnel were heli-lifted to Kompong Cham airfield to bolster defenses against enemy ground attacks.

During October there was again heavy fighting along the Prek Thnaot River. On 1 October the last elements of the 3d Division located south of the river were either withdrawn to the north bank or overrun. On 2 October, FANK was forced to abandon Kompong Toul and Kompong Kantout, suffering casualties of 26 killed, 51 wounded, and

30 missing. The 1st Division was ordered to reinforce on 3 October and committed its 1st Brigade in the zone of the 3d Division and its 48th Brigade, reinforced by one M-113 squadron, to move along Route 2. Between 4 and 20 October the FANK units conducted various maneuvers but no progress was made. Approximately two companies of enemy infiltrated north of the Prek Thnaot River in the 1st Brigade, 1st Division zone and remained lodged there as the month ended. A constant exchange of fire at long range and a lack of ground initiative by both forces characterized the combat action during October. During the last week, 3d Division elements moved south across the Prek Thnaot River at night and established a foothold on the southern banks. The continuous daily shelling of friendly positions by enemy indirect fire weapons caused casualties to already severely understrength FANK battalions which exceeded replacements received by the 1st and 3d Divisons.

The most significant activities in November were the losses of Tram Khnar, Srang, Tuk Laak, and Vihear Suor. The garrison at Vihear Suor was overrun and occupied by the enemy on 30 November. *(Map 20)* FANK attempts to link-up with Vihear Suor since 11 November had faltered for many reasons. Losses at Vihear Suor were: two 105-mm howitzers, two 75-mm howitzers, six 81-mm mortars, six 82-mm mortars and an unknown amount of ammunition.

December was highlighted by FANK efforts on Route 4. On 18 December units of the 13th Brigade, the 28th Brigade and one M-113 squadron demonstrated the ability to react rapidly when the enemy interdicted Route 4 between Kompong Speu and Phnom Penh. FANK troops cleared the enemy from the road after 12 hours of fighting. On 3 December, the 1st Division was committed to the task of clearing the month-old interdiction of Route 4, west of Kompong Speu, extending from Sre Khlong (VT240520) north to Moha Saing (VT380621). In contrast to the action mentioned above, the 1st Division did not effectively use its available combat power. When the battle was joined with the enemy the commander complained of lack of air and artillery support. These assets were made available to him on a priority basis and the 20th Brigade was also placed under the 1st Division operational control. During the last week of December, the 13th Brigade was assigned the task of securing the north flank of the 1st Division to allow the 1st Division to concentrate force on a more narrow front. The Assistant Chief of Staff, FANK Operations, Major General Mao Sum Khem, was appointed overall commander of the Route 4 clearing operation. However, on 29 December, front-line units of the 1st Division withdrew approximately 2 km, giving up key terrain features previously secured. The situation was so tenuous in the 1st Division that Marshal Lon Nol saw fit to visit the front himself on 30 December 1973. Four newly arrived 155-mm howitzers, assigned to the 1st Division, were also displaced to provide more firepower to the defense effort. A third M-113 squadron was committed on 30 December, and Route 4 was reopened on 6 January 1974.

Dry Season Operations, January–July 1974

Military operations during the period January through July 1974 were highlighted by heavy enemy attacks northwest and northeast of Phnom Penh and with major FANK reactions to restore the defenses of the capital in these sectors. In addition, there was significant combat along the Bassac River corridor, and a major enemy effort against the city of Kampot. By this time the defenses of Phnom Penh were organized generally into four sectors. *(Map 22)*

On the night of 5 January an estimated two enemy regiments moved into the northwest sector, approximately 5-6 km from Phnom Penh. FANK reacted on the morning of 6 January by committing the 28th Brigade, reinforced with two M-113 squadrons. Heavy fighting ensued on 6 and 7 January in the vicinity of VT8079 and 100 enemy were killed in action. On 8 January the 1st Division was committed to the operation as its subordinate units became available from the Route 4 clearing operation. By 10 January, over 300 enemy had been killed in action with friendly losses of 2 killed and 56 wounded. Eleven prisoners were captured and 13 KC soldiers rallied at Bek Chan (VT7271) on 10 January. Fighting continued for 12 more days as the 28th Brigade, moving from the south and the 1st Division moving from the east attempted to reduce the enemy penetration. One brigade of the 7th Division was also committed to the operation to move south toward VT7684 in an attempt to seal off the penetration. This force never

Map 22 – Defense Sectors for Phnom Penh, January 1974

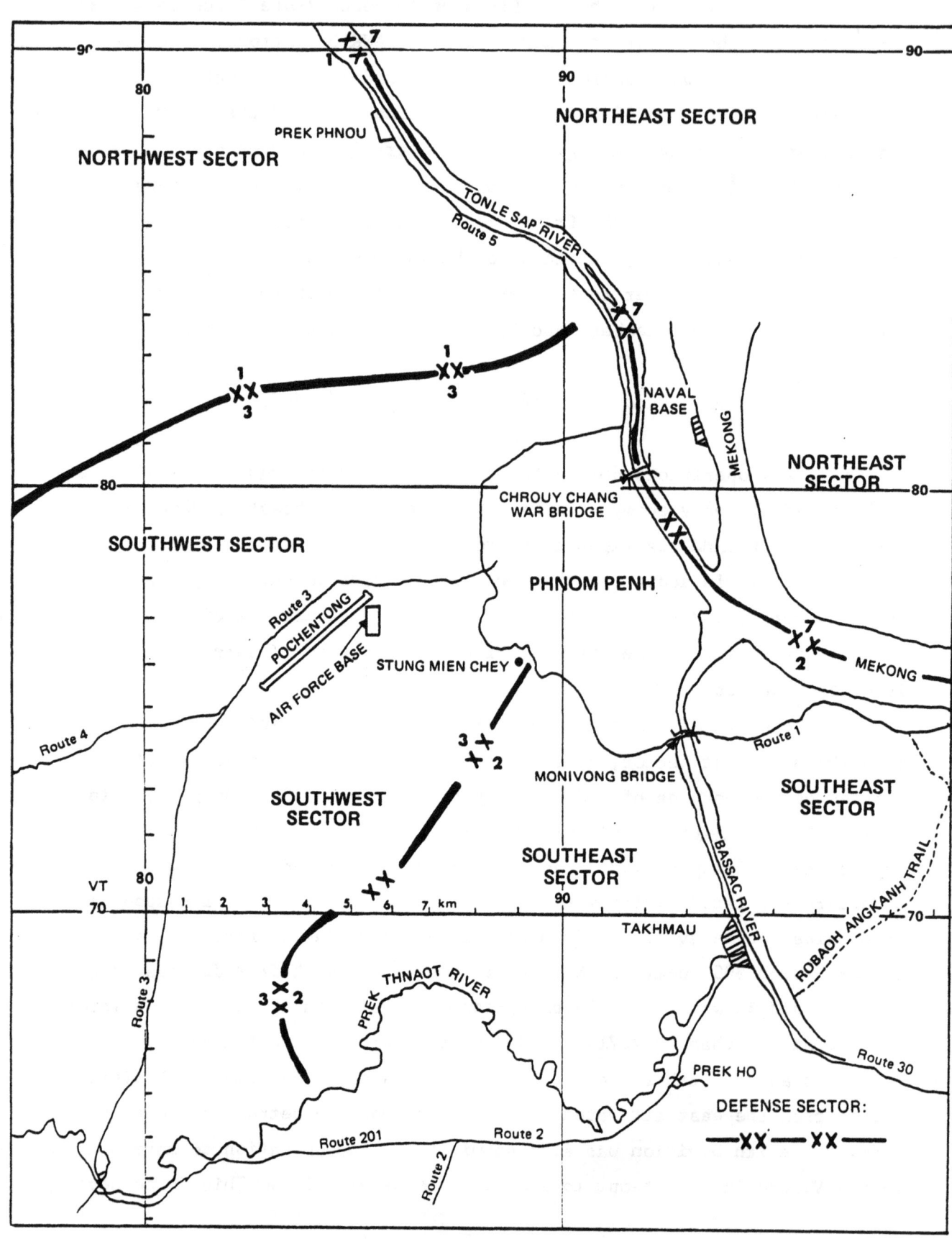

joined battle with the enemy, nor did it succeed in sealing off the penetration. Using his penetration as a firing base, the enemy was able to fire approximately 20 rounds of 75-mm RR fire and five 122-mm rockets against targets in the northwest part of Phnom Penh and Pochentong Airport. Casualties were light and negligible damage was caused by these shellings. Supported by heavy air and artillery strikes, the 1st Division succeeded on 22 January in breaking through the shoulders of the penetration and the enemy withdrew to the west. Casualties from the northwest sector fighting in the 1st Division zone were: 31 friendly killed and 175 wounded; an estimated 200 enemy were killed, 26 POWs taken and 70 weapons captured. In the 28th Brigade zone casualties were: 35 friendly killed and 268 wounded; an estimated 300 enemy were killed and 121 weapons were captured.

Attention shifted from the northwest to the southwest capital defense sector on 19 January when enemy elements infiltrated the 3d Division's frontline positions, causing the 334th Battalion to withdraw without orders. Adjacent battalions then withdrew from the south of Route 201 along Grid Line 63 to positions north of the Prek Thnaot River. Within 24 hours, much of the 3d Division front had withdrawn to positions north of the Prek Thnaot River, despite the fact that very little enemy pressure had been exerted. At least two battalion commanders were absent during the initial action and a breakdown of command and control resulted in this withdrawal of units, composed mostly of inexperienced recruits. The battalions of the 51st Brigade, securing the Bak Bridge (VT9064) sustained several killed in action on 20 January, indicating that the enemy had been able to move a sizable force as far north as the Prek Thnaot River. The most threatened area during the initial enemy penetration was in the vicinity of Prey Veng (VT8266) where the 15th Brigade CP and four 105-mm howitzers were positioned. On 20 and 21 January, FANK high command reacted to the newly developed threat by attaching two additional battalions from the 1st Division to the 3d Division and directing the 20th Brigade to move from Route 4 to the southwest sector. Upon arrival, the 20th Brigade was committed to reinforce the weakened 51st Brigade from VT8768 east to VT 8967. On 27 January, the 20th Brigade had a significant engagement with enemy forces at VT8867 but held its positions and inflicted losses of 39 killed on the enemy. Friendly losses were 17 killed and 25 wounded. An additional two battalions of the 81st Brigade, 1st Division were committed on 20 - 21 January to counterattack to the south and east of Prey Veng from VT8366 to VT8567. On 23 January the entire southwest sector was subdivided to significantly reduce the 3d Division's defensive sector and improve unity of command. The 1st Division was then committed to secure the Prek Thnaot from VT8466 east to VT9166. In an additional move to improve the command and control structure, FANK gave Brigadier General Yai Sindy responsibility for the area west of grid line 77 and formed a composite unit by placing the 12th, 23d and 28th Brigades under his command. On 30 January the situation had stabilized to the extent that the 20th Brigade was withdrawn from its positions on the Prek Thnaot River and moved to Prey Pring (West of Pochenton) in preparation for a new operation. On 1 February 74, the 1st Division's 1st Brigade replaced the 20th Brigade on the Prek Thoat River and as January ended it appeared that FANK had contained the enemy in the southwest sector and reestablished control of its units.

The FANK seized the dry season initiative from the enemy in February, pushing back the enemy in both the northwest and southern sectors of Phnom Penh. The KC, their penetration stopped by FANK in early February, shifted to 105-mm howitzer attacks on the city. One attack, on 11 February, caused civilian casualties of over 200 killed and wounded, with some 10,000 rendered homeless. FANK counterattacks late in February forced out the enemy from his January gains.

The 80th Brigade was moved to Phnom Penh on 6 February and committed on 9 February to clear the northwest sector in conjunction with the armor brigade, the 23d Brigade, the 28th Brigade and units of the 7th Divisiom. Enemy resistance was very determined from 9-14 February, until the 80th Brigade, reinforced with the M-113 squadron of the 7th Division, penetrated the enemy's primary defense lines. Once penetration occurred. the enemy effected an orderly withdrawal, while FANK units advanced methodically through the entire enemy-held area. Sweeps of the battle area after fighting ceased revealed that the enemy was equipped with M-72 light assault weapons (LAW), 75-mm RR and 57-mm RR and that much of the equipment was either new or in excellent condition. Fighting decreased progressively until 26 February when FANK units linked up north of Tuol Leap (VT7379). FANK losses during the period 6 - 25 February were 66 killed and 515 wounded in the northwest sector of Phnom Penh defenses.

The enemy continued to attack and harass convoy shipping throughout February and two incidents of mining occurred on the Mekong. Nine attacks by fire were reported on convoys which resulted in two killed and seven wounded, with the most significant on 18 February when the tug Bannock and the ammunition barge *Mt. Hood* received 75-mm RR fire and 12.8-mm machine-gun fire at WT2121. This subsequently resulted in the loss of approximately 1.4 million dollars of munitions and severe damage to the barge. The tug *Saigon 240* with ammunition barge 108-1 sustained several hits from B41 rockets which destroyed an estimated 50.3 tons of munitions. A total of 11 convoys transited the Mekong during February (6 to Phnom Penh and 5 from Phnom Penh). Twelve new PBRs were delivered to the Navy under U.S. military assistance.

During March, the major military activity shifted away from Phnom Penh and to the provincial capitals of Oudong and Kampot. The enemy was able to overrun Oudong, but the defenses of Kampot held.

Enemy pressure on Kampot commenced on 26 February with attacks north of the city. During the first week of March, several territorial companies and units of the 12th Brigade and the 68th Battalion abandoned defensive positions without authority. These actions combined with a dwindling water supply (the enemy had captured the city water works) caused an exodus of over 50% of the civilian inhabitants from the city. Enemy directed 107-mm rockets, 120-mm mortars and other lower caliber attacks against both tactical units/facilities and the civilian populace in Kampot City also added to the rapidly deteriorating situation. The 210th and the 68th Battalions were deactivated after approximately 300 troops deserted during the period 26 February - 2 March 74; the remaining troops were reassigned to the 12th Battalion. Effective support from Navy, Air Force, and artillery units during this critical time provided the FANK high command enough time to reinforce. The 20th and 12th Brigades were deployed to Kampot and directed to attack northeast, parallel to Route 3 to retake the Chakrei Ting Cement Factory (VT2080). Virtually no advance was made by either unit, however; rather, a defense posture developed once enemy strengths and dispositions were fully developed. During the period 2 - 10 March two more Army battalions, some Navy personnel, and six 105-mm howitzers were deployed to Kampot, and Major General Mhoul Khleng was sent to command all FANK units in Kampot. FANK/USAF aerial resupply operations increased appreciably; four new 105-mm howitzers were sent to Kampot to replace four older weapons. Early rain during mid-March somewhat alleviated the water problem (the Navy continued to resupply water reguarly); and finally, KAF priorities (airlift and tactical air support) were realigned to help the beleaguered and dwindling enclave. As of 3 April FANK defensive positions near Hill 169 (VS076752), which dominates the Kampot Airfield, had been abandoned after the enemy effectively isolated the positions. The 20th and 12th Brigades sustained significant casualties during the month, and by 2 April their effective strengths had been reduced to 664 and 827 respectively. The FANK high command sent Major General Fan Moung, Assistant Chief of the General Staff for Operations, to Kampot on 2 April to assess the situation and immediately after his arrival it was decided to make an all out effort to further reinforce Kampot. FANK losses in fighting at Kampot during March were 158 killed, 828 wounded. The enemy suffered 282 killed, 3 captured, and 25 weapons captured.

But the most significant action during March was the fall of Udong, a place of religious and histotical significance.[3] The attack commenced in earnest at 3:00 A.M. on 3 March and by 8:00 A.M. that same day, the territorial battalions defending Oudong had been forced to withdraw from positions northwest and southwest of the city in order to establish a small perimeter generally southeast of Oudong at VU7306. *(Map 23)* Two 105-mm howitzers were reportedly destroyed by FANK on 16 March in a small position at VU7205; when these howitzers were destroyed the FANK units at this position

---

[3] Oudong was the Royal capital of Cambodia until the arrival of the French in the 19th Century.

Map 23 — Oudong Area of Operations, March 1974

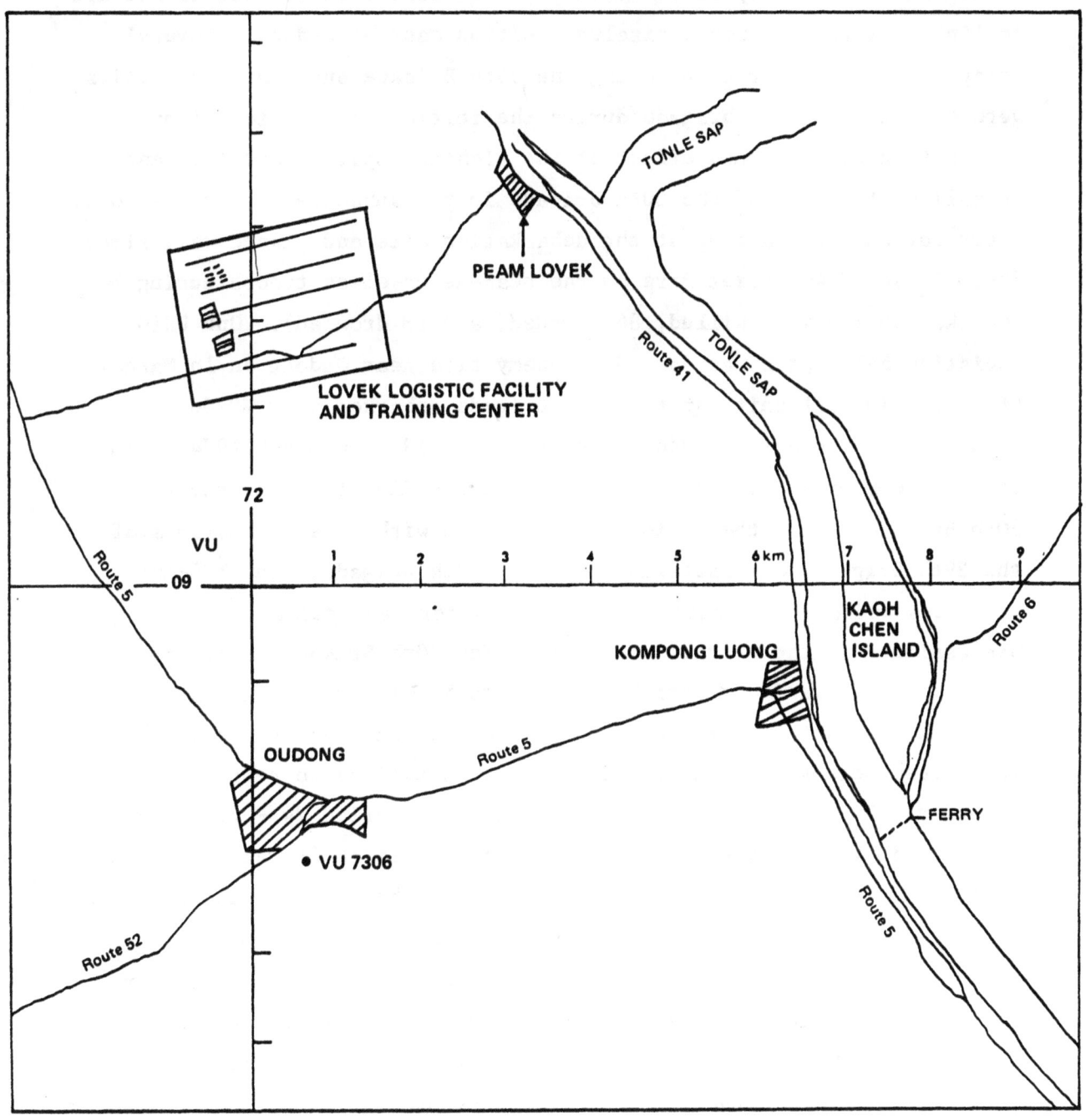

also withdrew north to join the previously mentioned perimeter at VU7306. Total troop strength at this location was then estimated at 700 troops, plus approximately 1500 civilians. An unknown number of civilians were killed or captured by the enemy upon entering the city. FANK reacted by moving the 45th Brigade, 7th Division to Lovek (VU7212) on 16 March and the 80th Brigade up the Tonle Sap River to debark in the vicinity of VU7807 and attack from east to west to attempt to link up with the then encircled position east of Oudong. Several delays were encountered in moving the 80th Brigade and heavy casualties were sustained by the brigade during the initial debarkation efforts. This action had a marked effect of the fighting spirit, attitude and overall performance of the 80th Brigade in the subsequent linkup effort. Enemy forces were waiting at the debarkation site and placed well aimed 75-mm RR and B 40 rocket fire on the near-defenseless troops during debarkation (25 were killed, 86 wounded, and 13 drowned). One UH1G logistics helicopter was downed by enemy fire near Oudong on 16 March. After the initial units of the 80th Brigade debarked near VU7808 the remainder of the brigade did not close until 19 - 20 March 1974. Continued enemy presence was sufficient to cause FANK to reinforce the 80th Brigade during the period 20 - 28 March with three battalions of the 39th Brigade, one battalion from the 28th Brigade, four 105-mm howitzers and one M113 squadron. Priority for tactical air support was assigned to the overall operation. The 80th Brigade commander allowed the forwardmost attacking units to become overcommitted as the linkup effort progressed from east to west and was unable to reinforce them because he had committed three battalions to rear area security. The FANK attack faltered during the period 24 - 27 March and FANK was in the process of further reinforcements on 28 March when the encircled position was overrun by the enemy. The final collapse of the encircled position was accelerated when an enemy-fired 75-mm RR round which impacted directly the unprotected ammunition storage area near the northwest corner of the perimeter, and caused detonations of 81 and 105-mm ammunition. Other contributing factors were the arrival of approximately 2,500 refugees into the already overcrowded perimeter during the night of 27 - 28 March; there was inadequate food, water and medical

supplies and a general atmosphere of fear that a recurrence of
previous enemy attacks was inevitable. When the ammunition exploded,
uncontrollable panic ensued, the perimeter was ruptured, and, within
30 minutes, enemy ground attacks overwhelmed the defenders. A company commander, who escaped, related that as the enemy entered the
perimeter, previously wounded FANK soldiers were machine gunned and
several FANK soldiers killed their own families and then themselves
to avoid being captured. The fate of 4,000 civilians was unknown;
650 military and civilian personnel returned to safety. Lon Nol
ordered that Oudong be retaken. However, the pressure at Kampot
at month's end caused conflicting priorities, and the enemy remained
in control of the Oudong area on 31 March 1974. Results of fighting
prior to 28 March were as follows: 328 enemy killed in action, 91
individual weapons and 15 crew served weapons captured; 50 FANK killed
and 240 wounded.

During April, the enemy continued his attacks north of Phnom Penh,
focusing on Kompong Luong. Following the capture of Oudong in March,
FANK forces remaining along the river were directed to establish a
defensive position on the Tonle Sap. On 20 April, enemy ground pressure
along the river bank increased sharply and several positions fell back.
Pressure continued. On 21 April enemy infiltrators overran key
friendly positions along the Tonle Sap River bank, effectively encircling the Kompong Luong garrison. FANK forces withdrew and by
2:30 P.M. on 21 April the first elements linked up with the Lovek
Garrison defenders. The defeat added valuable psychological momentum
to the new provincial phase of the enemy's dry season offensive and
representd his second significant military victory of the dry season.
FANK troop and materiel losses along the Tonle Sap in April were heavy:
approximately 600 military personnel were unaccounted for: four 105-mm
howitzers were lost; all heavy weapons (mortars and machine guns);
two M-113's, one bulldozer, one POL truck, and several other pieces
of engineering equipment were abandoned. Three Navy river craft were
beached. Kompong Luong and a sizeable stock of ammunition was abandoned
and later bombed by the Air Force. Subsequently, the FANK high command
decided to withdraw the civilian population and military garrison from

Sala Lek Pram to Lovek, consolidating assets into a single defensive position. Approximately 15,000 civilians and 2,000 military personnel moved into the Lovek garrison on 26 April. The month drew to a close with a highly vulnerable group of civilian and military personnel in that small isolated place. The population of 52,405 consisted of 5,260 military, 15,488 military dependents, 22,383 civilians, 8,383 refugees, and 891 para-military personnel. Heavy enemy shelling on Lovek (by 105-mm howitzer, 75-mm RR and 82-mm mortar fire) began on 30 April.

In Kampot, April opened with FANK forces being pushed deeper into the city, giving up approximately three km on the north and west of the city. *(Map 24)* By 10 April, the western perimeter had collapsed to within 1.5 kms of the heart of the city. The Naval Infantry had given up the southeast sector, and the enemy had stopped the flow of supplies and reinforcements by sea to Kampot. During the same period, enemy artillery struck the 105-mm howitzer positions ammunition storage area, destroying approximately 3,500 105-mm howitzer rounds and rendering eight 105-mm howitzers inoperable. Two battalions of reinforcements arrived and their immediate deployment in the southeast sector appeared to switch the offensive momentum from the enemy to FANK. After two days of heavy fighting on 8 and 9 April, the 28th Brigade reported 86 enemy killed, while the 20th Brigade in the west claimed another 100 enemy killed. Enemy initiatives diminished as fresh FANK ground forces began to slowly advance and push the enemy away from the city. The garrison military strength increased from 3,018 on 1 April to 4,006 on 9 April. The two remaining battalions of the 28th Brigade arrived, along with replacements for losses in other units. By 25 April, the Kampot military strength exceeded 4,561. Enemy mortar attacks diminished in intensity and frequency as advancing government forces reestablished the northern perimeter, pushed the west perimeter out 2.5 km from the city, and on 30 April, reoccupied Kbal Romeas on the east and reopened the river supply route. For the period 3 March to 3 May, in the Kampot area, FANK suffered 416 killed (25 civilians), 2,363 wounded (88 civilians) and 79 missing in action while the enemy suffered an estimated 2,363 killed in action.

Map 24 — The Battle for Kampot, March-April 1974

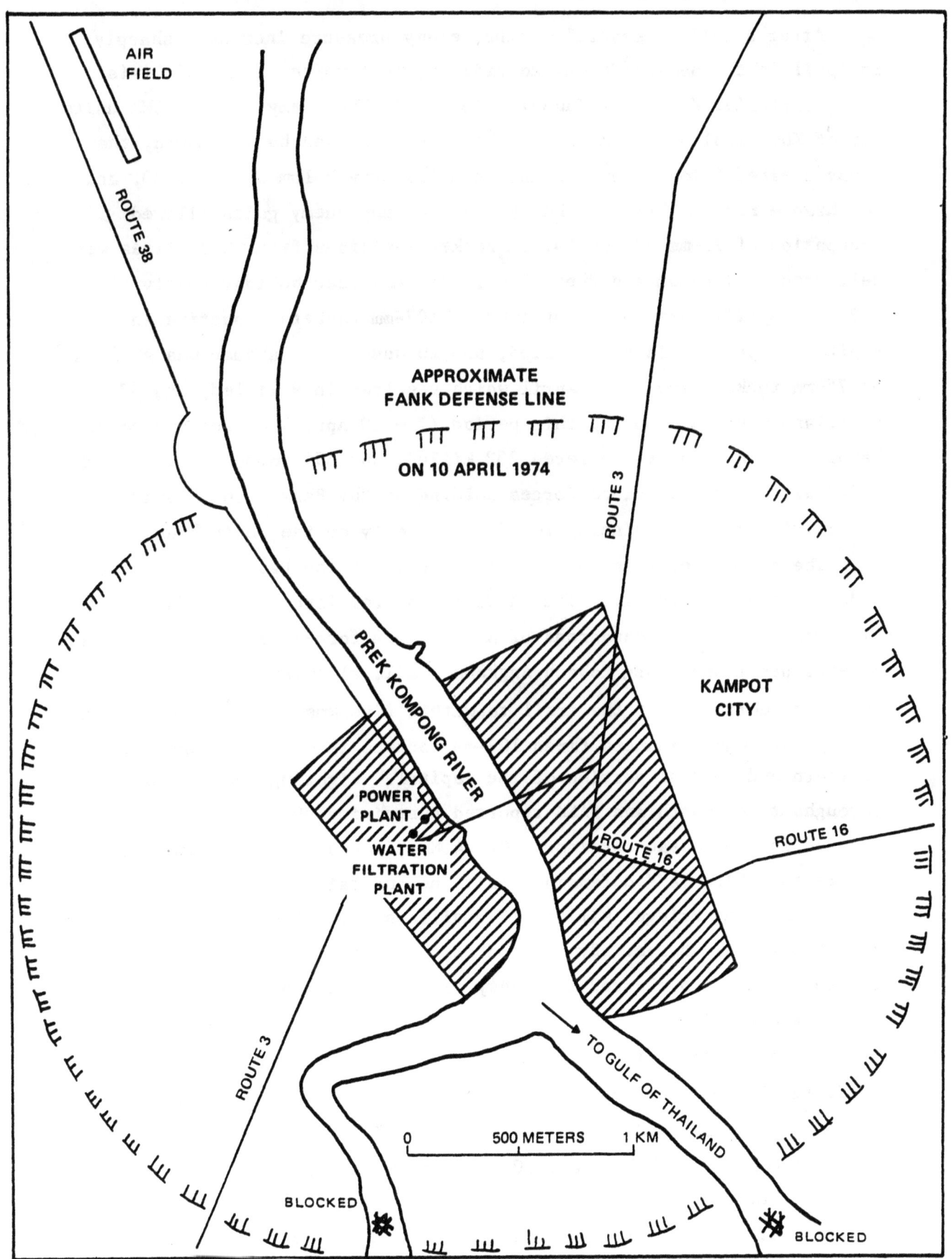

After a lull of several months, enemy pressure increased sharply in April in the Bassac/Mekong corridor against units of the 2d Division and territorial forces of Kandal. *(Map 25)* The enemy forced FANK units out of Kbal Kaol and Prek Pau in the first week and by mid month, the enemy cleared Anlong Chen Island, occupied Svay Rolum on Route 30, and Koh Krabie Krom. There was heavy fighting and enemy gains allowed occupation of 75-mm RR and 107-mm rocket positions from which fires were delivered on Takhmau and Phnom Penh. The new year holiday festivities (13 - 15 April) were interrupted by 11 107-mm rockets impacting in the capital, resulting in four killed, and 20 wounded. Takhmau was shelled by 75-mm rocket fire on 29 April which resulted in 9 killed, and 37 civilians wounded. During this period (7 - 30 April) of intense combat, Kandal Province forces suffered 232 killed, and 354 wounded. The month ended with Kandal Province forces holding on the Bassac south bank and 2d Division forces beginning to advance slowly on the north bank.

The enemy operations begun during April in the Bassac/Mekong corridor continued into May. The 2d Division, reinforced by Kandal provincial units and three squadrons of M-113s, was forced to evacuate/abandon several positions along Robaoh Angkanh Trail, allowing the enemy to penetrate northwest of the trail to within five kms of Phnom Penh. From this point, enemy gunners fired 107-mm rockets into Takhmau and the southern and central portion of the capital. Fighting was intense throughout the month and FANK reported sustaining 39 killed and 389 wounded in the Bassac corridor. On 24 May, a small enemy element infiltrated behind FANK defensive positions and raided a village south of the Monivong Bridge, killing 12 civilians, wounding 23, and burning approximately 12 homes. By the end of the month, FANK forces had closed the gap and cleared the enemy from positions northwest of the Boraoh Angkanh Trail.

In other actions in the southeast sector, Route 1 was interdicted on 21 May by an estimated battalion-size force for a day and a night; by 22 May, traffic had returned to normal. The 43d Brigade of the 2d Division reported 8 killed and 30 wounded in the clearing operation. Brigadier General Dien Del, Commanding General 2d Division, became governor of Kandal Province, in addition to his other duties, effective 15 May.

Map 25 — Operations Along the Bassac River, April-July 1974

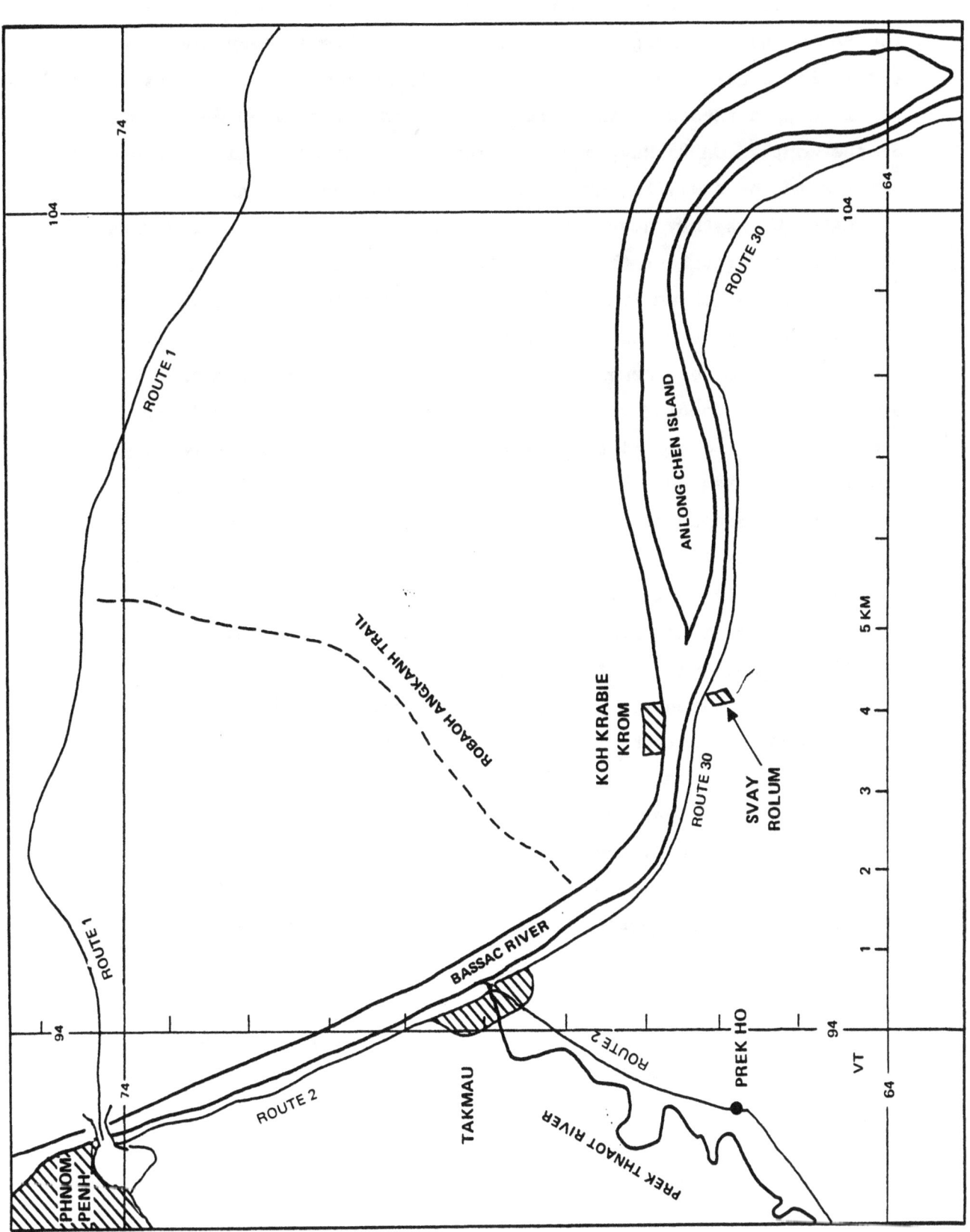

North of Phnom Penh, FANK was able to stabilize the situation during a month of hard fighting in May. The primary action was the FANK initiative of the 7th Division/5th Brigade conducting operations toward the north, along Route 5 in order to relieve enemy pressure on the isolated garrison at Lovek. FANK attacks and enemy counterattacks resulted in a seesaw battle between Kruos and Prek Taten during most of the month. On 25 May, ground forces overcame enemy flank pressures, penetrated the enemy forward defensive lines, and overran an enemy battalion CP as they advanced 2.5 km north of Prek Taten. Fighting was intense throughout the month with FANK sustaining 10 killed, 107 wounded, while accounting for 144 enemy killed and 6 POWs.

The highly vulnerable and densely populated garrison at Lovek was at the mercy of enemy gunners who shelled the garrison both day and night throughout May. Enemy ground attacks, primarily in the south and northwest, attempted to gain an early victory. The training center was lost on 4 May and the southwest defensive line was faltering when the 80th Brigade counterattacked to halt the enemy's advance. Ten days later on 14 May the training center and southern perimeter had been retaken. Limited friendly ground operations were conducted during the month in the most critical area along the southern defensive line. The military strength of the garrison, 4,305 troops, precluded maintaining a firm defensive posture in the northwest and southwest, while at the same time attacking east with the 80th Brigade to establish a beachhead on the Tonle Sap. Evacuation of the 15,000 - 20,000 civilian refugees was dependent upon this operation; reinforcement of the 80th Brigade was planned by the FANK high command; however, execution was not successfully accomplished. The arrival of Brigadier General Mey Sichan on 3 May as the Lovek operation commander resulted in rapid stabilization of the situation and a strengthening of the garrison's defensive posture. Both friendly and enemy initiated activities during the month resulted in 50 FANK killed, 319 wounded, and about 100 enemy killed. The month closed with enemy pressure diminishing and FANK attempting limited offensive action to the south and east.

June saw continued FANK success north of the capital. In that area, the 5th Brigade, reinforced by the 7th Brigade, progressed slowly north during the first 10 days of June. Between 10 and 14 June, ground forces moved north against decreasing enemy resistance with 50 enemy killed in action during the period and only light casualties reported by FANK. The high command dealt the enemy a decisive blow by reinforcing with the 15th Brigade on 15 June. On 19 June the 15th Brigade reoccupied Kompong Luong, leaving the enemy in disarray. The combined operations for the period 17 to 19 June netted FANK 314 enemy killed and, 21 POW's, while sustaining 21 killed and 47 wounded. During consolidation and reorganization, enemy reinforcements arrived and interdicted Route 5 on 28 June south of Kompong Luong in both the 15th and 7th Brigade zones. The 15th Brigade cleared the road on the same day, sustaining 5 killed and 14 wounded, and reporting 15 enemy killed. The major enemy force was located in the 7th Division zone and the high command again decided to mass combat power, reinforcing with two battalions and one M-113 squadron. FANK attacked on 28 June with elements from 3 brigades. Route 5 was cleared on 29 June, with an additional 114 enemy killed, 5 POW's and FANK units sustained a total of 4 killed, 13 wounded, and two M-113's damaged. A 5th Brigade operation on the Tonle Sap east bank at the same time accounted for 10 additional enemy killed. The month closed with FANK forces firmly entrenched on Route 5 and in Kompong Luong.

There was success as well at Lovek, whose garrison was able to end its isolation. A heavy enemy attack on 8 June against the northwest and southwest sections of the Lovek perimeter was repulsed by the counterattacking 80th Brigade. On 12 June, Lovek forces attempted to move east to link up with ground forces who had established a beachhead for the evacuation of the civilian population to Kompong Chhnang. After two and one-half days of no progress, they broke through and reached the Tonle Sap. Consolidation of the beachhead at Peam Lovek and evacuation of approximately 10,000 civilians was accomplished by 24 June.

FANK success north of the capital continued into July. The highlight of the month was the breakthrough by the 7th Division and 4th Brigade of the enemy's defensive line north of Phnum Chetares (VU7503) on 6 July and the successful link-up with the forces from Lovek in

Oudong on 9 July. Total enemy losses during the period 22 April to 9 July were 1,366 killed in action, 45 captured, 18 ralliers (to include the commander of the KC 114th Battalion and two of his lieutenants), 105 crew-served weapons and 308 individual weapons. Friendly losses were 104 killed and 786 wounded. The loss of Oudong was not only a tactical defeat for the enemy but a psychological defeat as well. Enemy reactions to this FANK victory were expected and FANK was prepared. On 16 July a major enemy force moved in behind two FANK battalions located southwest of Oudong and attempted to cut them off and destroy them. Fortunately, the 145th Brigade and the 2d M-113 Squadron were located in Oudong; they struck the enemy force from behind, causing it to flee the battle area. Friendly losses were 4 killed and 11 wounded, while enemy losses were 150 killed and 6 POW's and 43 weapons captured. During the period 16 - 23 July FANK forces along Route 5 were reinforced and consolidated their gains so that on 23 July an offensive west of Oudong could be launched in conjunction with the 80th Brigade and 8th M-113 Squadron attacking out of Lovek. On 23 - 24 July FANK forces moved more than 3 km west of Oudong against moderate enemy resistance. On 28 July, 2 battalions of the 28th Brigade moved by Navy craft to the east bank of the Tonle Sap River and secured a beachhead near Prek Kdam (VU7905). In conjuction with this move, forces from Lovek moved down the west bank of the Tonle Sap and linked up with the 36th Brigade, then sweeping north from Kompong Luong. No enemy contact was made.

The Wet Season, August - December 1974

The 1974 wet season was, relatively speaking, a period of lessened military activity throughout Cambodia as a whole, although there was some heavy fighting east and south of the capital.

The northeast sector was a very active sector in August as enemy attacks occurred in almost all areas. The month began with an enemy force holding part of Route 61 fifteen kms northeast of Phnom Penh, and a government force at Muk Kampul (VT9897) encircled. On 2 August, the 23d Brigade and 1st M-113 Squadron conducted a forceful attack against enemy positions astride Route 61 and, aided by effective air and artillery support, broke through the enemy's main defenses and linked up with the beseiged garrison at Muk Kampul on 3 August. Government losses in actions along Route 61 during the period 26 July to 3 August were 15 killed and 106 wounded, while enemy losses were 212 killed and 45 weapons captured. As FANK forces were mopping up along Route 61 on 4 August, an enemy force struck four outposts on the east bank of the Mekong River, manned by unprepared and poorly trained troops from Vihear Suor Military Subdivision. These attacks were supported by attacks against Prek Tamerk (WT0198) and Khnar Kar (WT0783). The four outposts fell apparently without much resistance, as a result of poor leadership and curtailed basic training of unit personnel. A counterattack on 5 August by reinforcements from the Parachute Brigade, 23rd and 84th Brigades retook the positions on 5 August with little or no enemy resistance. Friendly losses were: 39 killed, nine wounded, 105 missing and 175 weapons lost. Additionally, four heavy pieces of engineer equipment were damaged. No enemy casualties were reported. On 8 August, the enemy again attacked Muk Kampul and interdicted Route 61 south of this position. Quick reaction by elements of the 23rd Brigade, supported by M-113s, opened Route 61 that same day, leaving 121 enemy dead on the battlefield and capturing 16 weapons; friendly losses were only one killed and three wounded. Further enemy attacks against Route 61 and around Muk Kampul during the period 10 - 20 August were ineffective. After 20 August the enemy apparently gave up or postponed further offensive action against Muk Kampul and instead decided to attack Prek Tamerk on the east bank of the Mekong River northeast of Muk Kampul. FANK forces were well prepared and heavy enemy attacks against Prek Tamerk on the nights of 21 - 22, 26 - 27, and 30 - 31 August resulted in over 80 enemy killed and 71 weapons captured. Friendly losses were 11 killed and 29 wounded. Reportedly, the enemy penetrated the outer defensive perimeter around Prek Tamerk on the night of 21 - 22 August by claiming to be refugees who desired sanctuary. As August ended, government forces in the northeast sector returned Route 61 to government control and successfully countered determined enemy efforts to extend KC control in that area.

August was also a very active month in the southeast sector, as both government and enemy forces launched offensives to secure control of key positions along the Bassac River and in the Bassac corridor. FANK objectives were to deny the enemy areas from which rocket attacks could be launched against the capital. On 7 August a joint 1st Division/2d Division operation was launched in the Bassac corridor. On 8 August, 1st Division units succeeded in moving south from Route 1 to Prek Thmei (WT0067), a key enemy position on the Bassac River. During the night of 8 - 9 August, enemy gunners fired 10 107-mm rockets from the Bassac corridor, but all landed far south of Phnom Penh. On 9 August the 1st Division units linked up with 2d Division units advancing along the east bank of the Bassac, but enemy harassing attacks against the rear and flank of 1st Division units caused nine killed and five wounded. On 12 August an enemy attack forced the 2d Division elements out of Prek Thmei, and on 15 August forced 2d Division units back as far as two kms. However, the 2d Division was able to reconstitute a defense line and keep 107-mm rockets from reaching Phnom Penh and disrupting armed forces day celebrations. Another enemy attack on the west bank of the Bassac on the night of 20 - 21 August forced a 2d Division unit back about one km.

FANK reinforcements moved into the area on 21 August for a major offensive along the Bassac River and stabilized the situation. This operation involved 17 infantry battalions and four M-113 squadrons from four divisions and was the first major FANK offensive action of the rainy season. The objective of the operation was to extend government control in the Bassac region and establish a new defensive line between Route 1 and the Bassac River further away from the capital. On 23 August, a brigade from the 1st Division established a beachhead on Anlong Chen Island in the Bassac River, against heavy enemy resistance. FANK forces on the island then made slow progress against stiff enemy resistance, as did the government units along both banks of the Bassac River. Meanwhile, elements of the 3rd Division, attacking south from Route 1, advanced toward the Bassac River and reported reaching the east bank on 29 August. Although enemy resistance was determined, the greatest obstacle to movement was the difficult terrain and flooding that inundated many areas and severaly restricted the use of vehicles and M-113s. As August came to a close, units attacking along the Bassac River were still over five kms from the elements that had reached the river from Route 1, and progress was disappointingly slow. Moreover, enemy counterattacks and harassing fire against advancing government units were beginning to produce significant government casualties, including one M-113 destroyed. However, the main objectives of the operation had been realized by the end of the month.

In the northwest sector, the Route 5 operation was effectively terminated and the Lovek commander assumed command of forces in the Lovek/Oudong/Kompong Luong area; the 5th Brigade commander assumed responsibility for Route 5/Tonle Sap from Kruos (VT8293) north to Prek Kdam and the 7th Division commander assumed responsibility for the area west of Route 5 and northwest of Phnom Penh. In the latter part of August, activities in the northwest sector were centered west of Tuol Leap (VT3779). On 22 August, KC gunners fired four 107-mm rockets at the Kantuok ammunition depot (VT7873), west of Phnom Penh. The rockets failed to hit the depot and caused no damage but triggered a government operation to the west and south of Tuol Leap in order to expand the outer defensive perimeter and prevent the enemy from firing more rockets at this vital installation. On 30 August the enemy fired one 122-mm rocket from southeast of Tuol Leap at Kantuok. Again, the rocket missed the depot and caused no damage, but the fact that enemy rockets could reach Kantuok increased the pressure on the 23d Brigade and 7th Division to further expand FANK control to the west. Thus, as August drew to a close, government forces were attempting to push west of Tuol Leap.

Enemy attacks against Mekong River convoys continued during August, but their intensity, by comparison with previous months, was lessened due to more frequent clearing operations. The majority of the attacks came from the west bank in the vicinity of Phu My, and consisted of: 75-mm RR; B-40/B-41 rocket; 12.8-mm machine gun fire. The cargo ship *HAY AN* was sunk.

In September, the Bassac operation in the southeast sector continued to grind out slow progress -- progress often measured in meters per week. *(Map 26)* Severe flooding continued to hamper maneuver and resupply. The enemy was well entrenched in ideal defensive positions along most avenues of approach and had heavy automatic weapons, rocket and other fire support. By the end of the month Task Force Alpha, consisting of three brigades of the 1st and 2d Divisions, a battalion of the 7th Division, two Kandal provincial battalions, and one M-113 squadron had reached Russei Srok (WT040673) on the north bank, WT042667 on the island, and WT025660 on the south bank. Task Force Bravo, consisting of the 43rd Brigade of the 2d Division, two battalions and one M-113 squadron were moving west across the corridor. They were stopped just short of the east bank at WT067653. This gap on the east bank between Russei Srok and Task Force Bravo provided the enemy a corridor through which he resupplied his units and infiltrated behind attacking forces. On 23 September, a reserve battalion of the 78th Brigade was driven from Prek Thmei (WT014625) by an enemy force in sampans, but the position was reoccupied the same day.

Attacks against Mekong River convoys were at a lower level in September than August; four convoys reached Phnom Penh during the month.

In October, the Bassac operation continued, making slow progress. On 2 October, an enemy counterattack in the Task Force Bravo area caused FANK to withdraw 1 km to the east, and continued enemy pressure prohibited friendly progress on either axis. On 19 October, heavy enemy attacks were directed toward Task Force Bravo, in an apparent attempt to cut the friendly locations at the Sophi bridge site. Repeated enemy ground attacks failed to dislodge the FANK defenders, as Khmer air support was of high order. On 24 and 25 October, elements of the

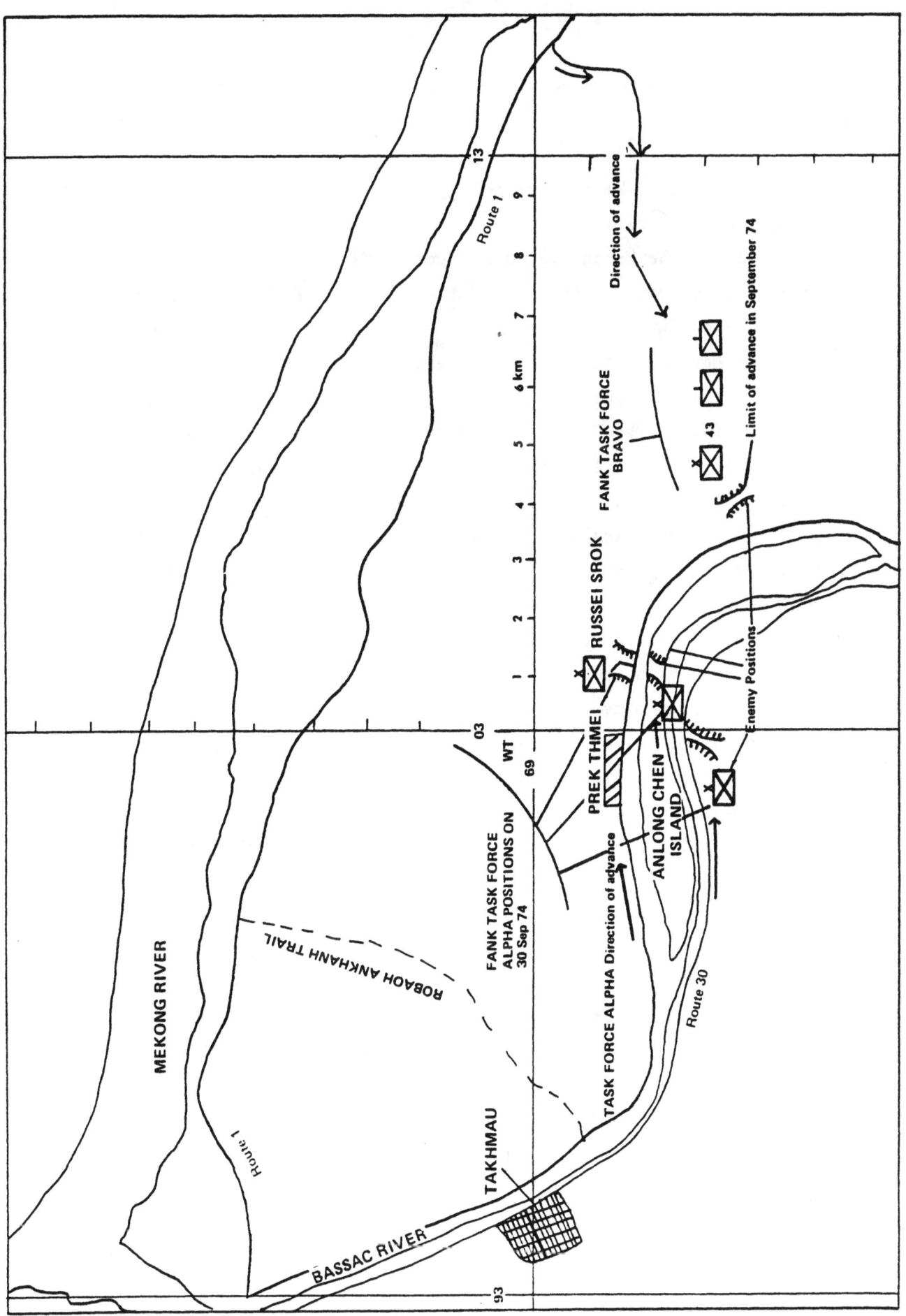

Map 26 — Operations in the Bassac — Mekong Corridor, September — December 1974

43rd Brigade conducted a sweep operation near the Sophi bridge site and killed 81 enemy during the two-day operation. The enemy continued its ground attacks and shellings against Task Force Bravo's area, failing however to take any friendly positions and paying a heavy price for their efforts.

The use of the Mekong was again unrestricted in October. Four convoys made the round trip from Vietnam to Phnom Penh, sustaining nine attacks by fire, light cargo damage, and no personnel losses.

During November, the northeast sector was the scene of a heroic defense by FANK of a position which blocked that area to the enemy for rocket positions. The FANK garrison at Barrong Khnar Kar, 14 kms northeast of the capital (WT070835) defeated an estimated 2-3 enemy regiments. The enemy, from Regiments 152, 153 and 182, (over 2,000 men as verified by prisoners and captured documents) hurled themselves against the small garrison on the morning of 10 November. The FANK defenders repulsed the first attack, suffering 4 killed and 28 wounded. However, on the following day, the determined enemy succeeded in overrunning two company-sized positions on the northern portion of the perimeter. Thirty-nine FANK soldiers were reported missing, including an unknown number killed in action. FANK reinforced the garrison with elements of the 128th Battalion and the complete 2d and 4th airborne battalions. Enemy attacks were launched almost daily against friendly positions for the next 13 days; however, government defenders successfully defeated each one. Friendly artillery and air support largely were responsible for over 400 attackers killed during this period. On 25 November, the garrison undertook to retake those positions lost on the 11th. In two days of heavy fighting, another 160 enemy were killed in action and the lost positions were retaken. November ended with FANK forces mopping up small pockets of resistance and with the enemy quitting the field. Final results of the 20-day battle were 558 enemy killed, 9 captured, 16 FANK soldiers killed and 185 FANK wounded. The defenders of Barrong Khnar Kar did themselves proud, and the KC incurred an expensive defeat.

In the southeast sector, the FANK operations in the Bassic area continued to "slug it out." On 5 November heavy enemy attacks against 72nd Brigade elements in Task Force Bravo of the operaton resulted in 3 battalions retreating 1 km to the north. Friendly casualties were not high; however, the loss of terrain was significant. The enemy shifted his attention to Task Force Alpha on the east bank of the Bassac, which had taken 600 meters from the enemy during mid-month assaults. On the night of 24 November heavy enemy attacks into the rear of the 78th Brigade of Task Force Alpha resulted in a retreat of 700 meters to the west of three of its battalions. FANK defensive positions were quickly consolidated but on the early morning of 27 November, enemy attacks against the 78th Brigade again forced it to retreat to the west. FANK reinforced the area with 2 battalions of the 28th Brigade, and by the end of the month the situation appeared to be under control. Total casualties for the Bassic Operation during the month of November were 94 FANK killed, 499 wounded, while only 34 enemy were killed. The enemy probably lost more; however, FANK inability to sweep the battlefield precluded an accurate body count. The enemy launched several 107-mm rocket attacks from the southeast sector towards the capital city; however, none impacted within the city limits during the month.

Although there was some increase in harrassment of Mekong convoys during November, the combined efforts of the Navy, Air Force, and Naval Infantry made possible four round-trip operations from RVN. On a resupply mission by river to Kompong Cham there were unfortunate losses, however. On 21 November, the enemy carried out a violent attack north of Phnom Penh. Of 316 tons of ammunition, 1,000 tons of rice, 50 tons of salt and 100 tons of POL shipped, only 25 tons of ammunition, 100 tons of POL and 25 tons of salt arrived. Enemy forces sank 2 ammunition junks, 1 USAID tug, 2 rice barges and 1 Navy monitor. Eight navy personnel were lost.

The Bassac Operation in the southeast sector was again the scene of heavy fighting in December. Early in the month, the enemy attacked the 78th Brigade and succeeded in completely decimating it. FANK declared the unit ineffective and retired its colors, transferring remaining personnel to other units. The 24th Brigade, an independent brigade, was selected to replace the 78th Brigade in the 2d Division. A few days later the enemy attacked the 24th Brigade, defending in the Task Force Bravo area between Route 1 and the Bassac, forcing that unit to retreat in disorder with heavy casualties. By the 20th of the month FANK had reinforced the Task Force Alpha units with elements of the Airborne Brigade, who moved aggressively and enjoyed great success against the enemy. By 24 December, a defensive line was consolidated between Route 1 and the east bank of the Bassac River. The main FANK effort was then directed along the west bank of the Bassac. In order to clear the region and finally end the operation, four division commanders (1, 2, 3 and 7) cooperated in an operation which had their M-113 squadrons attacking abreast to sweep the last remainder of the enemy from the horseshoe portion west of the Bassac River, killing 63 enemy, and by 31 December terminating the Bassac Operation.

There were five Mekong convoys to Phnom Penh during December, four of which were subjected to some enemy attack. Two ships sustained significant damage.

CHAPTER VII

Closing Months, January - April 1975

The year of 1975 opened on the most somber of notes for the young Khmer Republic. The war had gone on for five years, during which Cambodia the Monarchy and "oasis of peace" had become Cambodia the Republic and "oasis of war." It was a period when all of the unhappy things of the world had been poured out on Cambodia: a war of aggression carried out by foreign forces, the VC/NVA, and a civil war, pitting Khmer against Khmer. While we had gained some allies on the international scene, these could not compensate for our losses on the battlefield. The morale of the FANK sank lower and lower, as the great sacrifices of yesterday's battle brought no relief, but, rather, presaged even greater hardship. Each year had seen the circle tighten around the population centers and particularly around the capital. Each year had seen the military capabilities of the enemy more than keep pace with those of the FANK, notwithstanding heroic efforts and generous military assistance.

By 1975 it was also clear to the various elements of the republican side that our internal political divisions could no longer be ignored if we were to have any hope of salvaging the situation for the Khmer Republic. The divisions between the political party in power, the Socio-Republican Party of Marshal Lon Nol, and the other parties were becoming deeper and deeper. No reconciliation was found. In his leadership Marshal Lon Nol was completely isolated from his companions of the early hours: General Sirik Matak, Mr. Cheng Heng, Mr. In Tam. The Chamber of Deputies and the Senate, with their Presidents, expressed their disagreement over the way in which Marshal Lon Nol carried out his responsibilities as chief executive of the country. Throughout 1974 and into the beginning of 1975 this discontent on the part of the legislative branch manifested itself by several investigations into the conduct of certain cabinet members. The criticism of military and administrative matters became more and more violent, followed by social crises manifested particularly by dishonesty in the supply of food and in the almost vertical rise in prices. But the greatest damage from this internal crisis was complete division or non-cooperation between civil and military authorities. These two groups accused each other, on the slightest pretext, of the ills of the century and placed all blame on each other. The principle of all for one and one for all, advocated by Marshal Lon Nol, produced no result and this great wound became more and more open.

In this situation of political and military asphyxiation, the storm-tossed Khmer ship of state passed the helm to a new team and redoubled its efforts to find a negotiated settlement of the war.

Peace Initiatives

The Paris cease fire agreement for South Vietnam was signed on the 27th of January 1973 and the Joint Communique of Paris of 13 June specified the obligation of all parties concerned in the South Vietnam cease-fire to apply strictly Article 20 of those accords, an article which pertained specifically to Cambodia.

On the 29th of January 1973 Marshal Lon Nol seized the occasion to offer to the Khmer enemy a unilateral cease fire in place, as a means to finding a negotiated peace. In his radio message of 29 January he asked that the VC/NVA lay down their arms and that the Khmer communist forces rejoin their national community with a guarantee of general amnesty. The FANK for their part, suspended offensive operations against the enemy and limited themselves to defensive actions. The reactions to this peace offer varied. In certain national and foreign circles, the offer was seen as a "trial balloon", launched toward the Vietnamese Communists and the Khmer with a view to measuring the level of their goodwill and sincerity to observe the cease-fire agreement; it was also a gesture on the part of the Khmer Republic to demonstrate to international opinion its own desire to find national reconciliation. For others this gesture toward peace was interpreted as a sign of weakness and was a factor which demoralized the FANK and caused them to loose their combat initiative. There was a feeling that it was useless to try to negotiate with the other side unless the FANK were in a strong position and this seemed all the more useless as 1973 was also the time when the fundamental policy of the United States had already shown an intention to carry out progressive disengagement from the Indochinese Peninsula.

As a result, this first peace initiative achieved no favorable response from the enemy who, rather, redoubled his political and military efforts at the expense of the Khmer Republic. If the FANK could congratulate themselves on the number of Khmer who rallied to the republican side during the years 1973 and 1974, giving thereby a favorable psychological lift to its cause, the same was not true in the practical world. The question of rallying created enormous social, economic, and political difficulty. The flood of refugees who fled the combat zones along with the ralliers drained the fragile economy of the Khmer Republic. Their feeding alone posed for the government an almost insoluble problem. This says nothing of the problem of security in the friendly camp, which was certainly endangered by the enemy practice of introducing its own agents among the groups of refugees. In a sense people viewed these massive rallyings to the Khmer Republic cause as a sort of bad joke, played on us by the Communists for the purpose of giving us more mouths than we could feed. At the same time the enemy could be freed from these groups who would be unable to play the role or make the contribution to the enemy effort which the enemy sought.

For our part we accepted the refugees with open arms. Whether traitor or not, these refugees were first of all human beings and it was up to the authorities to judge whether they properly belonged to the friendly or enemy group. Nevertheless, what did seem to lend support to this off-hand judgment was the fact that the vast majority of these refugees and ralliers were almost entirely made up of old people, wounded people, women and young children.

Thus we have the results of our first peace initiative. If the effect of the Paris Accords was to bring a certain calm to South Vietnam, permitting the antagonists to begin the processes of the cease-fire, it was altogether different on the battlefield of Cambodia. Months went by and the level of combat mounted, while Marshal Lon Nol persisted in his efforts to achieve peace as shown by the following chronology:

1. On 6 July 1973, he called for strict application of Article 20 of the Paris Accords, cease-fire between the forces of all parties, a withdrawal of all foreign troops from Cambodian territory, as well as their weapons and ammunition, a reactivation of the International Control Commission (ICC) for Cambodia, and discussions between the Khmer parties with a view to finding national reconciliation.

2. On the 9th of July 1974, the Khmer Government addressed once more an appeal to the Khmer Communist forces to commence peace talks without prior conditions. No favorable response came from the appeal of 9 July 1974, nor from appeals made at three additional times during 1974. Lon Nol reiterated his call for peace talks on 15 August during the course of Armed Forces Day celebrations, again on 9 October, on the occasion of the 4th anniversary of the Khmer Republic and finally on the 30th of November, after the victorious vote in the United Nations which maintained the seat of the Khmer Republic in the General Assembly and marked the adoption by that organization of a resolution asking the various parties to the Cambodia conflict to enter into negotiations.

In the absence of any positive response to these peace offers, the Khmer Republic began during 1974 and into 1975 to enlarge its foreign contacts, in order to gain additional sympathizers for its cause. Previously, the Khmer Republic had neglected this aspect of its diplomacy and there were many countries who simply did not understand the principle causes for the fighting in Cambodia. In line with this we made particular representations to the Arab nations and to the countries of Southeast Asia, and Latin America. We were, of course, greatly helped by the very effective work of the United States and its allies on our behalf.

Enemy Strategy

The reactions of the enemy to our peace initiatives were in keeping with his overall strategy. The GRUNK of Prince Sihanouk became more intransigent as it found its international position reinforced among non-aligned countries, in Africa, and among the European communist countries. It drew strength as well from those Khmer within Cambodia who by now had come to be known as opportunists, those who would await and see what sort of deal might be made with the GRUNK in the event of the latter's victory.

In Chapter VI, I discussed the campaigns carried out by the enemy during the period 1972 to 1974. The objective of the Khmer Communists, an objective supported by the VC/NVA even though these latter had signed the cease-fire agreement for South Vietnam, remained always to isolate Phnom Penh from the other zones held by the FANK. With this being accomplished the capital and the other provincial centers survived only with the resources at their own disposition; communications with the capital and resupply from outside were possible only by air-drop. The zones of insecurity grew to the point that it prevented almost all normal activity by the population and by FANK forces who continued to hold certain important positions. After isolating the capital, the enemy massed the majority of his forces around the capital and began to carry out a campaign of harassment by rocket and mortar, both day and night. Beginning in January, the enemy carried out heavy attacks on Route 1, along the Mekong. During this same month the enemy was able to mine the Mekong, thereby blocking the passage of our resupply convoys and all Naval operations. At the same time, the air base at Pochentong was not spared; there, harassment of the airfield continued on a daily basis at the rate of some 30 to 40 rounds per day. In spite of this pounding this remarkable air base remained in service to both civil and military aircraft until the 15th of April, two days before the fall of Phnom Penh. It should be noted that the shipments of U.S. aid in rice, gasoline and military equipment, were carried out by cargo aircraft beginning on

16 February 1975, and these continued until the end of the first week of April.

FANK Change of Command

I returned to Phnom Penh on 20 February 1975 from New York after my assignment as a member of the Delegation of Khmer Republic to the 29th Session of the United Nations of 1974. I should note here that since the summer of 1972 I had spent all of my time attached to the Ministry of Foreign Affairs in the capacity of roving ambassador, and much of my time traveling abroad. During these two or more years I had not had the opportunity to follow the military situation closely, nor had I had a great deal of contact with the senior members of FANK.

Thus, it was a great surprise to me that starting only days after my return a good number of FANK general officers, including division and military region commanders and directors of logistic services came to see me. They wanted to make me aware of the political situation within the country and more particularly the military problems at that time. The one theme in the conversations of these officers, who, I might add, came to see me at my house time after time, was the request that I accept the idea of returning to military command and taking the posts of Chief of the General Staff and Commander-in-Chief of FANK. They confessed to me that they could no longer carry out their responsibilities in such an atmosphere of internal division and disagreement between the civil and military authorities of the same regime; and, in the circumstances they dared not try to exercise their responsibility of command any longer. At the same time, I was contacted as well by civil authorities, such as Mr. Long Boret, Prime Minister, and certain members of his cabinet who held responsible positions in the Socio-Republican Party. These latter contacts had the same objective, that is, that I consent to assume the functions of Chief of the General Staff and Commander-in-Chief of FANK.

These visits and entreaties went on for a month and I found myself in a real dilemma. Finally, with a clear conscience I agreed. Thus, it was in a troubled atmosphere, charged with military and political tensions, that I relieved my friend, Lieutenant General Sosthene Fernandez, on 12 March 1975 at a ceremony presided over by Marshal Lon Nol and carried out with complete simplicity. As an interested party to this change of command I abstain here from all comment and confine myself to the facts of the matter. Marshal Lon Nol was not a stranger to this question either, because on two occasions during the month of February 1975 he had sounded me out, and asked me to take on this new mission. I accepted this post with complete understanding of what lay before me but again in good conscience because I had told my military and civilian friends quite frankly that it was my conviction that I would not be able to redress the military situation which then existed. The picture of the Khmer Republic which came to mind at that time was one of a sick man who survived only by outside means and that, in its condition, the administration of medication, however efficient it might be, was probably of no further value.

Thus, it was no great shock when I had my first briefing on the situation only hours following the change-of-command ceremony to see that the general military situation throughout Cambodia consisted of little more than defeats everywhere, due to various reasons: the lack of resupply; inefficiency; misunderstandings; and discontent, provoked by the conduct of certain senior officers.

Military Operations

The fighting for Phnom Penh was by this time concentrated within a radius of some 15 kilometers of the capital. In the northwest, the 7th Division, whose units were primarily Khmer Krom, was in an increasingly difficult position. Its front had been cut in several places, particularly in the region of Toul Leap where the situation had changed hands several times. The 3rd Infantry Division, located on Route 4 in the vicinity of Bek Chan, some 10 kilometers west of Pochentong was cut off from its own command post at Kompong Speu.

In the south, the 1st Division handled the defense, along with the 15th Brigade of Brigadier General Lon Non; it was the calmest part of the front at that time. In the region of Takhmau, Route 1, and the Bassac, the 1st Division was subject to continued enemy pressure. East of the capital were the parachute brigade and the troops of the Phnom Penh Military Region. The Naval base and the Air Force base were defended by their own forces. The key position of Neak Luong on the east bank of the Mekong was completely isolated following many attacks. As for the state of the Air Force and the Navy, these two services were on their last gasp. Their best efforts simply could not satisfy the requirements stated by the ground forces. The general logistic situation for FANK was increasingly critical and the resupply of ammunition for the infantry could not be carried out except in a sporadic way.

The rapidly worsening situation of March was capped on the night of 1 April by the fall of Neak Luong, despite ferocious resistance and following many days of siege. *(Map 27)* This development opened the gates of the capital to the south and two days later all friendly positions on Route 1 above Neak Luong and held by the mostly Khmer Krom 1st Division, fell one after the other, in the course of heavy combat. All intervention, whether by road or by the Mekong, was impossible. The Mekong itself was mined in several places, and the capture of six 105-mm howitzers at Neak Luong was a further menace to Phnom Penh.

North of the capital, in the 7th Division area, enemy attacks came every day, and despite air support carried out day and night, there was no improvement in the situation there. Several counterattacks by FANK, carried out to retake certain lost positions, met with no success. The losses suffered by this division grew and grew every day and the evacuation of its sick and wounded by helicopter was no longer possible. The last reserves of the high command, reconstituted hastily by taking the battalions of the former Provincial Guard, were rushed to the north, only to be completely dispersed by the enemy after several hours of combat. Finally, a great breech was

Map 27 – Final Assault on Neak Luong and Closing of the Mekong, March 1975

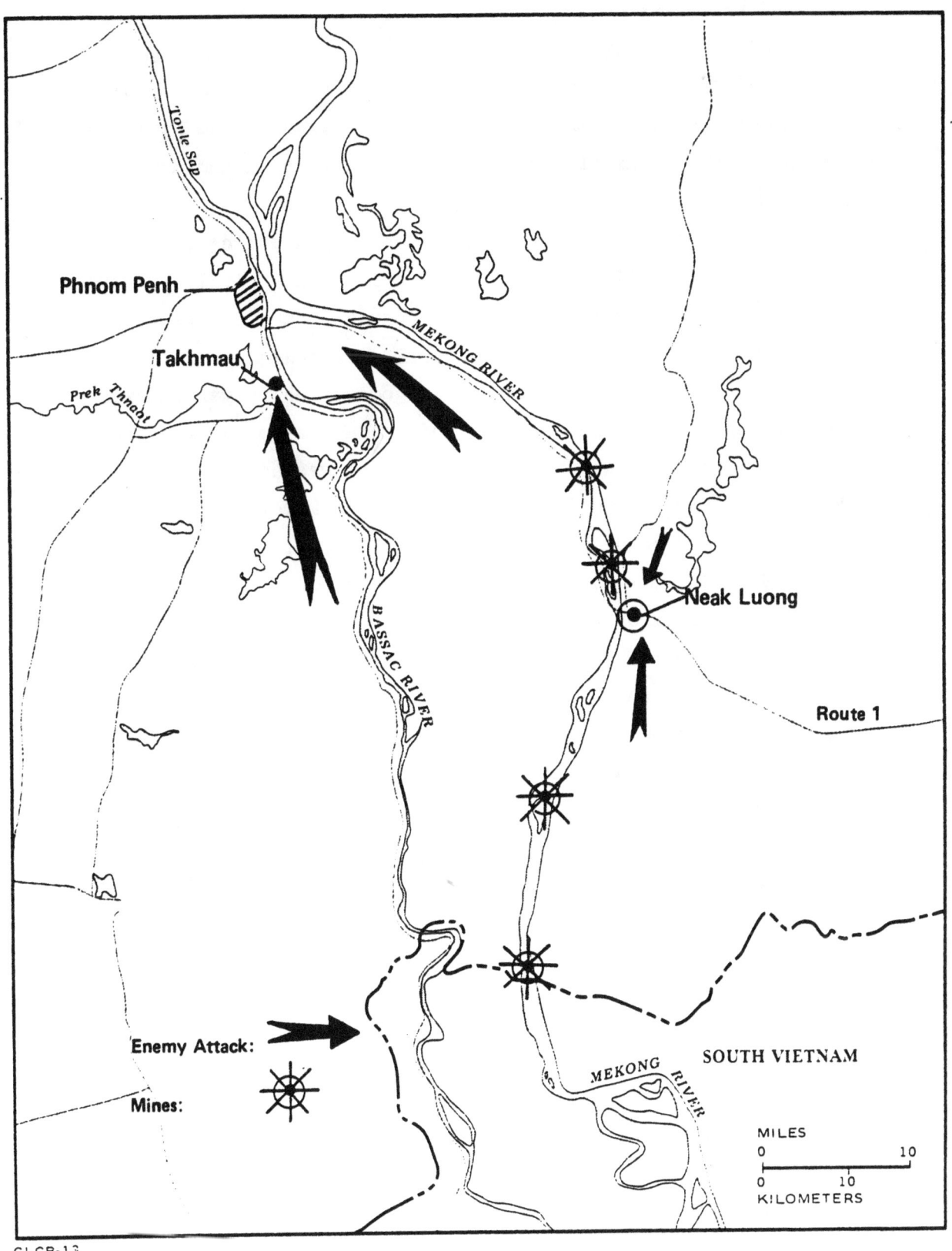

opened in the north defenses without hope of closing it. To the west, the troops of Brigadier General Chantaraingsei's 3rd Division, despite reinforcements, were unable to make junction with their own elements at Kompong Speu and to retake the position at Toul Leap. An error of computation which caused FANK artillery fire to land on 3rd Division elements during this operation had a very bad effect on the morale of that unit.

The situation I have described above developed during the period from 3 to 12 April 1975, a period during which civilian refugees never ceased to flow toward the capital, coming from all directions. The authorities, civil and military as well, were submerged and no one knew where to lodge them. Schools, pagodas, public gardens were completely occupied by these refugees and there was no way for the authorities to determine who was friend and who was enemy.

The unravelling of the five-year war of the Khmer Republic came, for all practical purposes, to its end on the day of 15 April when the town of Takhmau, the air base at Pochentong, and the dike running east/west to the north of Phnom Penh, all of which formed the last ring of defense around the capital, were overrun by enemy assault. *(Map 28)* The last units of the FANK, whose resupply of ammunition was no longer possible, the aerial resupply of U.S. assistance having been completely halted on 14 April, continued to fight to their last bullet. The intervention of the parachute brigade, brought back from the east of the Mekong, had no effect on the situation to the west of the capital. The brigade tried to move west but was able to get no further than 6 kilometers down Route 4.

The Departure of Lon Nol

The departure of Marshal Lon Nol from Phnom Penh on 1 April 1975 was, in effect, a final gesture on the part of all concerned in our efforts to move Cambodia toward peace. The various responsible elements in Cambodia, the National Assembly, the FANK, the leaders of Lon Nol's own Socio-Republican Party, had begun to wonder in 1974 whether or not

Map 28 — The Battle for Phnom Penh, April 1975

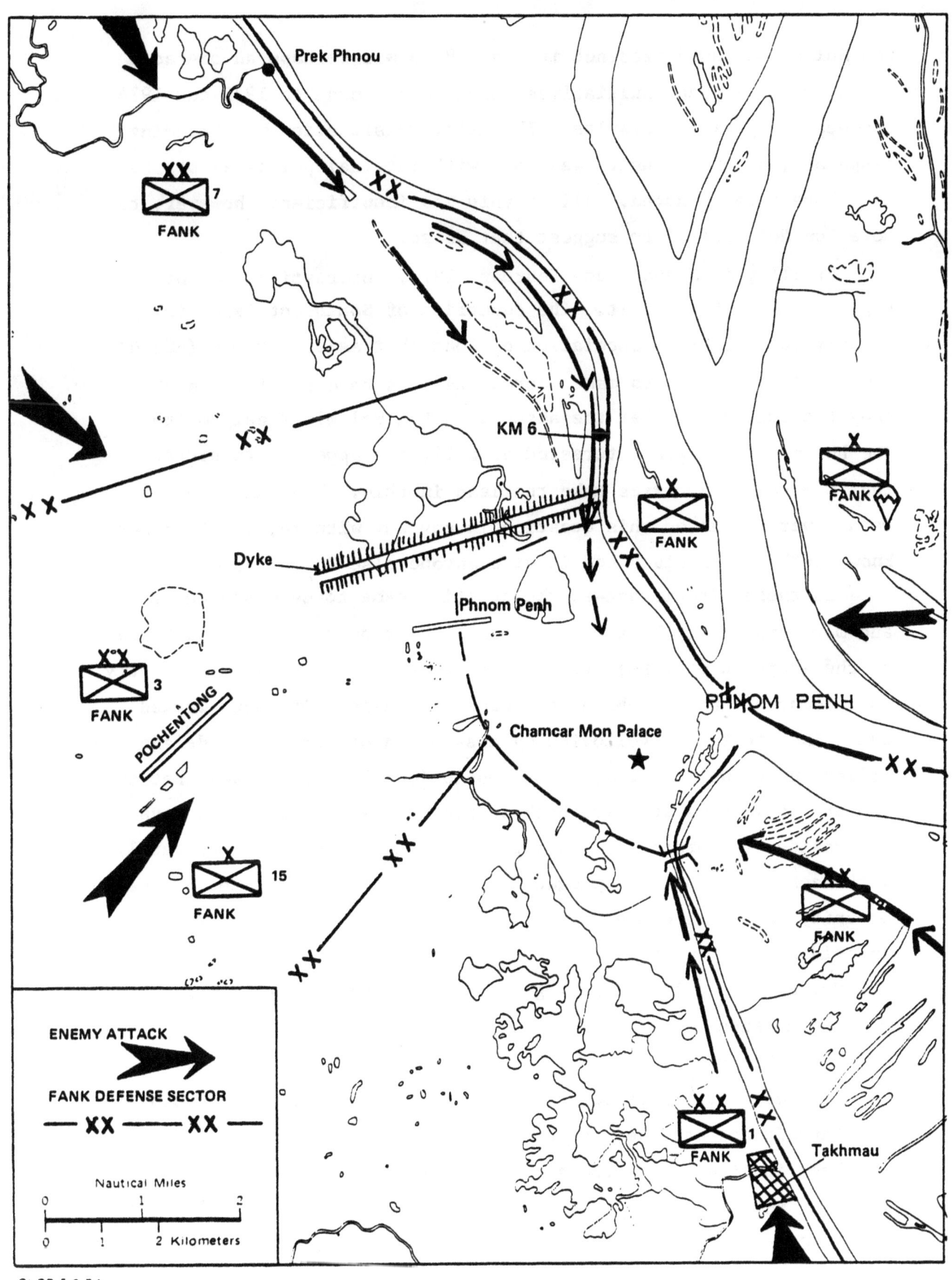

Lon Nol's continued presence in Phnom Penh was perhaps an obstacle to peace. The peace initiatives which he had made in 1973 and 1974 produced no positive results. The military situation was becoming desperate, and the country was torn with internal political strife, as I have already noted. All of this was insufficient, however, to move Lon Nol himself to suggest that he go.

Finally, in January and February 1975, international opinion began to make itself felt. The countries of Southeast Asia, particularly those of the Association of Southeast Asian Nations (ASEAN) and Japan, all began to make representations to our officials that they too considered that the absence of Lon Nol might help matters. The United States was interested as well, but appeared to prefer that the ASEAN countries take the lead in this. U.S. Ambassador Dean never discussed this question in any way with me, and I do not know whether Dean discussed it with anyone else in our government.

In these circumstances, the question came to be discussed more and more explicitly by the above-mentioned groups, leading in March to the adoption of formal resolutions that Lon Nol leave the country on a temporary basis, while the terms of a cease-fire were worked out. In late March, following my assumption of command, a delegation called on Lon Nol to present the resolution; he was shocked that the country would thus turn its back on him, and asked for a few days to consider the proposal. During this time, Lon Nol met separately with each member of the delegation in an effort to test the degree of unity among his detractors. Finding them both collectively and individually of one mind in support of the resolution as submitted, Lon Nol agreed to leave, asking that those remaining work for an honorable peace -- not simply capitulate -- and, failing that, continue the struggle.

The departure ceremony at the Chamcar Mon Palace was devoid of all fanfair and attended by Khmer only, the diplomatic corps having not been invited. From the grounds of Chamcar Mon, helicopters took Lon Nol, his family and party to Pochentong, where they boarded an Air Cambodia craft. Ambassador Dean was at Pochentong when the group arrived. From Phnom Penh, Lon Nol traveled to the U.S. base at Utapao, Thailand, where a plane sent by the Government of Indonesia waited to take him to Bali. After several days in Bali, during which Lon Nol had an interview with President Suharto, the President of the Khmer Republic traveled to Hawaii to continue medical treatment for the effects of his 1971 stroke.

CHAPTER VIII

The Final Days of the Khmer Republic

My taking office, after the departure of Marshal Lon Nol, a departure desired by both the Khmer and the United States Embassy, gave evidence of a real effort on the part of both the Khmer Government and the United States to reach a peaceful and honorable solution to the struggle. The government called for a purge of certain key people. Although it was a little late in the game, this was carried out but not without difficulty. Everyone rejoiced, especially the civilian population from the highest placed to the most humble. It was thought, not unreasonably, that real negotiations would take place and that peace was at hand. The troops were tired of fighting, the ammunition supply was running low, supplies were increasingly difficult to deliver to the troops at the front as the battle raged around the besieged capital. People waited for a miracle which only the United States Congress could provide -- a favorable vote to continue military air support. Everyone hung on the radio listening for news from the United States. Alas, the decision -- a negative one -- was announced soon and caused an immediate and general panic. Nevertheless, President Ford did say that supplies would continue to be provided in accordance with the remaining credits of the original FY75 U.S. MAP.

Departure of the U.S. Embassy

On April 12, 1975, the American Embassy evacuated its staff, its Cambodian personnel, including their families, and Acting President Saukham Khoy (with whom Washington had some further plans) by helicopter in plain daylight. This spectacular evacuation, considered by many to be a flight, as neither the Government nor the National Assembly knew about the mission of General Saukham Khoy, marked the beginning of the end for the Khmer Government. Not only was this a surprise, but it was also a moral shock of vital importance, as subsequent events proved. The U.S. plan was to evacuate certain other Khmer officials as well whose lives, according to U.S. Ambassador John Gunther Dean, were in danger. General Sisowath Sirik Matak was invited to join the exodus, as were General Lon Non, Mr. Long Boret, Pan Sothi, Long Botta, and General Saukham Khoy. General Sirik Matak courteously declined the invitation, as well as General Lon Non and Mr. Long Boret. All of these personalities were contacted separately by the U.S. Embassy. Mr. Long Boret, for example, did not know that General Saukham Khoy had been contacted or, if he had been, he thought that the latter had refused.

To the great surprise of the Americans, the entire Cabinet and all other military and civilian leaders decided to stay with their people (only one lower echelon member of the government, Undersecretary of Sports Mr. Long Botta, joined the fleeing party). The declaration of Prime Minister Long Boret, announcing the continuation of the fight, gave the keynote to the days to come. Even those who saw no more hope rejected the offer. Former Premier Sisowath Sirik Matak's widely circulated and moving letter explained eloquently why he chose to remain.

And, indeed, all was not yet lost. Not only Phnom Penh but almost all provincial capitals (except those in the east occupied by the North Vietnamese) were in the hands of the government, packed with millions of refugees who voted against Communism with their feet. Some reliable estimates put the number of the population under government control at six million and under Khmer Rouge control at one million. The Phnom Penh airfield was still in friendly hands (there was also a smaller one used by military planes), and an aerial bridge, much smaller than that of Berlin, could still have had the necessary effect. In fact, considerable quantities of food, ammunition, and medical supplies were parachuted every day by American planes, even after the evacuation.

The Last Government

Events accelerated rapidly following the U.S. departure. On 12 April at 8:30 a.m., the Council of Ministers met in the office of Prime Minister Long Beret. It was decided that a sort of general assembly should be convoked, consisting of the highest functionaries and military leaders, members of the Cabinet, the President of the Senate par interim (Mr. Tep Hun), the President of the National Assembly (Mr. Ung Bun Hor), the representative of the Republican Party (Mr. Op Kim Ang). The President of the Democratic Pary (Mr. Chau Sau), although invited, decided not to participate. From 2:00 p.m. the general assembly sat during the greater part of the day in the Chamcar Mon Palace. It finally adopted a unanimous resolution asking the transfer of power to the military and condemning Mr. Saukham Khoy for not handing over his office in a legitimate way. At 10:00 p.m. the Presidents of both Houses convoked all members to ask them to confirm the resolution, which they did unanimously.

At 11:00 p.m. the general assembly continued its session, accepted the decision of the two Houses, and elected the members of the Supreme Committee:

    Lt. General Sak Sutsakhan
    Maj. General Thong Van Fanmuong
    Rear Admiral Vong Sarendy
    Brig. General Ea Chhong
    Mr. Long Boret, Prime Minister
    Mr. Hang Thun Hak, Vice Prime Minister
    Mr. Op Kim Ang, Representative of the Republican Party

At 12 midnight I went to the General Staff to check the new developments at the front. The military situation had deteriorated sharply during the day. The Khmer Rouge threatened the capital from all sides. The fall of Neak Luong on the Mekong, an important communication center, was particularly disturbing. In the north our front was cut at several points by the massive attacks of the Communists, in spite of the fierce resistance of certain of our units. The airport, Pochentong, was in immediate danger of being taken; therefore, the small military airport of Stung Mean Chey had to be designated as an emergency landing place for the planes and helicopters bringing ammunition and supplies.

April 13th, the Cambodian New Year, would have been celebrated with public festivities, sermons in the pagodas, family outings; this time, however, no official celebration took place. The Khmer Rouge continued to bombard Phnom Penh. At 9:00 a.m. the Supreme Committee of seven had its first session and elected me as its President. The vote was unanimous. The General Assembly sat from noon until late that night. It approved the election unanimously, and thus I had to assume power, being in a way both the head of the government and an interim Chief of State. I was fully conscious of the heavy responsibility laid upon me. I was faced with a desperate situation, one which in all sincerity exceeded my imagination. The progressive decline in morale among our soldiers during the previous weeks, as contrasted with the enthusiasm they showed during the five years of fighting, was frightening.

But I was equally conscious that during these five cruel years too much blood had been shed on Khmer soil, too many human lives had been sacrificed. So in the first hours of my assumption of power I arrived at the conviction that at any price I must find a way to an honorable peace immediately. It was in this spirit, completely devoid of illusions, bitterness or pride, that I decided to make our last peace offer to Prince Sihanouk. Late that night I called my first meeting of the Council of Ministers. The Council of Ministers—this time consisting of both the Supreme Committee and the Cabinet—composed a message to the nation to be read by me on Radio Phnom Penh. Other decisions included certain political and military measures, channeling the ever increasing stream of refugees into schools, pagodas, their feeding, the reshuffling of the cabinet, reinforcing the troops in Phnom Penh by flying in (through the smaller military airport) a few battalions from different provinces, etc. But one of the most important resolutions was the formation of an Ad Hoc Committee to prepare peace overtures with either Prince Sihanouk or the Khmer Rouge. Its chairman was Long Boret.

On April 14th the military situation was becoming increasingly precarious. That morning the Cabinet met at my office at the General Staff. It was important that I remain with my command post without interruption and equally important that the Cabinet follow the events closely, having contact with all fronts there. At 10:25 a.m., a tragic thing happened: a young Khmer pilot, won over by Communist propaganda, dropped four 250-pound bombs from his T-28 fighter bomber. Two of the bombs exploded about 20 yards from the office where we were meeting, but none of us were hurt. However, the bombs killed seven officers and N.C.O.s and wounded twenty others. The session continued. Our main task was to direct the refugees, now pouring in from all points of the compass, into hospitals, pagodas, schools, the university, etc. The atrocities committed against them in the neighboring villages left them no alternative other than to escape into the city.

That afternoon another one of our bastions fell, Takhmau, the capital of Kandal Province, which was only 11 km from Phnom Penh. The loss of this key town, a key point in our defense perimeter, had a demoralizing effect. Several counterattacks were initiated but to no avail. Soon a fierce battle was in progress in the southern suburbs. The Cabinet met again that evening, as it had every night. The mood was gloomy.

On 15 April almost everyone in Phnom Penh knew that President Ford had dropped his request for the $333 million additional aid for Cambodia, in anticipation of Phnom Penh's imminent fall. Even the front-line soldiers were able to hear Khmer-language broadcasts of the Voice of America. It is true that, seeing the determination of the people to continue the fight, he reversed his stand, but the damage could not be repaired by then. Even in this last moment the morale could have been boosted by active American help. Numerical strength was on the government's side. The air bridge was functioning (although faltering), and aid even as low as $50 million could have provided the army with ammunition, with about 20 surplus planes and a few dozen old tanks—all waiting to be delivered in Thailand. These could possibly have turned the tide of the battle.

The 15th began with the enemy pressing in from north and west. The number of the refugees quadrupled, quintupled, multiplied tenfold! Our police force was no longer sufficient to direct the refugees, despite the many students who offered their assistance. In fact, the Khmer Rouge used the terrorized people, peasants with their families, as a shield as they advanced. Rockets and shells rained on the city. In the north and west, fires started to flare up; depots of food, fuel and arms were on fire; and the population found itself in ever-increasing disarray. The fighting went on. The climax of the day's battle—so catastrophic for us!—was the fall of the Pochentong airport. Of course, at that time it could no longer be used by planes, but ammunition and food could still be dropped on it. Even greater were the consequences for the troops' morale. A few relief operations were undertaken but in vain. Our reinforcements did not arrive in time, and the enemy succeeded in cutting off the main arteries, preventing their use for relief operations.

I could not maintain contact with my family during those days. Leaving at 7:00 a.m. and returning around 2:00 or 3:00 a.m. the following day, I saw practically nobody. Anyway, I was too tired to discuss anything with anybody in the family. Besides, starting at 6:00 a.m., visitors were announced regularly, visitors I could not refuse to see. I ate on the run at impossible hours and hardly slept. I did not even visit my poor sick father, confined to his room. Always rushing, pressed and pushed from all sides, I just had time to tell my wife to be ready with the children for a forced departure. I did not think I would be able to join them for a long time. However, destiny decided differently.

One More Effort to Negotiate

On 16 April, our early morning Cabinet meeting was devoted entirely to the mechanics of sending the peace offer to Peking as quickly as possible. Prime Minister Boret drafted it, asking for peace from Prince Sihanouk, so that every problem could be discussed in an atmosphere of serenity. But above all, the Khmer people needed peace. To this end we were ready for an immediate ceasefire and transfer of power to GRUNK and to FUNK. We had two channels to forward the offer. We used the good offices of the representative of the UN and the International Red Cross, Mr. Scheller; he promised to forward it personally to Peking via Geneva. The second channel was the representative of the France Press who had rapid access to Peking and who also promised to pass on the offer.

In the meantime, the military situation was becoming worse. The morale of the population, of our functionaries, and of the military cadres was disastrously low. On the other hand, the leadership, aware of the peace offer they made, still nurtured some hope.

All afternoon we waited for the answer from Peking. By 11:00 p.m. an answer still had not arrived. We realized then that the Khmer Rouge did not want to accept our offer. We decided to have another meeting of the Ministers at my command post.

The 17th of April 1975

It was already 2:00 a.m. on the 17th of April when we agreed that, as our appeal had not been accepted and we did not want to succumb to the Communists, we would establish a government in exile (i.e., outside of Phnom Penh but still in Cambodia). We would transfer the Cabinet, the Supreme Committee, and even members of the Assembly to the north to the capital of Oddar Mean Chey Province. We planned to continue resisting there. The only way to leave the capital was by helicopter. We agreed to rendezvous the members of the Government at 4:00 a.m. in the garden in front of the Pagoda Botum Vaddey. We waited there for over an hour, but the helicopters we ordered to report there did not show up. The dawn was breaking over the eastern horizon. We said to ourselves that our plan was ruined and were ready to leave when our liaison officer appeared and announced that there were no more helicopters. All of them had left the city on operational missions and were prevented from returning. Even the few still in Phnom Penh the day before had left during the night.

Due to this shocking turn of events, we returned to Premier Long Boret's house. It was about 5:30 in the morning, and we decided to resist to the death in Phnom Penh itself. After 6:00 a.m., while we held our meeting, the Minister of Information, Thong Lim Huong, brought the cable just arrived from Peking; our peace appeal had been rejected by Sihanouk. At the same time they branded the seven members of the Supreme Committee as chief traitors, in addition to the seven who had taken power in 1970. There was no longer any hope for peace for the Khmer people.

A little before 8:00 a.m. a strange calmness descended on the house of Long Boret. The rest of the Cabinet, the Deputees and Senators all left the session without saying a word, leaving us alone, Long Boret and me. This was the moment when General Thach Reng arrived to plead with us to yield to reason, to face the facts and leave with him, as he still had his men of the Special Forces and a few helicopters at his disposal. It was exactly 8:00 a.m. when I sent my aide-de-camp to tell my wife to join me with the children and Mrs. Sisowath Sirik Matak at the Olympic Stadium on the Boulevard ex-Moniret, renamed Boulevard Samapheap after 1970. I left the house of the Prime Minister in my official car and Long Boret in his. I arrived at the stadium at 8:10. My family was already there, and we boarded the helicopter General Thach Reng kept ready. When Long Boret arrived, he boarded our helicopter too, accompanied by Mr. Thong Lim Huong, Minister of Information. Both joined us while the pilot (without a copilot and used to flying only transport planes) tried to start the motor -- without success. It was decided to exchange the battery with that of another of the helicopters standing nearby. At this moment, Mrs. Long Boret, their two children, his sister and the family of Mrs. Diep Dinar, General Secretary of the Senate, and a good friend of the couple, arrived in the center of the stadium, loaded with luggage. Mr. Long Boret, followed by his faithful companion, Thong Lim Huong, left us to join the newcomers in another helicopter. His decision was normal, and I did not try to detain him; there were still two more helicopters and two pilots ready to take charge. At 8:30 a.m. our machine took off, and while we gained altitude I saw Mr. Long Boret and his family wander from one helicopter to the other. This was my last view of our Prime Minister. I never knew exactly what happened to him afterwards.

We should have landed at Kompong Chhnang to get fuel, but the base radioed us not to land. So we continued our flight. Later, a little after my arrival in Thailand, I understood that the base was in the hands of defeatist officers and N.C.O.s who arrested all personalities of the Republican regime. I escaped this way a fate which would have cost my life. At 9:30 a.m. we arrived in Kompong Thom for refueling and to change pilots. Through establishing contact by radio with Phnom Penh, we understood that the enemy penetrated into the Headquarters of the General Staff and was engaged in the act of ordering all the personnel present to undress. Afterwards I heard the voice of General Mey Sichan who addressed the nation and all the troops in my name asking them to hoist the white flag as the sign of peace. Mey Sichan was interrupted while delivering his short message by a Khmer Rouge who yelled that they came as victors, as masters, and not as negotiators.

The troops in Kompong Thom and Siemreap were still loyal to their commanders and decided to resist. But the Governnor, General Teap Ben, and his family had to leave the city with us. There were two helicopters leaving Kompong Thom. In Siemreap the Governor and Commanders of the Military Region promised to protect our trip towards the frontier. He planned to join us later, but we heard that he was killed the same night.

At 1:30 p.m. we arrived in Oddar Meanchey, the last stop before crossing the Thai border. After a gloomy lunch and a short meeting with all the officers present, General Teap Ben offered to make the necessary steps to obtain entry visas for all those who wanted to leave. He returned to the Headquarters of the region at about 5:30 p.m. It was almost dark. Departure was scheduled for next morning very early. There were other groups which came from Kompong Som, Kampot, Phnom Penh, and Kompong Thom. They were mostly members of families of Air Force officers.

However, the night brought another alarming surprise for us. The nightmare began at about 10:00 p.m. and lasted until the early hours of the next morning. No one closed his eyes; all were on the watch waiting for the least noise. The population of the place, after getting wind of my presence, demanded that the governor hand me over into their custody. Finally, a compromise was reached, and Colonel King Saman came to see me to get my assurance that he might first accompany his own family to the frontier. His wife and his numerous children then left in the middle of the night by car. The Colonel returned afterwards to the gathering of the region's civilian authorities and calmed them down by some miracle I cannot even imagine. This made it possible for us to carry out our original plan.

On April 18 the expedition began at 5:00 a.m. sharp. The only incident occurred when the guards at the airport did not want the groups walking on foot to pass. But they became reasonable after they received a large sum of money. In total darkness, the C-123 took off with a cargo of people weary from grief, lack of sleep, and fear. The trip was sad and silent, all of us lost in our thoughts, barely aware of what we had just experienced. The arrival at Utapao marked the end of the nightmare, but only for us, a few individuals.

CHAPTER IX

Analysis and Conclusions

During the early hours of its war, the Khmer Republic entertained the hope of resolving this grave problem by peaceful means, especially those means that could be undertaken by that great international organization, the United Nations. As a full member of the United Nations, Cambodia had, in fact, hoped that this organization would do for Cambodia what it had done for South Korea and Israel by committing its own security troops for the maintenance of peace. Unfortunately, our hopes did not come true. Of the five years of agony, and the many relevant events, both internal and external to Cambodia, I believe it useful to comment here on two decisions taken by the United States for reasons which related as much to the situation in that country as to the situation in Cambodia. They are not the decisions of initiative, the decisions to send U.S. troops into the communist sanctuary areas of Cambodia in 1970, or to accord the FANK a very generous military assistance; rather they are decisions of termination, the decisions to terminate its cross-border operations on 30 June 1970 and to terminate its presence in Phnom Penh on 12 April 1975. In both cases, the significance to Cambodia far exceeded their importance to the United States.

When President Nixon announced his decision to commit U.S. forces in Cambodia, an intervention which was designed to destroy the war potential of NVA/VC forces installed in Cambodia there was reason for the Cambodian leadership to feel immediately relieved and content. Indeed we witnessed, in the wake of this intervention, a marked, though temporary, decrease in combat capabilities on the part of the enemy. Knowing, however, that this important intervention

by U.S. forces was both limited in time and scope, the enemy avoided
confrontation and was thus able to conserve his main forces while
waiting out the deadline for U.S. withdrawal, only 60 days later. If
a careful analysis were made of this aspect of the problem and from
an enemy viewpoint, one might say that the enemy made a well-
calculated move when his forces took the areas east of the Mekong
River (Stung Treng, Kratie, Kompong Cham, Prey Veng and Svay Rieng)
and used them as sanctuaries, firmly established this time deep in
Cambodian territory. For friendly troops no longer occupied this part
of Cambodia and in a certain sense intervention operations by U.S.
and RVN forces in Cambodia merely pushed these mobile and viable enemy
sanctuaries deeper inside this abandoned part of Cambodia.

On the Cambodian side, we observed that these operations consisted
of frontal, rather than enveloping maneuvers. This gave the enemy
ample opportunity for seeking refuge deeper inside Cambodia. Therefore,
this part of Cambodia was effectively cut off and isolated from the
rest of the country. The local population who stayed behind were
thus caught in the grip and remained under the total control and
domination of the enemy. Although the U.S. Air Force continued
to apply its efforts to this region, enemy forces were nevertheless
able to bring in reinforcements, organize themselves and eventually
change the outlook of this war of aggression against Cambodia into
one of civil war between Communist and Republican Khmer. If, in
fact this operation was conducted solely within the framework of
Vietnamization as the U.S. command had intended it, then it might
be considered a success, because it largely contributed to the
achievement of Vietnamization within the time limits imposed by the
U.S. Government. On the other hand, the withdrawal of U.S. troops
would be possible only if the RVNAF were capable of taking over.
It was difficult at the time to tell that the RVNAF had that capability.
For one thing, the NVA/VC sanctuaries were solidly anchored along the
entire western border of South Vietnam. For another, the armed forces
of South Vietnam were compelled to extend themselves precariously in
order to fill the voids created by the departure of U.S. combat units.

As far as the FANK Command was concerned, however, and within the framework of its war efforts against the NVA/VC forces, the destruction or even occupation of that part of Cambodia which was under enemy control, if done on a temporary basis only, did not end the problem for FANK. For, while these temporary effects were sought by the U.S. command, in view of their absolute necessity for Vietnamization to succeed, their repercussions fell with all their weight onto the FANK, who were from the beginning not sufficiently prepared to confront an enemy of this size. To avoid massive bombings by U.S. and RVN forces, the enemy fell back deeper and deeper inside the Cambodian territory. These bombings and attacks by friendly forces also caused the complete evacuation of these areas by the civilian population, whereupon the enemy immediately moved in. The result of all this was that a sizable part of the Cambodian territory was lost to the enemy.

But if the destruction of these enemy sanctuaries had been followed by the permanent U.S. occupation of the recovered territory, it would have been much more beneficial to Cambodia, as well as to South Vietnam because, as we can now see, the enemy was able to reconstitute his forces and renew his activities from the destroyed sanctuaries. In addition, we have also to consider the psychological impact created by this operation which marked the last episode of the presence of U.S. combat troops in South Vietnam. The publicity with which the U.S. disengagement was made largely benefited the enemy, who took advantage of it to sap the morale of the civilian population and troops alike in Cambodia, as well as in South Vietnam. As a result, there was a certain lowering in morale on our side; during the same period, the other side, encouraged by ever-increasing support and assistance, became more aggressive and began to prepare for its eventual and final victory. The departure of U.S. troops on 30 June 1970, in the midst of this critical period, and during which the last decisive card was to be played thus resulted in a void so great on the allied side that neither the FANK nor the RVNAF were ever able to fill it.

Turning now to 12 April 1975, the departure of the U.S. Embassy was based on a U.S. judgment that the fall of Phnom Penh was imminent.

Clearly, the defense of Phnom Penh was related both to the will of the FANK to resist and their means to do so. Up to that point, the U.S. had been supplying the means. But here the internal situation in the U.S. came into play. The needs of the FANK were jeopardized by the most unfortunate Watergate scandal, which considerably weakened the prestige of the U.S. Executive Branch of government vis-a-vis the U.S. Congress and the American public. In a certain sense, the departure of President Nixon sealed the fate of the non-communist side in Indochina. Note that the U.S. Congress would not grant credits for additional help to Cambodia or South Vietnam in April 1975, even though this was known to be vital.

While I had no illusions about the situation or my ability to influence events when I accepted military command in March, I came to have some hope a little later, after taking office. It seemed that if there had been a little time and had the U.S. Government supported me, there never would have been a 17th of April so bloody and barbaric; in fact, there would have been no 17th of April. I still had several loyal and patriotic commanders of battalions who wanted, like I did, to purge the country of its most unhealthy elements. The young people, idealistic as everywhere, also approached me. The population saw a new ray of sunshine rise on the horizon, - warm, promising, stable and comforting after all the devastating storms that had raged since the beginning of the war. Morale began to surface, slowly, still hesitant but confident and hopeful of a better future. And it is appropriate to remind the Western reader that a few days before the catastrophe, a far-away people, small, because epic struggles in the past had weakened it, and great by its works of art, was still resisting, almost in its entirety, a foreign ideology which brought destruction to its social and cultural fabric and death to millions of its citizens.

With the fall of Cambodia there died a millennial civilization and -- irony of fate -- there was reborn -- in this 20th century -- a cynical demagoguery. While our plane hovered over the western plains of my country, I realized that it was not a question only of a little nation, submerged under a murderous rule, but world totalitarianism, engulfing new territories on its march for the domination of the world. Will humanity stand still and simply watch the genocide committed against one poor, defenseless nation after the other, without reacting at all?

APPENDIX A

The Delegations to the Summit Conference
of the Indochinese Peoples, April 25, 1970[1]
(The Canton Summit)

*Joint Declaration of the Summit Conference of the
Indochinese Peoples, April 25, 1970*

The summit conference of the Indochinese peoples was held on April 24 and 25, 1970, in a locality of the Lao-Vietnam-China border area, on initiative of Samdech Norodom Sihanouk, Head of State of Cambodia and President of the National United Front of Kampuchea (FUNK). The three peoples of Indochina were represented by four delegations:

The delegation of the Cambodian people comprised:

Samdech Norodom Sihanouk, Head of State of Cambodia, President of the National United Front of Kampuchea, head of delegation.
Samdech Penn Nouth, private advisor to the Head of State, delegate of FUNK, deputy head.
Mr. Huot Sambath, Ambassador Extraordinary and Plenipotentiary, delegate of FUNK.
Mr. Sarin Chhak, Ambassador Extraordinary and Plenipotentiary, delegate of FUNK.
Mr. Chau Seng, delegate of FUNK.
Mr. Thiounn Mumm, delegate of FUNK
Mr. Roeurng Mach, delegate of FUNK

The delegation of the Lao people comprised:

His Highness Prince Souphanouvong, President of the Lao Patriotic Front, head of delegation.
Mr. Khamsouk Keola, Chairman of the Committee of the Alliance of Lao Patriotic Neutralist Forces, deputy head.
Mr. Phoumi Vonvichit, Secretary General of the Central Committee of the Lao Patriotic Front, deputy head.
Mr. Khamphay Boupha, Member of the Central Committee of the Lao Lao Patriotic Front.
Mr. Oun Heuan Phounsavath, Deputy Director of the Information Bureau of the Lao Patriotic Front in Hanoi.

---

[1] Quoted in Caldwell, Malcolm and Lek Tan, Cambodia in the Southeast Asian War, New York, Monthly Review Press, 1973. (pgs. 363-365).

The delegation of the people of the Republic of South Vietanm comprised:

Lawyer Nguyen Huu Tho, President of the Presidium of the Central Committee of the South Vietnam National Front for Liberation, President of the Advisory Council of the Provisional Revolutionary Government of the Republic of South Vietnam, head of delegation.
Lawyer Trinh Dinh Thao, Chairman of the Central Committee of the Vietnam Alliance of National, Democratic and Peace Forces, Vice-President of the Advisory Council of the Provisional Revolutionary Government of the Republic of South Vietnam, deputy head.
Mrs. Nguyen Dinh Chi, Vice Chairman of the Thau Thien-Hue Revolutionary People's Committee, Vice Chairman of the Committee of the Alliance of National, Democratic, and Peace Forces for Hue City, member of the Advisory Council of the Provisional Revolutionary Government of the Republic of South Vietnam.
Mr. Le Quang, member of the Central Committee of the South Vietnam National Front for Liberation, Vice-Minister for Foreign Affairs of the Provisional Revolutionary Government of the Republic of South Vietnam.
Professor Nguyen Van Hieu, member of the Central Committee of the South Vietnam National Front for Liberation, Ambassador of the Republic of South Vietnam to Cambodia.
Mr. Vo Dong Giang, member of the Central Committee of South Vietnam National Front for Liberation.

The delegation of the people of the Democratic Republic of Vietnam comprised:

Mr. Pham Van Dong, Prime Minister of the Democratic Republic of Vietnam, head of delegation.
Mr. Hoang Quoc Viet, Member of the Presidium of the Central Committee of the Vietnam Fatherland Front, deputy head.
Mr. Hoang Minh Giam, Member of the Presidium of the Central Committee of the Vietnam Fatherland Front, Minister of Culture of the Democratic Republic of Vietnam.
Mr. Nguyen Co Thach, Vice Minister for Foreign Affairs of the Democratic Republic of Vietnam.
Mr. Nguyen Thuong, Ambassador of the Democratic Republic of Vietnam to Cambodia.

APPENDIX B

The Members of FUNK and GRUNK[1]

Government of the National United Front of Cambodia (FUNK):

Head of State and President: Samdech Norodom Sihanouk

Political Bureau of the Central Committee:

    President: Samdech Penn Nouth
    General Secretary: Thiounn Prasith
    Members: Chan Youran
             Chau Seng
             Chea San
             General Duong Sam Ol
             Hou Yuon
             Hu Nim
             Huot Sambath
             Khieu Samphan
             Sarin Chhak
             Thiounn Mumm

Central Committee:

Ang Kim Khoan	General Duong Sam Ol
Chan Youran	Hak Seang Layny
Chau Seng	Han Mat
Chea San	Hay Kim Seang
Chem Snguon	Hou Yuon
Chou Chet	Heng Pich
Hu Nim	Ong Meang
Huot Sambath	Samdech Penn Nouth
Mme Ieng Thirith	Poc Doeus Komar
In Sokan	Ros Thol
Kiet Chhon	Sarin Chhak
Keo Meas	Seng Chongkal
Khieu Samphan	Sien An
Kong Sodip	Sor Thouk
Koy Toum	Suong Sikoeun
Krin Lean	Thiounn Mumm
Ly On	Thiounn Prasith

---

[1] Quoted in Caldwell, op. cit. (pgs. 384-386).

Princess Monique Sihanouk
Ngo Hou
Ngo Taing Tykea
Ok Sakun
Tiv Ol
Toch Kham Doeun
Ung Panharith
Van Pinny

Royal Government of National Union of Cambodia (GRUNK)

    Prime Minister: Samdech Penn Nouth
    Vice-Prime Minister and Minister of National Defense: Khieu Samphan
    Minister Delegate to the Presidency of the Council of Ministers: Kiet Chhon
    Minister of Foreign Affairs: Sarin Chhak
    Minister of Information and Propaganda: Hu Nim
    Minister of Interior, Communal Reforms, and Cooperatives: Hou Yuon
    Minister of Economy and Finance: Thiounn Mumm
    Minister in charge of Special Missions: Chau Seng
    Minister in charge of the Coordination of Struggle for the National Liberation: Thiounn Prasith
    Minister of Popular Education and Youth: Chan Youran
    Minister of Equipment and Military Armament: General Duong Sam Ol
    Minister of Justice and Judiciary Reforms: Chea San
    Minister of Public Works, Telecommunication, and Reconstruction: Huot Sambath
    Minister of Public Health, Religious, and Social Affairs: Ngo Hou
    Minister without Portfolio: H.R.H. Norodom Phourissara
    Vice-Minister of Foreign Affairs: Poc Doeus Komar
    Vice-Minister of National Defense: Kong Sodip
    Vice-Minister of Interior and National Security: Sor Thouk
    Vice-Minister of Information and Propaganda: Tiv Ol
    Vice-Minister of Economy and Finance: Koy Thuon
    Vice-Minister of Popular Education and Youth: Mme Ieng Thirith
    Vice-Minister of Public Health, Religious, and Social Affairs: Chou Chet

High Military Command of the People's National Liberation Armed Forces of Cambodia

    President: Khieu Samphan, Commander-in-Chief
    Vice President: Salot Sar, Chief of the Military Conduct of the Army
    Vice President: Nuon Chea, Chief of the Political Conduct of the Army
    Vice President: So Vanna, Deputy Chief of the Military Conduct of the Army
    Members: Thieun Chhith, Chief of the Conduct of the Military Materiel
            Son Sen, Chief of the Joint Chiefs of Staff

Committee of FUNK of Phnom Penh, Capital of Cambodia

    President: H.R.H. Norodom Phourissara
    Vice-President: Thiounn Thieunn
    Vice-President: Mme Khieu Ponnary, Women's Representative
    Members: Toch Phoeun, Civil Servants' Representative
             Phouk Chhay, Youth and Students' Representative
             Nguon Eng, Workers' Representative
             Ros Chet Thor, Writers and Journalists' Representative

APPENDIX C

Major Items of U.S.-Furnished Equipment in FANK
(Total Inventory by Year)

Army Item	1972	1973	1974
Rifle M-16	41,351	69,224	158,115
Carbine, Cal 30	52,616	83,515	83,515
Machine Gun M-60	18	18	859
Machine Gun Cal 30	2,278	4,531	6,220
Mortar 60-mm	815	1,170	2,223
Mortar 81-mm	97	196	503
Grenade Launcher M-79	6,971	7,735	20,481
Recoilless Rifle 106-mm	7	33	304
Howitzer 75-mm	20	47	57
Howitzer 105-mm	69	134	208
Howitzer 155-mm	0	0	24
Ambulance 1/4T & 3/4T	41	139	380
Truck Dump 2-1/2T & 5T	0	24	76
Truck 2-1/2T Cargo	496	982	1,838
Truck 3/4T Cargo	0	441	758
Truck 1/4T Utility	220	647	1,264
Personnel Carrier M113	21	46	185
Personnel Carrier M106	3	7	17
Telephone TA1 & TA312	1,037	4,298	9,629
Radio AN/PRC 10	2,206	4,750	4,843
Radio AN/PRC 25	1,975	3,207	5,023
Radio AN/URC 46, 47	85	152	320

Navy Item	1972	1973	1974
Patrol Boat River (PBR)	39	43	64
Armored Troop Carrier (ATC)	2	14	14
ATC (Refueler)	0	2	3
ATC (Recharger)	0	1	1
Command & Communications Boat (CCB)	0	1	2
Monitor with Flamethrower (ZIPPO)	0	1	1
Assault Support Patrol Boat (ASPB)	0	4	4
Minesweeper River (MSR/MSM)	0	6	5
Monitor	0	5	6
Landing Craft Medium (LCM6)	19	22	30
Landing Craft Medium (LCM8)	0	5	5
Combat Salvage Boat (CSB)	0	1	1
Landing Craft Utility (LCU/YFU)	1	4	4
Patrol Craft Fast (PCF)	0	4	20
Floating Crane (YD)	0	1	1
Mobile Support Base (MSB)	1	2	2
Infantry Landing Ship (LSIL/LCI)	2	2	2
Patrol Craft (YTL)	2	2	2
Yard Tug Light (YTL)	2	2	3
Drydock	1	1	1
Total Craft	69	123	171

Air Force Item	1972	1973	1974
T-28B/D	16	48	64
O-1D/A	17	31	37
AU-24	0	14	14
AC-47	3	6	14
C-47	10	15	11
U-1A	16	7	1
C-123K	0	0	8
UH-1H	14	19	34
UH-1GS	0	0	10
T-41	0	14	18
Total	76	154	211

APPENDIX D

FANK Order of the Day, 5 October 1971

Officers,
Noncommissioned Officers,
Men,
of CHENLA II

In order to liberate our compatriots from the yoke of the enemy, and to fall upon the communist VC/NVA aggressors, CHENLA II was launched the 20th of August last on my instructions.

In six weeks of violent combat, during which you confirmed once more your determination to defend Khmer soil, you have overcome the enemy and destroyed his finest regiments.

The enemy has been put to flight, leaving on the field irreparable losses: four VC/NVA regiments were practically put out of action, and the materiel captured is even more considerable.

The losses inflicted on the enemy bear witness to the importance of your victory:

- 3,634 VC/NVA put out of action, of which 952 bodies were left on the battlefield
- 287 weapons captured, including 18 crew-served, of which two were 75-mm
- A large quantity of ammunition
- An important stock of food and fuel
- A great number of vehicles
- An important stock of latex

The morale of the enemy is, therefore, surely very low, and from this moment more than 100,000 of our compatriots return to the peace of the Khmer family, and the quietude of republican law.

Officers,
Noncommissioned Officers,
Men,

Your exploits have exceeded our hopes, and you have held high the flag of the Republic. You have earned the praise of the Fatherland.

Humbly do I bow before your dead. Their sacrifices are not in vain.

I salute your colors, and I address to you my most affectionate congratulations.

Nevertheless, still further sacrifices will be asked of you that the Nation may survive.

Now, forward, to victory.

                                      Done at Phnom Penh, 5 October 1971
                                      Marshal Lon Nol, Commander-in-Chief
                                      and Chief of the General Staff, FANK

                                                    /s/   Lon Nol

Glossary

ARVN	Army of the Republic of Vietnam
ASEAN	Association of Southeast Asia Nations
CINPAC	Commander-In-Chief, Pacific
COMUSMACV	Commander, U.S. Military Assistance Command, Vietnam
COSVN	Central Office (for) South Vietnam
DAO	Defense Attache Office
DATT	Defense Attache
DRV	Democratic Republic of (North) Vietnam
FANK	Forces Armees Nationales Khmeres (Khmer Armed Forces after 18 March 1970)
FARK	Forces Armees Royales Khmeres (Khmer Armed Forces prior to 18 March 1970)
FAO	Foreign Assistance Office (FANK)
FNL	Front for National Liberation
GKR	Government of the Khmer Republic
GVN	Government of (South) Vietnam
ICC	International Control Commission (First Indochina War)
KAF	Khmer Air Force (after 18 March 1970)
KC	Khmer Communists
MAAG	Military Assistance Advisory Group
MACV	Military Assistance Command, Vietnam
MAP	Military Assistance Program (U.S. grant military assistance)
MEDTC	Military Equipment Delivery Team, Cambodia
MILSTRIP	Military Standard Requisitioning Procedures (U.S.)
MNK	Marine Nationale Khmère (Khmer Navy after 18 March 1970)

MR	Military Region
MRK	Marine Royale Khmère (Khmer Navy prior to 18 March 1970)
NLF	National Liberation Front
NVA	North Vietnamese Army
POL/MIL	Politico/Military Counselor
PRC	People's Republic of China
PRG	Provisional Revolutionary Government (Viet Cong)
RVN	Republic of Vietnam
RVNAF	Republic of Vietnam Armed Forces
SEATO	South East Asia Treaty Organization
TCN	Third-Country National
UN	United Nations
USAF	United States Air Force
USAID	U.S. Agency for International Development
USN	United States Navy
VC/NVA	Viet Cong/North Vietnamese Army
VNAF	Vietnam Air Force
VNN	Vietnam Navy

www.ingramcontent.com/pod-product-compliance
Lightning Source LLC
Chambersburg PA
CBHW080543170426
43195CB00016B/2659